The
Promise
of
Educational
Psychology

Learning in the Content Areas

Richard E. Mayer

University of California, Santa Barbara

Merrill
an imprint of Prentice Hall
Upper Saddle River, New Jersey   Columbus, Ohio

Library of Congress Cataloging-in-Publication Data

Mayer, Richard E.
    The promise of educational psychology : learning in the content
areas / by Richard E. Mayer.
       p.   cm.
    Includes bibliographical references (p.   ) and index.
    ISBN 0-13-913013-6
    1. Educational psychology. 2. Learning. I. Title.
LB1051.M3915   1999
370.15—dc21   98-9789
                                            CIP

Cover art © 1998 C. Herscovici, Brussels/Artists Rights Society (ARS), New York
Editor: Kevin M. Davis
Production Editor: Julie Anderson Peters
Production Coordinator: Betsy Keefer
Text Designer: Fred Pusterla Design
Production Manager: Laura Messerly
Illustrations: The Clarinda Company
Director of Marketing: Kevin Flanagan
Marketing Manager: Suzanne Stanton
Advertising/Marketing Coordinator: Krista Groshong

This book was set in Veljovic Book by The Clarinda Company and was printed and bound by R.R. Donnelley & Sons. The cover was printed by Phoenix Color Corp.

 ©1999 by Prentice-Hall, Inc.
Simon & Schuster/A Viacom Company
Upper Saddle River, New Jersey 07458

Credits and Acknowledgments

p. 50: From Samuels, S. J. (1979). The method of repeated readings. *The Reading Teacher,* 32, 403-408. Reprinted with the permission of the International Reading Association and S. J. Samuels.

Credits continue on page 272.

Printed in the United States of America

10 9 8 7 6 5 4 3 2 1

ISBN 0-13-913013-6

Prentice-Hall International (UK) Limited, *London*
Prentice-Hall of Australia Pty. Limited, *Sydney*
Prentice-Hall Canada Inc., *Toronto*
Prentice-Hall Hispanoamericans, *S. A., Mexico*
Prentice-Hall of India Private Limited, *New Delhi*
Prentice-Hall of Japan, Inc., *Tokyo*
Simon & Schuster Asia Pte. Ltd., *Singapore*
Editora Prentice-Hall do Brazil, Ltds., *Rio de Janeiro*

Dedicated to the memory of my first teachers,

James

and

Bernis Mayer

What does a child need to know in order to read a printed word, to understand a text, to write a high-quality essay, to solve a math problem, or to discover a scientific principle? Which kinds of instruction help students to learn the knowledge they need to be successful on academic tasks? These are the kinds of questions addressed in this book—questions about the psychology and pedagogy of school subject areas. They represent what is most promising about the field of educational psychology, namely, progress in the study of learning and teaching in the content areas.

If you are interested in promising and exciting advances in the field of educational psychology, then this book is for you. The two promising themes of the book are *learning and teaching in specific subject areas,* such as reading, writing, mathematics, and science, and *detailed analyses of the cognitive processes of individual students* that are required to accomplish real academic tasks.

The first chapter serves as an introduction that defines and provides an historical overview of educational psychology. The other five chapters explore learning and instruction in the subject areas of reading fluency, reading comprehension, writing, mathematics, and science. Each chapter begins by analyzing the kinds of knowledge and cognitive processes that are needed to perform academic tasks in the domain under discussion, such as writing an essay or solving a word problem. Then the text examines how students learn each type of knowledge or cognitive process, and how instruction can help them learn more effectively.

The Promise of Educational Psychology is intended as a brief introduction to educational psychology. It can be used as a stand-alone textbook in a wide variety of courses, or as a supplement to more traditional educational psychology textbooks. The book is written at an introductory level and does not assume that the reader has any previous experience in psychology or education. Rather than trying to mention all relevant studies in an encyclopedic manner, I have opted for examining a few representative studies in enough detail for you to understand them. Rather than blindly producing long lists of recommendations for instruction, I have opted for showing how a few representative recommendations can be derived from research and applied to instruction. Finally, instead of covering all of the traditional areas in educational psychology—including development and assessment—I have focused mainly on learning and instruction in five basic subject areas.

This book differs from some other educational psychology books by trying to show more clearly the connection between psychology and education. In contrast to textbooks that tell you how to implement instructional recommendations while ignoring psychological research, this book carefully documents how instructional recommendations can be derived from useful research. In contrast to textbooks that emphasize general psychological research and theory but then are unable to relate them adequately to instructional recommendations, this book focuses on learning and instruction in academic domains. My goal is for you to be able to see how psychological theories and research influence the development of better instructional practices and how real instructional problems influence the development of better psychological theories and research.

The Promise of Educational Psychology has been a pleasure to write because it invigorated me with a growing optimism for the connection between psychology and education. I hope that you enjoy reading this book as much as I have enjoyed writing it.

ACKNOWLEDGMENTS

I wish to thank Kathryn W. Linden, Purdue University; Michael S. Meloth, University of Colorado; Gary Phye, Iowa State University; and Paul R. Pintrich, University of Michigan for their reviews.

I am indebted to my publisher, my teachers, my colleagues, my students, and my family. I thank Kevin Davis and his colleagues at Merrill/Prentice Hall for their patience and support during the course of this project. I also appreciate the production services of Betsy Keefer and the copyediting services of Sherry Babbitt. My mentors at the University of Michigan (where I received my Ph.D. in psychology in 1973) include my graduate adviser, James Greeno, as well as Robert Bjork, Bill McKeachie and Art Melton. Colleagues with whom I have had the privilege of collaborating at Indiana University (where I served from 1973 to 1975) and at the University of California at Santa Barbara (where I have served since 1975) include Betsy Brenner, Dorothy Chun, Priscilla Drum, Richard Duran, Mike Gerber, Mary Hegarty, Yukari Okamoto, Frank Restle, and Russ Revlin. It also has been my honor to work with such colleagues at other institutions as Joan Gallini, Kenneth Kiewra, Jill Larkin, Joel Levin, Hidetsugu Tajika, Clare Weinstein, Richard White, and Merlin Wittrock. I also appreciated the opportunities to spend sabbaticals at the Learning Research and Development Center at the University of Pittsburgh and at the Center for the Study of Reading at the University of Illinois, and to make extended visits to the Aichi University of Education in Japan and the Universidad Nacional Autonoma de Mexico. I have been fortunate to be able to work with an outstanding group of graduate students and postdoctoral scholars over the years, and I appreciate the many helpful suggestions of undergraduate students in my course on educational psychology. I particularly wish to thank my wife, Beverly, for her support and encouragement, and just for bringing so much happiness into my life; and my children Ken, David, and Sarah for reminding me to keep the book interesting and for keeping my life so interesting. I am grateful to my parents, who were my first teachers and who regularly asked me how the book was going. With special memory for them, I dedicate this book to my parents with love.

Richard E. Mayer
Santa Barbara, California

CONTENTS

CHAPTER 1

Introduction to Learning in the Content Areas

CHAPTER OUTLINE

After exploring a classic educational study, this chapter defines educational psychology, summarizes its history, and explains how it can help to answer questions about educational practice. The chapter also provides an organizational structure for the rest of the book.

"WILD BOY"

Suppose a child were allowed to develop without any social contact with other people. This experiment could be viewed as providing a child with the ultimate in educational freedom. What would the child be like? Is society needed to help children develop to their fullest potential as human beings? Take a moment to provide some predictions in Figure 1–1.

These questions were at the heart of a historic educational experiment that began in 1800 in Paris. The experiment involved only one student, an adolescent boy, named Victor, and his teacher, a physician named Dr. Jean-Marc Itard. Victor had been discovered living in the forest of Aveyron in France. Apparently, the boy had grown up in the forest, without any human contact. When captured, the boy was completely naked, dirty, and inarticulate. He seemed insensitive to temperature and pain, and was incapable of maintaining attention. He ate his food raw, using only his hands. Although physically healthy, he was totally unsocialized. The public showed great interest in the boy, and he become popularly known as the *enfant sauvage de l'Aveyron*—that is, the "wild boy of Aveyron." Dr. Itard was convinced that the boy, whom he named Victor, could be taught to become a civilized member of society. For the next five years, the doctor worked with his student, often having to develop new materials and instructional techniques.

Dr. Itard's educational program was based on several principles. First, he believed that the needs and characteristics of the student should dictate the educational program, an approach that can be called "learner-centered." Instead of letting the curriculum determine what the student will learn, in lock-step fashion, the teacher must be free to shape instruction to suit the needs of the student. Second, he argued that education depends on the student having had acquired certain "readiness skills" through natural interactions with the physical and social environment. For example, a student must have experiences with objects before learning their language names. If a student lacks appropriate sensory experiences, then these experiences must be provided as prerequisites to more academic components of an educational program. Third, he believed that the student had to be motivated to learn. According to Dr. Itard, Victor had successfully learned to cope in the wild because his survival depended on it. Now, the doctor introduced new needs for Victor so that the boy would be motivated to learn social skills. Finally, Dr. Itard believed that instruction often requires the development of new instructional devices and techniques. Many of the materials and techniques of behavior modification that he developed became the basis for subsequent programs to teach deaf and retarded students.

How far did Victor progress during the five years of instruction? He learned to master basic social skills, such as dressing himself, sleeping in bed without wetting, and eating with utensils; to use his senses, including sight, sound, and taste; to show affection; and to try to please others. Although he

FIGURE 1-1

What would
it be like for a
child to grow
up without
any human
contact?

Suppose that a child grew up from birth to age twelve in a forest, without any human contact. What do you think the child would be like at age twelve? For each pair of attributes listed below, place a check next to the one you think would apply.

_____ physically weak and unhealthy

_____ attentive to stimuli

_____ responsive to pain

_____ responsive to temperature

_____ interested in other people

_____ enjoyed a broad variety of food tastes

_____ had developed a form of oral language

_____ had developed a form of gesturing language

_____ had developed a form of written language

_____ had developed basic arithmetic skills

_____ had invented many useful tools

_____ was well mannered with people

_____ longed for human affection

_____ would be able to learn basic social skills swiftly

_____ would be able to learn basic language skills swiftly

_____ physically strong and healthy

_____ unattentive to stimuli

_____ unresponsive to pain

_____ unresponsive to temperature

_____ uninterested in other people

_____ restricted to a very few food tastes

_____ hadn't developed a form of oral language

_____ hadn't developed a form of gesturing language

_____ hadn't developed a form of written language

_____ hadn't developed basic arithmetic skills

_____ hadn't invented useful tools

_____ wasn't well mannered with people

_____ was not interested in human affection

_____ wouldn't be able to learn basic social skills swiftly

_____ wouldn't be able to learn basic language skills swiftly

never learned to speak effectively, he did learn to communicate using written language. However, Victor did not reach full self-sufficiency and spent the rest of his life under the supervision of a caretaker. His lack of complete success has been attributed to many causes, including the absence of appropriate stimulation during critical periods of his development, the limitations of Dr. Itard's methods (including his insistence than Victor use spoken rather than sign language), and the possibility that Victor was born mentally retarded. Thus your predictions in Figure 1-1 are correct if you checked each of the attributes on the right and none on the left.

As we leave the "wild boy," let's consider what we have learned about the nature of education. Some of the broader educational issues addressed by Dr. Itard were summarized by Lane (1976): (1) society (including formal instruction) is crucial for human development: "the moral superiority said to be natural to man is only the result of civilization . . . [and without society, man] pitifully hangs on without intelligence and without feelings, a precarious life reduced to bare animal functions" (p. 129); (2) people learn to satisfy their needs: "in the most isolated savage as in the most highly civilized man, there exists a constant relation between ideas and needs" (p. 129); (3) instructional programs should be based on science: "the progress of education can and ought to be illuminated by the light of modern medicine, which of all the natural sciences can help most powerfully toward the perfection of the human species" (p. 129); and (4) instructional programs should take into account the individual characteristics of each student: progress will be made "by detecting the organic and intellectual peculiarities of each individual and determining there from what education ought to do for him" (p. 129).

The conclusions of Dr. Itard, written nearly 200 years ago, can serve as a starting point for this book on the promise of the future of educational psychology. Like Dr. Itard's research, this book is based on a *learner-centered approach* in which the learner is at the heart of all learning (Lambert & McCombs, 1998). In taking a learner-centered approach, the first fundamental goal is to describe and understand the cognitive processes and knowledge used by learners in carrying out academic tasks. What are the cognitive processes that a skilled reader engages in while reading a textbook lesson? What are the cognitive processes that a skilled writer engages while composing an essay? What are the cognitive processes that a skilled mathematician engages in while solving a mathematics problem? What are the cognitive processes that a skilled scientist uses in investigating a new phenomenon? These are the kinds of cognitive questions that are addressed in this book. In short, we seek to understand what skilled readers, writers, mathematicians, and scientists know.

The second fundamental goal of a learner-centered approach is to understand how to help students to develop the cognitive processes that skilled practitioners use to perform academic tasks. How can we help a beginning reader to know what a skilled reader knows? How can we help an aspiring writer to know what a skilled writer knows? How can we help novice mathematics and science students to acquire the knowledge needed to think like skilled mathematicians and scientists? These are the kinds of instructional questions that are addressed in this book. In short, we wish to understand the kinds of learning experiences that foster cognitive growth in learners.

In summary, this book takes a learner-centered approach to educational psychology by examining the cognitive issue of determining the cognitive processes that students use on academic tasks and the instructional issue of how to help students develop the appropriate cognitive processes for academic tasks. The remainder of this chapter explores some of the basic issues in educational psychology.

WHAT IS EDUCATIONAL PSYCHOLOGY?

A DEFINITION OF EDUCATIONAL PSYCHOLOGY

What is educational psychology? Based on the learner-centered perspective described in the previous section, educational psychology can be defined as a branch of psychology concerned with understanding how the instructional environment and the characteristics of the learner interact to produce cognitive growth in the learner. In particular, educational psychology focuses on the scientific study of techniques for manipulating human cognitive processes and knowledge states. There are three major components in this definition:

1. Educational psychology is a science, namely a branch of psychology.
2. Educational psychology investigates the instructor's manipulation of the environment.
3. Educational psychology investigates resulting changes in the learner's cognitive processes and knowledge structures.

As a discipline, educational psychology is poised between teaching and learning (i.e., between the instructional manipulations provided by the teacher and the changes in knowledge and behavior created in the learner). *Teaching* refers to the teacher's construction of environments for the student that are intended to foster changes in the learner's knowledge and behavior. For example, Gagne (1974) defines instruction as "the arrangement of external events to activate and support the internal processes of learning" (p. vii). *Learning* refers to changes in the learner's knowledge that arise from experience. In his classic textbook *Principles of Teaching Based on Psychology,* Thorndike (1906) recognized that the central theme in education is an externally manipulated change in the learner:

> The word education is used with many meanings, but in all its usages it refers to changes. No one is educated who stays as he was. We do not educate anybody if we do nothing that makes any difference or change in anybody. . . . In studying education, then, one studies always the existence, nature, causation or value of change of some sort. (p. 1)

In summary, teaching and learning are inevitably connected processes that involve the fostering of change within the learner.

In his provocative little book *Experience and Education,* Dewey (1938, p. 25) described the relationship between teaching—the process of providing students with useful experiences—and learning—the students' acquisition of knowledge. "All genuine education comes about through experience," he argued. However, he added an important warning that "all experiences are not genuinely or equally educative." Unfortunately, many instructional manipulations are what Dewey (1938) calls "mis-educative":

Some experiences are mis-educative. Any experience is mis-educative that has the effect of arresting or distorting the growth of further experiences. . . . Every experience lives on in further experiences. Hence the central problem of an education based on experience is to select the kind of present experiences that live fruitfully and creatively in subsequent experiences. (p. 25)

Thus instructional manipulations result in changes in the learner's knowledge. Since all learning involves connecting new information to existing knowledge, it is crucial to help students develop knowledge structures that can support the acquisition of useful new information. If students have not acquired knowledge, they cannot successfully connect incoming information with it.

BEHAVIORIST VERSUS COGNITIVE APPROACHES TO EDUCATIONAL PSYCHOLOGY

This definition of educational psychology raises the question of what is learned by students—a behavioral change or a cognitive change—and points to the classic tension between behaviorist and cognitive approaches to learning. Although this book is based on a cognitive approach, it is useful to examine both positions.

A behaviorist approach to educational psychology is summarized in the top of Figure 1–2. As you can see, the behaviorist approach involves deter-

FIGURE 1–2 Two approaches to educational psychology

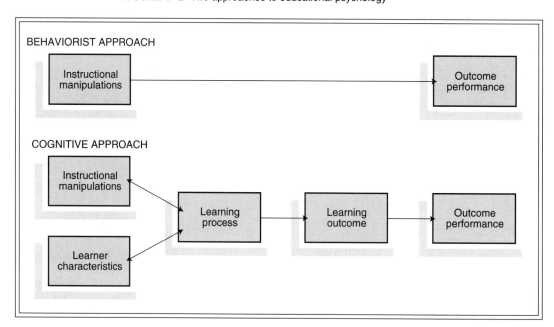

mining the relationship between two factors—instructional manipulations and outcome performance. Both correspond to externally observable events: instructional manipulations refer to the nature of the stimulus that is presented to the learner, while outcome performance refers to the nature of the response that the learner gives on tests. According to this approach, the goal of educational psychology is to determine how instructional manipulations affect changes in behavior. Thus the main question here is: What is the relationship between instructional manipulations and outcome performance?

In contrast, a cognitive approach to educational psychology is summarized in the bottom of Figure 1–2. As you can see, the cognitive approach involves determining the relationships among external factors (e.g., instructional manipulations and outcome performance) and internal factors (e.g., learning processes, learning outcomes, and learner characteristics such as existing knowledge and skill). The cognitive approach attempts to understand how instructional manipulations affect internal cognitive processes such as paying attention, encoding, and retrieving; how these processes result in the acquisition of new knowledge; and how new knowledge influences performance, such as on tests. According to the cognitive approach, the goal of educational psychology is to explain the relationship between stimulus (i.e., instructional manipulation) and response (i.e., outcome performance) by describing the intervening cognitive processes and structures. Thus, the main question here is: What are the internal cognitive processes and states that allow us to understand the relationship between instructional manipulations and outcome performance?

The distinction between these two approaches to educational psychology is certainly not new. For example, in his classic book *The Nature of Intelligence,* Thurstone (1924) argued against behaviorist approaches to education:

> A brand of educational psychology is being taught to prospective
> teachers in which they are drilled in the jargon of establishing
> "bonds" between stimuli and the desired behavior. It would be
> more appropriate to describe the normal impulses of children,
> and the methods by which children may be induced to express
> these impulses in ways that are profitable. (p. 165)

In essence, Thurstone asserted that there is more to learning than helping students build stimulus-response (S-R) connections; indeed, the internal processes of the learner play a central role in the education process.

Thurstone's complaint, and those of modern cognitive educational psychologists, have had little impact on educational practice until fairly recently. However, during the past twenty-five years, there has been an explosion of research and theory on the workings of the human mind works (Mayer, 1981a, 1992). One useful product of this cognitive revolution has been the development of a framework for describing the cognitive factors underlying the teaching/learning process.

By using a cognitive approach, this book offers an integrated approach to educational psychology that may be described as follows:

Useful: If we find out that instructional method A results in more learning that instructional method B, it is useful to also know why this is so in order to determine when to use the methods, how to modify them, and so on.

Current: The cognitive approach is a more recently developed perspective that enhances and interprets earlier behaviorist work.

Widespread: Because the cognitive approach has come to dominate most fields of psychology, including the study of how we perceive, learn, remember, and think, it can also be applied successfully to educational psychology.

FACTORS IN THE TEACHING/LEARNING PROCESS

Table 1–1 summarizes some examples of factors that might be involved in the teaching/learning process. The factors are as follows:

Instructional manipulations: The sequence of environmental (i.e., external) events, including the organization and content of instructional materials and behaviors of the teacher. The instructional manipulations include both what is taught and how it is taught, and depend on the characteristics of the teacher and on the curriculum.

Learner characteristics: The learner's existing knowledge, including facts, procedures, and strategies that may be required in the learning situation, and the nature of the learner's memory system, including its capacity and mode of representation in memory.

Learning processes: The learner's internal cognitive processes during learning, such as how the learner selects, organizes, and integrates new information with existing knowledge.

Learning outcomes: The cognitive changes in the learner's knowledge or memory system, including the newly acquired facts, procedures, and strategies.

Outcome performance: The learner's performance (i.e., behavior) on tests that measure the amount of retention or the ability to transfer knowledge to new learning tasks.

TABLE 1–1 Examples of factors in the teaching/ learning process	Instructional Manipulations	Learner Characteristics	Learning Processes	Learning Outcomes	Outcome Performance
	Repeating a lesson	Existing knowledge	Selecting information	Rote learning	Retention
	Providing examples	Existing information-processing strategies	Organizing information	Meaningful learning	Transfer
	Asking questions		Integrating information		

Adapted from Mayer (1984)

Because the cognitive approach involves several factors that are internal to the learner—learner characteristics, learning processes, and learning outcomes—it is clearly learner centered. Since these factors are not directly observable, they can only be inferred from the learner's behavior. Thus a major challenge of the cognitive approach is to devise methods of study that allow us to make correct inferences about internal processes and states in the learner.

A BRIEF HISTORY OF THE RELATIONSHIP BETWEEN PSYCHOLOGY AND EDUCATION

What is proper relationship between psychology in education? How does the psychologist's view of learning affect the educator's approach to instruction? In this section we explore the historical evolution of three paths for the role of psychology in education, and three views of learning and instruction.

THREE ROADS FOR PSYCHOLOGY IN EDUCATION

Psychology involves studying how people learn and develop, whereas education involves helping people to learn and develop. What do you think should be the relationship between psychology and education? Check one of the answers below:

_____ Psychologists should conduct laboratory research about learning and development, and explain the resulting theories to educators; educators should apply this scientific research to their instruction.

_____ Psychologists should conduct laboratory research about learning and development without concern for educators; educators should develop instruction that meets the practical needs of their students without examining irrelevant psychological theories.

_____ Psychologists should study how people learn and develop in real educational situations, basing their research on the challenges of educators; educators should base their instructional decisions on psychological theories of how students learn and develop.

If you chose the first answer, you have opted for a one-way street that runs from psychology to education. If you chose the second answer, you have selected a dead-end street on which psychology and education do not meet. If you chose the third answer, you have decided on a path that seems to be a two-way street running from psychology to education and from education to psychology.

These three kinds of paths represent three phases in the history of psychology in education in the United States (Mayer, 1992, 1996a). By the 1890s psychologists, who had recently given birth to what Gardner (1985) has called "the mind's new science," were struggling to keep their infant science alive. At the same time educators, who faced the daunting new task of providing universal compulsory education, were struggling to professionalize the practice of teaching. The rise of psychology and education in the late nineteenth century led to the question of what should be the proper relationship between psychologists and educators. In short, what should be the path between the science of psychology and the practice of education? The answer to this question has passed through three major phases: (1) a one-way street—a phase of naive optimism during the early 1900s in which psychological advances would be applied directly to improving education, (2) a dead-end street—a pessimistic phase during the mid-1900s in which the paths of psychology and education failed to cross, and (3) a two-way street—the rebirth of optimism during the latter part of the 1900s in which educational issues shape psychological research and psychological research informs educational practice. These three paths are summarized in Table 1–2.

PHASE 1: ONE-WAY STREET FROM PSYCHOLOGY TO EDUCATION. At the start of this century, educational psychologists were optimistic that psychological science could improve educational practice. They viewed educational psychology as the "guiding science of the school" (Cubberly, 1920, p. 755)—a discipline that borrowed its research methods from psychology and its research agenda from education. In his classic book, *The Principles of Teaching Based on Psychology,* Thorndike (1906) proclaimed:

> The efficiency of any profession depends in large measure upon the degree to which it becomes scientific. The profession of teaching will improve (1) in proportion as its members direct their work by the scientific spirit and methods, that is by honest, open-

TABLE 1–2	Phase	Direction of Relation	Period	Emotional Tone	Vision for Psychology and Education
Three paths for psychology and education	Phase 1	One-way street	Early 1900s	Naive optimism	Psychology is applied to education; education is recipient of psychology
	Phase 2	Dead-end street	Mid-1900s	Pessimism	Psychology ignores education; education ignores psychology
	Phase 3	Two-way street	Late 1900s	Cautious optimism	Education shapes psychological research; psychology shapes educational practice

minded consideration of facts, by freedom from superstitions, fancies, and unverified guesses, and (2) in proportion as the leaders in education direct their choices of methods by the results of scientific investigation rather than general opinion. (p. 206)

As the first editor of the *Journal of Educational Psychology* in 1910, Thorndike envisioned that educational psychologists would apply the exact methods of science to the problems of education. Thus began this 100-year-old vision that the "proper application of psychological findings might lead the way to better instruction in all schools" (Woodring, 1958, p. 6).

Yet even during the optimism of the early 1900s, educational psychologists recognized that psychology was not likely to be able to satisfy the needs of educators. In his famous lectures on psychology for teachers, which he later published as *Talks to Teachers,* the great American psychologist William James (1899/1958) admitted his doubts as follows:

The desire of the schoolteachers for a completer professional training, and their aspiration toward the professional spirit in their work, have led more and more to turn to us for light on fundamental principles. . . . You look to me . . . for information concerning the mind's operation, which may enable you to labor more easily and effectively in the several classrooms over which you preside. . . . Psychology ought certainly to give the teacher radical help. And yet I confess that, acquainted as I am with the height of your expectations, I feel a little anxious lest, at the end of these simple talks of mine, not a few of you may experience some disappointment at the net results. (p. 22)

James acknowledged two obstacles blocking the application of psychology to education. First, he correctly observed that the psychology of the late 1800s lacked a sufficient data base and that much work needed to be done to test psychological theories. Second, James (1899/1958) warned that psychological research results and theories would not necessarily translate directly into prescriptions for classroom practice: "You make a great, a very great mistake, if you think that psychology, being a science of the mind's laws, is something from which you can deduce definite programmes and schemes and methods of instruction for immediate classroom use" (p. 23).

PHASE 2: DEAD-END STREET FOR PSYCHOLOGY IN EDUCATION. Despite the aspirations of the early educational psychologists, the discipline of educational psychology was in serious trouble by the mid-1900s. Educators and psychologists became pessimistic concerning whether educational psychology would be able to assume its role as the guiding science of education. Psychologists busied themselves studying learning by using experiments with laboratory animals, such as rats running in mazes, or human learning of senseless material in rigid laboratory settings, such as memorizing lists of nonsense syllables—issues that seemed far removed from the world of education. Educators focused on practical issues, such as whether one method was better than another for teaching a given skill, while failing to base educational decisions on a coherent theory of how students learn.

Grinder (1989) has identified three reasons for the decline of educational psychology in the mid-1900s:

Withdrawal: Educational psychologists lost interest in contributing to educational policy.

Fractionation: Educational psychologists failed to achieve a coherent theoretical perspective.

Irrelevance: Educational psychologists focused on research issues far removed from the problems of schooling.

In short, during this dead-end phase, psychology and education became disconnected.

PHASE 3: TWO-WAY STREET BETWEEN PSYCHOLOGY AND EDUCATION. Something happened in the late 1950s and early 1960s that brought about a new phase of optimism to educational psychology. That something was the "transition from behavioral to cognitive psychology" (DiVesta, 1989, p. 39), or what Scandura et al. (1981) called the "shift from S-R [stimulus-response] to information processing" theories (p. 367). The cognitive revolution in educational psychology highlighted "the learner as an active participant in the learning process" (DiVesta, 1989, p. 54). It also encouraged research into how real students learn in real classroom settings, with a particular focus on the individual learning strategies used to learn school material such as reading, writing, or arithmetic. This view allowed the discipline of educational psychology to overcome the withdrawal, fractionation, and irrelevance that had plagued it.

In a recent historical review, Mayer (1992) asked, "Can educational psychology regain its position as the guiding science of education?" (p. 406). In many ways, this book provides the latest installment in educational psychology's quest to become the place where psychology and education meet. During the first part of this century, educational psychology failed largely because it lacked the research tools and data base necessary to improve education; during the middle part of the century, educational psychology failed because it was unwilling to build theories that were relevant to improving education; but during the last part of this century, educational psychology has acquired both the research tools and theories that are relevant to improving education. After nearly 100 years, there again is cause for optimism concerning the vision of educational practice based on scientific theory as well as psychological theories of real human learning.

The road between psychology and education has become a two-way street. The road runs from education to psychology: By providing the research agenda, education challenges psychology to develop theories about real people in real situations, rather than theories that are limited to how people learn contrived tasks in artificial laboratory settings. This road travels from psychology to education. By developing useful theories of human learning, cognition, and development, psychology provides the basis for making informed decisions about educational practice. In summary, "educational psychology—rather than being the place solely to apply psychological theories that have been developed elsewhere—is an exciting venue for shaping and testing the dominant psychological theories of the day" (Mayer, 1993, p. 553).

THREE METAPHORS OF LEARNING

How would you complete the following sentence? Learning is like:

_____ Strengthening a connection (i.e., adding new behaviors to your repertoire)

_____ Adding files to a file cabinet (i.e., adding new facts and skills to your knowledge base)

_____ Building a model (i.e., understanding how to fit pieces of information together into a structure)

If you chose the first answer, you seem to view *learning as response strengthening*—the idea that learning involves adding new responses to an ever-growing collection. If you chose the second answer, you view *learning as knowledge acquisition*—the idea that learning involves transferring knowledge from the teacher's head to the student's head. If you chose the third answer, you view *learning as knowledge construction*—the idea that students actively create their own learning by trying to make sense of their experiences.

These three views of learning represent three persistent metaphors that have been developed over the history of psychology in education—metaphors that have been invented by psychologists and applied by educators. Examining your personal metaphor of learning is worthwhile because educational practice can be influenced by the educator's underlying metaphor of learning. Table 1–3 summarizes three common metaphors

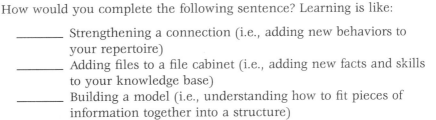

TABLE 1–3

Three metaphors of learning

Learning	The Learner	The Teacher	Typical Instructional Methods
Response strengthening	Passive recipient of rewards and punishments	Dispenser of rewards and punishments	Drill and practice on basic skills
Knowledge acquisition	Information-processor	Dispenser of information	Textbooks, workbooks, and lectures
Knowledge construction	Sense-maker	Guide for understanding academic tasks	Discussion, guided discovery, and supervised participation in meaningful tasks

for learning—learning as response strengthening, learning as knowledge acquisition, and learning as knowledge construction.

LEARNING AS RESPONSE STRENGTHENING. The first metaphor to gain broad acceptance in psychology was learning as response strengthening, which evolved throughout the first half of the 20th century and was based largely on research on laboratory animals. According to this view, learning is a mechanical process in which successful responses to a given situation are automatically strengthened and unsuccessful responses are weakened. In this way, learning is seen as the strengthening or weakening of the association between a stimulus (S) and a response (R). Thus, the term "response strengthening" includes the idea of both strengthening and weaking of responses, or more properly, of stimulus-response (S-R) associations. For example, the S-R association to be strengthened in reading may be the one between the printed word "cat" and its corresponding sound; in writing, between the spoken word "cat" and its corresponding spelling "c-a-t"; and in arithmetic, between "4 + 4 = " and "8." Accordingly, the learner becomes a passive recipient who is completely shaped by reinforcements in the environment, and the teacher becomes a feedback dispenser who delivers rewards and punishments.

The learning-as-response-strengthening view suggests educational practice in which the teacher creates situations that require short responses, the learner gives a response, and the teacher provides the appropriate reward or punishment. For example, the teacher may ask, "What is 750 divided by 5?" If the student responds with the correct answer (i.e., 150), the teacher says, "Right, good job." If the student responds with an incorrect answer (250, for example), the teacher may say, "No, you need to review the worksheet." As you can see, drill-and-practice is a popular method of instruction that is consistent with the learning-as-response-strengthening metaphor. When they accept the learning-as-response-strengthening metaphor, educators emphasize teaching of basic skills in reading, writing, and arithmetic.

LEARNING AS KNOWLEDGE ACQUISITION. The second metaphor, learning as knowledge acquisition, developed during the 1960s and 1970s as research shifted from studying animal learning in laboratory settings to studying human learning in laboratory settings. According to this view, learning occurs when information is transferred from a more knowledgeable person (such as a teacher) to a less knowledgeable person (such as a student). In this way, learning is like filling a void, i.e., like pouring information into a student's memory. Within this metaphor, the learner becomes a processor of information, and the teacher becomes a dispenser of information. Information is a commodity that the teacher gives to the student.

The learning-as-knowledge-acquisition view suggests educational practice in which the teacher presents new information for the student to learn. For example, the teacher may ask students to read a section in their science textbooks on how electricity flows in a circuit and then test them on the material. As you can see, the goal of instruction is to increase the amount of knowledge in the learner's memory, so textbooks and lectures offer popular methods of instruction. When educators call for covering material in the curriculum, they are working under a learning-as-knowledge-acquisition metaphor.

LEARNING AS KNOWLEDGE CONSTRUCTION. The third metaphor is learning as knowledge construction, the idea that learners actively build their own mental representations as they attempt to make sense of their experiences. This view grew out of research on human learning in realistic settings conducted since the 1970s and 1980s. Learning occurs when people select relevant information, organize it into a coherent structures, and interpret it through what they already know. Resnick (1989) expresses this view as follows: "Learning occurs not by recording information but by interpreting it" (p. 2). According to this view, the learner is a sense-maker and the teacher is a guide who assists students as they seek to understand how to perform academic tasks. The focus is on helping the learner to build cognitive strategies for academic learning tasks.

The educational practices suggested by the learning-as-knowledge-construction view include group discussions and supervised participation in meaningful academic tasks. For example, in learning how to write, students may discuss how they plan what to say and the teacher may offer suggestions along the way. Instead of emphasizing the product of learning, such as how much is learned, this view emphasizes the process of learning, such as strategies for how to learn and understand. When educators take a learner-centered approach, they are operating within the learning-as-knowledge-construction metaphor.

There is merit to each of these metaphors and the instructional methods they suggest (Mayer, 1996a). However, in this book I rely most heavily on the learning-as-knowledge-construction metaphor because I believe it offers the most potential benefit for improving education and promoting the promise of educational psychology. By emphasizing knowledge construction, I do not mean to diminish the value of learning basic skills, such as facts and procedures. However, according to the knowledge-construction metaphor, basic skills should be learned in the context of larger academic tasks rather than in isolation. For example, Ohm's Law could be learned as part of a project involving the design of a real electrical circuit rather than memorizing the formula in isolation.

A CLOSER LOOK AT THE LEARNER-CENTERED APPROACH

This book is concerned mainly with influencing the intellectual growth of the learner and more specifically with understanding how instructional manipulations affect changes in the learner's knowledge, including changes in cognitive strategies and memory structure. Because the learner's construction of knowledge is at the center of the educational process, the essence of education is to effect changes in the learner's knowledge as manifested in changes in academic, motor, social, and personal behavior.

KINDS OF KNOWLEDGE

Cognitive psychologists have found it useful to distinguish among several kinds of knowledge, including the following (Mayer, 1981a, 1992):

Semantic knowledge: A person's factual knowledge about the world, including what Gagne (1974) calls verbal information. Examples include knowing the capital of California and the number of sides in a square.

Conceptual knowledge: A person's representation of the major concepts in a system. Examples include being able to answer questions such as, "What is difference between the units column and the tens column in 39 + 45?"

Schematic knowledge: A person's knowledge of problem types such as being able to distinguish between word problems that require the use of a time-rate-distance formula and those requiring a formula for computing interest.

Procedural knowledge: A person's knowledge of an algorithm, or list of steps, that can be used in a specific situation, including what Gagne (1974) calls "intellectual skill." An example is being able to use the procedure for long division in order to solve the problem, $234,234/13 = $ _____. Other examples include being able to classify objects, such as different geometric shapes, into categories, or being able to change a word to plural form using the rule "Add s."

Strategic knowledge: A person's possession of a general approach for how to learn, remember, or solve problems, including the self-monitoring of progress in the use of the strategy. Gagne (1974) refers to this kind of knowledge as "cognitive strategy." Examples include being able to design and monitor a plan for composing an essay, or to decide on a technique for memorizing a list of definitions.

In subsequent chapters, we shall explore how each kind of knowledge is related to school tasks. Although there are other kinds of knowledge, including affective, motoric, personal, and social knowledge, this book will focus mainly on those listed above, which have been the object of most of the research.

KINDS OF MEMORY STORES AND LEARNING PROCESSES

If knowledge construction is at the center of educational psychology, then the learner's memory system is where the action is! Figure 1–3 describes the basic architecture of the memory system. As you can see, there are three main components indicated as rectangles:

FIGURE 1–3 An information-processing model of the memory system

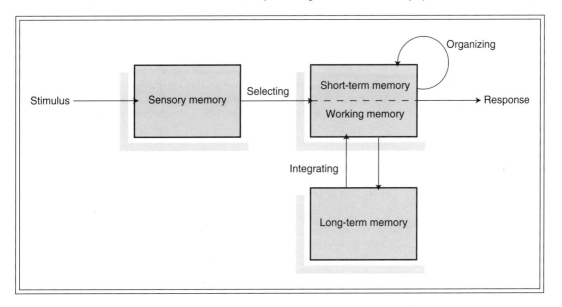

Sensory memory: Incoming information is accepted by the sense
receptors which is held very briefly in a sensory memory store.
According to the classic model, the capacity of sensory memory
is unlimited, the mode of representation is sensory, the duration
is very brief (e.g., a half-second for visual information), and loss
occurs due to time decay.

Short-term memory: If you pay attention to the incoming information before it decays, you may be able to transfer some of it to
short-term memory (STM), which corresponds to active con-
sciousness or awareness. According to the classic model, the
capacity of short-term memory is extremely limited (e.g., you
can actively think about only five or so different things at one
time), the mode is acoustic or related to some other modification of the sensory input, the duration is temporary (e.g., items
are lost after about 18 seconds unless they are actively
rehearsed), and loss is due to new information displacing existing items in STM. In addition, a portion of STM, known as
working memory, can be used for performing mental manipulations such as mental arithmetic.

Long-term memory: If you encode the information from STM into
long-term memory (LTM), some of it may be retained perma-
nently. LTM has unlimited capacity, including the three kinds of
knowledge listed above; can retain information for long periods;
and loses information when other information interferes with
retrieving the target information.

In addition to these three components, the arrows in the figure represent basic learning processes:

> **Selecting** involves focusing attention on the relevant pieces of the presented information and adding them to STM, as indicated in Figure 1–3 by the arrow from SM to STM. In paying attention to some of the information that enters through your eyes and ears, you are selecting pieces of information for further processing in STM. Sternberg (1985) refers to this process as *selective encoding* and defines it as "sifting out relevant from irrelevant information" (p. 107).
>
> **Organizing** involves constructing internal connections among the incoming pieces of information in STM, as indicated in Figure 1–3 by the arrow from STM to STM. In constructing internal connections, the learner is "organizing the selected information . . . into a coherent whole" (Mayer, 1984, p. 32). Sternberg (1985) refers to this process as *selective combination,* and defines it as "combining selectively encoded information in such a way as to form an integrated . . . internally connected whole" (p. 107).
>
> **Integrating** involves constructing external connections between the newly organized knowledge in STM and existing relevant knowledge that the learner retrieves from LTM, as indicated by the arrow from LTM to STM. This process involves "connecting the organized information to other familiar knowledge structures already in memory" (Mayer, 1984, p. 33). Sternberg (1985) refers to integrating as *selective comparison,* and describes it as "relating newly acquired or retrieved knowledge . . . to old knowledge so as to form an externally connected whole" (p. 107).

The learner thus uses selecting, organizing, and integrating processes to construct new knowledge in short-term memory. Knowledge constructed in STM is transferred to LTM for permanent storage via the process of *encoding* which is represented by the arrow from STM to LTM.

COGNITIVE CONDITIONS FOR MEANINGFUL LEARNING

Now that we have briefly explored the kinds of knowledge and the architecture of the memory system, let's return more closely to the theme of this book—the promise of educational psychology. For example, suppose that we ask students to read a short lesson on how lightning occurs. Then we give them a retention test to measure how much of the presented information they remember and a transfer test to measure how well they can creatively apply what they learned to solve new problems. The retention test could include items such as "A lightning flash lasts about _____ microseconds" or "The amount of electrical potential in a lightning flash is _____ volts." The transfer test could ask, "How could you decrease the intensity of lightning?"

Some students will not remember much from the lesson or be able to answer transfer questions; they could be called the nonlearners. Others

TABLE 1–4	Type of Learner	Retention Performance	Transfer Performance
Three kinds of learners	Nonlearner	Poor	Poor
	Nonunderstander	Good	Poor
	Understander	Good	Good

Adapted from Mayer (1984)

will remember much of the information but will not be able to use it creatively to solve problems or make explanations; they could be called the nonunderstanders (or rote learners). Finally, certain students might be able to remember information and to use it creatively in solving novel problems; they are the understanders. Table 1–4 summarizes the differences in the performances among these three types of learners.

What conditions of learning create each of these kinds of outcomes? Gagne (1974) has made a useful distinction between two kinds of conditions of learning: *internal conditions* refer to the cognitive processes that are activated inside the learner at the time of learning, and *external conditions* refer to the instructional events that occur outside of the learner.

Mayer (1984, 1989, 1996b) has suggested that three major internal conditions must be met for instruction to foster meaningful learning: instruction must help the learner to select relevant information, to organize information, and to integrate information, as summarized in Figure 1–4. Based on these three conditions, three learning scenarios can be generated:

FIGURE 1–4 The three major conditions of meaningful learning

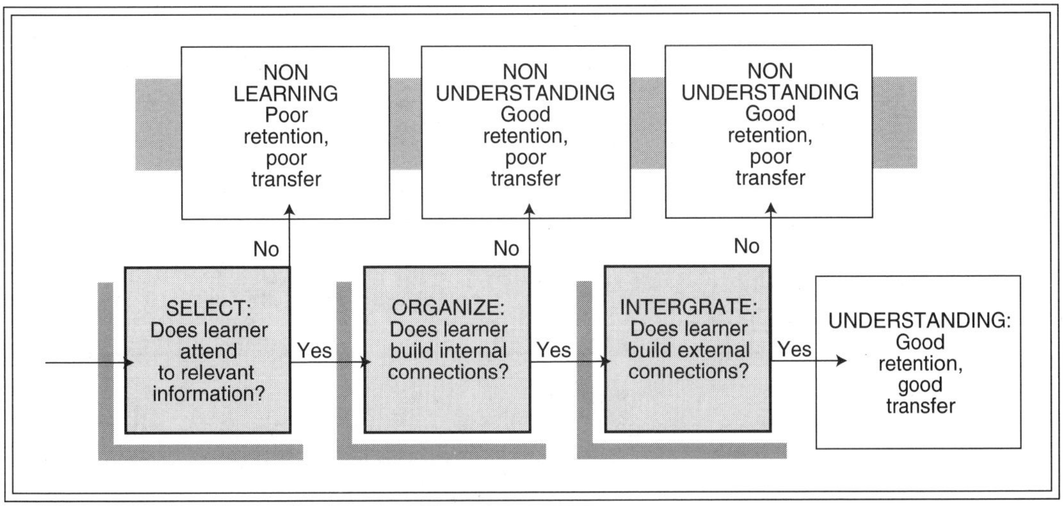

Nonlearning: If the first condition is not met, nothing will be learned. Thus even when a student may be actively thinking about all he or she knows about lightning, nothing will be learned if the student fails to read the passage carefully. This result is indicated by poor retention and poor transfer performance.

Nonunderstanding: If the first condition is met but the second or third condition is not, the student will learn in a nonmeaningful way. For example, in reading a passage on lightning, the second condition would be lacking if the learner fails to create a cause-and-effect chain among events in the process of lightning. Similarly, the third condition would be missing if the learner does not possess or activate relevant existing knowledge (e.g., the concepts of temperature imbalance and electrical imbalance), to integrate with the material. This result is indicated by good retention and poor transfer performance.

Understanding: If all three conditions are met, the student will learn in a meaningful way. For example, the new information about lightning will be organized into a coherent cause-and-effect structure and integrated with existing knowledge about temperature and electrical imbalances. The result is manifested in good retention and transfer performance.

Although these distinctions are much too vague to qualify as a theory of instruction, they do provide a framework for describing kinds of learning situations. The main theme, of course, is that meaningful learning depends on active cognitive processing during learning—that is, on the active construction of knowledge.

In addition, three external conditions required for instruction to foster meaningful learning are that: (1) the material is potentially meaningful; (2) the learner needs help; and (3) the test evaluates meaningful learning. If the material is not understandable (e.g., a random list of unconnected facts), no type of instruction can help the learner make sense of it. If the learner already knows how to select, organize, and integrate information in a lesson, then instruction aimed at inducing the learner to use these processes is not needed. Finally, if the test simply measures overall amount of information retained, it is not possible to show that meaningful learning has occurred.

WHAT IS THE PROMISE OF EDUCATIONAL PSYCHOLOGY?

From today's vantage point, 200 years after Dr. Itard's valiant efforts to teach Victor using learner-centered methods and 100 years after the beginnings of the scientific discipline of educational psychology, the future of educational psychology looks promising once again. Although education and psychology have had a rocky relationship in the past, today's educational psychology holds great promise for improving educational practice and advancing psychological theory.

The two most promising contributions of educational psychology are as follows:

Psychologies of subject matter, which focus on development, learning, instruction, and cognition within the context of specific subject areas.

Cognitive analyses of learner knowledge, which focus on the individual learner's specific cognitive processes and knowledge for academic tasks.

In short, the promise of educational psychology rests in its focus on the specific cognitive processes used by students on authentic academic tests.

The first promising contribution of educational psychology is a focus on psychologies of subject matter. In contrast to traditional experimental psychology's focus on developing general theories of how people learn, develop, or think, today's educational psychology seeks to build domain-specific theories within each subject area. For example, instead of asking general questions such as "How do people learn?" or "How do people develop?" or "How do people think?", we can ask, "How do people learn to solve mathematics problems?" or "How do people develop mathematical competence?" or "How do people think mathematically?" By examining cognition in the context of real academic tasks rather than in contrived laboratory tasks, we can develop more realistic theories of how people learn, develop, and think. These theories—based on cognition in academic contexts—are more relevant for guiding instruction. Although there has been sporadic interest in psychologies of subject matter throughout the 20th century—such as Huey's (1908/1968) *Psychology and Pedagogy of Reading* or Thorndike's (1922) *Psychology of Arithmetic*—the groundbreaking consensus to focus on specific subject domains has occurred only within the last 20 years (Shulman & Quinlan, 1996).

The second promising contribution of educational psychology is its focus on detailed analyses of the cognitive processes and knowledge in individual learners. In contrast to traditional experimental psychology's focus on comparing averages of one group against those of another, today's educational psychology seeks to describe the cognitive processes and knowledge required for success on a given task. Instead of asking "How much does group A know?", we can ask, "What does learner A know?" or "Which cognitive processes does learner A engage in?" By understanding the cognitive processes and knowledge of skilled students, it is possible to establish specific goals of instruction for less skilled students. In contrast to more gross measurements of what students know, cognitive analyses offer a level of precision that is helpful for guiding instruction. Like the focus on subject areas, the emphasis on detailed cognitive analyses has only arisen within the last 20 years.

Educational psychology has a unique and central role to play within the fields of education and psychology. To education, educational psychology can contribute a theoretical account of how the human mind works in academic settings, including how students learn, remember, and use academic knowledge. By constructing cognitive theories of academic learning, educational psychologists foster the development of more effective methods of instruction. In short, educational psychology offers an alternative to education's unproductive proclivity for basing instructional practice on undocumented fads. To psychology, educational psychology can contribute an ecologically valid context for generating and testing cognitive theories. By challenging psychologists to develop theories that can account for academic learning, educational psychologists insure the authenticity of cognitive theories. In short, education psychology offers an alternative to psychology's unproductive record of developing precise theories of artificial learning tasks.

In many ways, this book represents a progress report on recent advances in the cognitive psychology of subject matter. To explore these promising contributions of educational psychology, the remainder of the book is divided into five chapters, covering some selected academic tasks—learning how to read academic texts, learning how to comprehend academic texts, learning how to write academic essays, learning how to solve mathematics problems, and learning how to solve scientific problems. In each chapter, we begin with a cognitive analysis of the academic task, that is, we explore each of the cognitive processes required for success on that task. Then we examine instructional techniques for helping students to develop the ability to engage in these processes. In short, each chapter focuses on learning and teaching in a specific subject area: reading fluency, reading comprehension, writing, mathematics, and science.

CONCLUSION

The example of the "wild boy" of Aveyron raises issues concerning the role of education in human development. A boy raised in the wild without human guidance apparently failed to reach his full potential as a human being. This case suggests that natural experience—everyday interactions with the environment—must be supplemented by manipulated experience—instructional sequences designed by teachers. The example is important because it was one of the first to emphasize a learner-centered view of education.

Educational psychology is a branch of psychology concerned with understanding how the instructional environment and the characteristics of the learner interact to produce cognitive growth in the learner. Thorndike and Dewey both recognized that the central theme in education is an externally manipulated change in the learner. The definition of educational psychology requires a distinction between the behaviorist approach, which focuses solely on external conditions of learning such as instructional manipulations and outcome performance, and the cognitive approach, which adds internal conditions of learning such as learner characteristics, learning processes, and learning outcomes.

The history of the relationship between psychology and education includes three phases: a one-way street, in which educators were supposed to apply what psychologists created; a dead-end street, in which psychology and education went their separate ways; and a two-way street, in which psychology and education mutually enrich one another. In addition, the history of psychology and education includes the progression of three metaphors—learning as response strengthening, learning as knowledge acquisition, and learning as knowledge construction.

The learner-centered approach is based on the idea that instruction helps learners to bring about changes in their knowledge. Five kinds of knowledge are semantic, conceptual, schematic, procedural, and strategic knowledge. The architecture of the memory system includes memory stores—sensory memory, short-term memory, and long-term memory—and memory processes—selecting, organizing, and integrating. Instructional manipulations may result in no learning, nonunderstanding, or understanding. Understanding, or meaningful learning, requires that the learner pay attention, possess appropriate prerequisite knowledge, and actively organize and integrate the new information with existing knowledge.

The promise of educational psychology rests in determining the cognitive processes of successful students for various academic tasks and fostering the development of these processes in less successful students. Educational psychology offers insight into how the cognitive conditions for meaningful learning interact to result in intellectual changes in the learner. The remainder of this book examines cognition and instruction in the subject areas of reading, writing, mathematics, and science.

SUGGESTED READINGS

Berliner, D., & Calfee, R. (Eds.). (1997). *Handbook of educational psychology.* New York: Macmillan. (Systematically presents everything you ever wanted to know about educational psychology.)

Bruer, J. T. (1993). *Schools for thought: A science of learning in the classroom.* Cambridge, MA: MIT Press. (Reviews cognitive science research on learning in various content areas.)

Dewey, J. (1938). *Experience and education.* New York: Collier. (Provides a dose of Dewey's "child-centered" educational philosophy.)

Gagne, E. D., Yekovich, C. W., & Yekovich, F. R. (1993). *The cognitive psychology of school learning* (2nd ed.). New York: Harper Collins. (Summarizes modern cognitive research and its relation to the psychology of instruction.)

CHAPTER 2 Reading Fluency

CHAPTER OUTLINE

Learning to read is a fundamental national goal, because academic and economic success often build on the ability to read words quickly and effortlessly. Unfortunately, one out of five adults in the United States is functionally illiterate, and these people account for 75% of the unemployed and 60% of the prison population (Adams, 1990). This chapter is concerned with early reading instruction. In particular, this chapter focuses on four processes involved in learning to read: recognizing the sound units that comprise words, decoding the symbols on the page into pronounced words, accessing the meaning of each word in long-term memory, and integrating the words into a coherent sentence. Research and instructional implications are explored for each of these topics.

THE PROBLEM OF READING A WORD

Let's consider the task of reading words from a printed page, as you are doing now. How much time do you think that it takes you to read a typical word? The answer is that competent adult readers can read a word in a fraction of a second, usually less than one-quarter of a second (Crowder & Wagner, 1992; Just & Carpenter, 1980; Rayner & Pollatsek, 1989). The act of reading a word may seem so rapid and so automatic that it could not possibly involve much cognitive processing. However, in this introduction, I will try to convince you that the seemingly simple act of reading a word may indeed involve many cognitive processes.

WHAT COGNITIVE PROCESSES ARE INVOLVED IN READING A WORD?

First, say aloud each of the four words in the first row of Figure 2–1. Based on the sounds in the words, circle the word that lacks a sound that is present in the other three words. Now, follow this same procedure for each set of four words. This is a test of *phonological awareness,* that is, the ability to recognize that words are made up of component sounds. For example, in the first row of Figure 2–1 the sound unit (or *phoneme*) that is common to three words is /ng/, so the correct answer is "pain." The other answers are "fan," "treat," and "light." When Bradley and Bryant (1978) used a similar task to evaluate students' ability to recognize sound units in words, they found that good readers were successful but that poor readers often were not. It thus appears that an important process in reading is recognizing the separate phonemes that make up words as separate sound units.

FIGURE 2–1 Which word does not belong?

For each set of four words, circle the word that does not belong:

1. song   long   pain   wrong

2. hit   pit   fan   kit

3. boat   treat   bank   bunk

4. shoe   light   ship   sheet

FIGURE 2–2 Can you pronounce these words?

caws	fign
saif	shud
wight	phrend
hought	blud
frish	nal
ait	

Second, try to pronounce each "word" in Figure 2–2. If you are like most adult readers, you used a variety of pronunciation strategies and made errors on about one-tenth of the words (Baron, 1977). Some possible strategies are sounding out the letters and blending them together, finding a real word that rhymes with the nonsense word, and pronouncing a real word that is similar to the nonsense word. This word-pronunciation task highlights an aspect of reading that is referred to as *decoding,* which is the process of translating printed symbols into sounds.

Now, let's try another task that is related to reading. You will need a pencil and a watch with a second hand (you will have to record your starting time and ending time for this task). Remembering to record your times, circle each word in Figure 2–3 that is a member of the category "animal." If you are like most readers, you were able to accomplish this task without too much difficulty. For those of you who like to keep score,

FIGURE 2–3 Circle each animal word

house	mountain	zebra
rabbit	elephant	belt
tree	dog	deer
shoe	lamp	cloud
horse	bed	basket
table	shirt	mouse

Adapted from Baron (1977)

there were seven animals on the list, and it takes school children about 1 second per word to make decisions like the ones you made (Perfetti & Lesgold, 1979). This word-recognition task requires decoding as well as the process known as *meaning accessing*. Meaning accessing refers to searching long-term memory for the meaning of a word.

Let's try one more reading task, using Figure 2–4. Read each sentence, and then pick the one that is the easiest and the one that is the hardest to read. Sentence 1 is an excellent candidate for the hardest, because it requires moving your eye many times in order to read the words. Sentence 4 is an excellent candidate for the easiest, because it is presented in the most familiar format. However, you probably could learn to read sentences presented as words or phrases, such as sentences 2 and 3.

As this task demonstrates, reading involves moving your eye across the page to take in information. In addition to using the processes of decoding and accessing meaning, you must also put all the information in each sen-

FIGURE 2–4

Which sentence is the easiest and which is the hardest to read?

SENTENCE 1

R e c e n t
r e s e a r c h
h a s s h o w n
t h a t s a c c a d e
l e n g t h i s
a b o u t o n e o r
t w o w o r d s,
w h i c h
c o r r e s p o n d s
t o a b o u t
e i g h t l e t t e r
p o s i t i o n s
p e r f i x a t i o n.

SENTENCE 2

One
educational
implication
of
this
work
is
that
students

tence together. Figure 2–4 shows that the integration process may be easier if presentation formats allow the eye to take in a lot of information on each glance. The process of joining all of the words of a sentence into a coherent idea is known as *sentence integration.*

The four tasks you have just tried represent four kinds of processes in reading words: recognizing phonemes, decoding words, accessing meaning, and integrating sentences. In this chapter, a brief historical and theoretical overview are presented, followed by an examination of each of these four kinds of processes.

WHAT IS READING?

Any serious discussion of reading must confront the problem that reading means different things to different people. For example, reading researchers make a fundamental distinction between *learning to read* and

FIGURE 2–4 *(continued)*	can read faster if they can be taught to increase their saccade length. *SENTENCE 3* Training in speed reading can increase reading rates from less than 300 words a minute to more than 900 words a minute. *SENTENCE 4* However, many research studies have shown that there can also be a corresponding drop in readers' performance on tests of comprehension.

reading to learn (Adams, 1990; Chall, 1979; Singer, 1981; Weaver & Resnick, 1979). Learning to read involves learning how to translate printed words into another form, such as pronouncing and understanding words. Developing automaticity in this translation process is a dominant focus of reading instruction in grades K–3. Although many students may achieve reading fluency by the third grade, other children may complete junior high school without mastering basic reading skills (Singer, 1981). The present chapter deals with this phase of reading, which can be called *reading fluency.*

Reading to learn involves the use of reading as a tool for gaining specific knowledge in some subject domain. This activity includes comprehension and evaluation of entire passages. The acquisition of specific knowledge from reading is a dominant focus of reading instruction in grade 4 and thereafter. Chapter 3 examines techniques for improving students' success in extracting useful knowledge from text, which is called *reading comprehension.*

A HISTORY OF READING RESEARCH

In the early days of educational psychology, the question of how people learn to read was a fundamental research issue. In his classic book *The Psychology and Pedagogy of Reading,* Huey (1908/1968) summarized the importance of understanding the reading process:

> And so to completely analyze what we do when we read would almost be the acme of a psychologist's achievement, for it would be to describe very many of the most intricate workings of the human mind, as well as to unravel the tangled story of the most remarkable specific performance that civilization has learned in all its history. (p. 6)

Unfortunately, the early enthusiasm for experimental research on reading did not find a comfortable home in the psychology of the early 1900s. The behaviorist movement, which swept across the scene during the first half of the twentieth century, was not consistent with the study of underlying cognitive processes in reading. As Kolers points out in his introduction to a reissued version of Huey's book in 1968, "remarkably little empirical information has been added to what Huey knew" (p. xiv).

The rebirth of cognitive psychology in the 1960s brought with it a rebirth of interest in the psychological study of reading. During the past decades, many models have been proposed to describe the processes by which people understand written language. Although a review of all of the proposed models is beyond the scope of this book, most include the basic cognitive processes of recognizing phonemes, decoding words, accessing word meaning, and integrating sentences.

RECOGNIZING PHONEMES

WHAT IS PHONOLOGICAL AWARENESS?

Phonological awareness refers to knowledge of the sound units (phonemes) used in a language, including the ability to hear and produce separate phonemes. Following initial work by Mattingly (1972), Wagner and Torgesen (1987) define phonological awareness as "awareness of and access to the phonology of one's language" (p. 192). Sometimes called *phonemic awareness,* this knowledge includes the recognition that words are composed of sound units and that sound units can be combined to form words. For example, the spoken word "hat" consists of three phonemes: /h/, /a/, and /t/. Phonological awareness refers to the process of breaking a spoken word into its sound units—such as being able to discriminate the sounds /h/, /a/, and /t/ when the word "hat" is spoken—and to the process of producing and blending sound units to form spoken words—such as being able to produce and blend these three sounds when one wants to say the word "hat."

If you looked at a spectrogram showing the speech stream for a sentence such as "The cat in the hat is back," you would not see a series of neatly separated sound units. Instead, you would see continuous waves represcnting acoustic energy. Acoustic speech entering our ears comes as a continuous flow. The apparent segmentation that we hear is based on our cognitive processing, rather than on the acoustic properties of the utterance. The ability to segment a continuous flow into discrete sound units requires learning by the listener.

In standard American English there are approximately 42 basic sound units (i.e., "phonemes"), as summarized in Table 2–1, although regional differences in pronunciation and dialect can create more units. Interestingly, there are more than 26 phonemes in English because some letters can produce more than one sound. For example, "c" can be hard as in "cat" or soft as in "cent." Phonological awareness of English does not focus on awareness of the relation between letters and sounds (that skill is covered in the next section on decoding), but rather consists of representing these sound units in long-term memory.

What are the sounds in "cat"? Do these words rhyme: "cat, hat"? Listen and recite these words: "hat, fir, led." All are examples of tests of phonological awareness. Students are classified as phonologically aware if they are able to break a word such as "cat" into its three consituent sounds, distinguish between rhyming and nonrhyming words, and correctly reproduce spoken words. Other common tests include being able to tap out the number of sounds in a word (e.g., giving 3 taps for "hat"), to reverse the order of sounds in a word (e.g., saying /t/, /a/, and /h/ for "hat"), to add a sound to a word (e.g., adding "h" to "at" to get "hat"), to delete a sound

TABLE 2–1	Character	Common Spellings	Examples
Common sound units for English words	b	b	back
	c or k	c, k	cat, kitten
	ch	ch, _tch	chief, catch
	d	d	dog
	f	f, ph	fit, elephant
	g	g	give
	h	h	help
	j	j, _dge, ge, gi, gy	just, fudge, age, giant, gym
	l	l	lion
	m	m	milk
	n	n, kn	no, know
	ng	ng	sing
	p	p	pot
	r	r, wr	right, write
	s	s, c	sent, cent
	sh	sh, _t_, _c_	shoe, nation, special
	t	t	ten
	th	th	thin
	t͟h	th	that
	v	v	voice
	w	w	way
	wh	wh_	white
	y	y	yes
	z	s, _s	zebra, nose
	zh	_s_	vision
	a	a, a_e, ai_, -ay, ea, -ey	able, cape, train, day, steak, they
	e	e, ee, e_e, ea, _y, _i_	equal, feet, eve, each, baby, babies
	i	i, i_e, igh, _y, _ie, ai	I, bite, high, sky, pie, aisle
	o	o, o_e, oa, _ow, _oe	go, phone, boat, low, toe
	u	u, ue, you, u_e, _ew	using, cue, youth, use, few
	ā	a, au, ai	hat, aunt, plaid
	ah	a, al, o	father, calm, on
	aw	a, aw, au, o	tall, law, caught, soft
	ē	e, ea	bed, bread
	ī	i, ui, u, ea, ee, ie	sit, build, busy, dear, deer, pierce
	ū	u, o, ou, a, e, o	cup, some, couple, alone, loaded, wagon
	oo	oo, u, ew, ue, ou, o	too, rule, new, due, group, do
	o͞o	oo, u	book, full
	oi	oi, -oy	oil, toy
	ow	ow, ou	owl, ouch
	ar	ar	park, car
	ur	ur, ir, er, or, ear	hurt, stir, term, word, earn

Note: *This table does not include separate listings for q (as in queen) or for changes in sounds in unaccepted syllables. Pronunciation guides vary in listing from 41 to 45 sounds.*

Adapted from Open Court Phonics Kit (1983), Stein (1966), Carrell and Tiffany (1960), Clark and Clark (1977) from a word (e.g., taking away the first sound in "hat" to get "at"), and to blend sounds presented in isolation to form a word (e.g., saying "hat" when given the three sounds /h/, /a/, and /t/ separately).

RESEARCH ON PHONOLOGICAL AWARENESS

How does phonological awareness develop? To answer this question, Liberman and colleagues (Liberman, Shankweiler, Fischer, & Carter, 1974) tested four-, five-, and six-year-olds on their ability to segment words into phonemes and syllables. As shown in Figure 2–5, there was a developmental trend in which almost none of the four-year-olds recognized phonemes but almost all six-year-olds did. However, half of the four- and five-year-olds and almost all of the six-year-olds could break words into syllables. These results demonstrate that phonological awareness tends to develop in children in the years leading up to the primary grades.

Similar results were obtained when Juel, Griffin, and Gough (1986) tested the phonological awareness of a group of 80 children at several points across the first and second grades. Table 2–2 shows some of the items included on the phonological awareness test they used. Children correctly answered 35% of the items in fall of the first grade, 73% in spring of the first grade, 83% in fall of the second grade, and 86% in spring of the second grade. These results are consistent with the idea that phonological awareness increases across the primary school years.

FIGURE 2–5 The development of phonological awareness

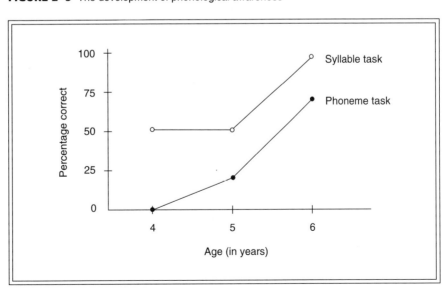

Adapted from Liberman, Shankweiler, Fischer, and Carter (1974)

TABLE 2–2	Task	Tester Says:	Child Says:
A test of phonological awareness	Segmentation	Say "no." What are the two sounds in "no"?	/n/ /o/
	Blending	Say /n/, /i/, /s/. What word is /n/ /i/ /s/?	"nice"
	Deletion of first phoneme	Say "top." Now say "top" without the /t/.	"op"
	Deletion of last phoneme	Say "same." Now say "same" without the /m/.	"sa" (as in "say")
	Substitution of first phoneme	Say "ball." Instead of /b/, begin the new word with /k/.	"call"
	Substitution of last phoneme	Say "park." Instead of /k/, end the word with /t/.	"part"

Adapted from Juel, Griffin, and Gough (1986)

What is the relation between phonological awareness and learning to read? Phonological awareness is a prerequisite for learning to read, so that students who lack skills in phonological awareness are likely to have difficulty in learning to read. This claim, which can be called the *phonological awareness hypothesis,* has been subjected to rigorous study (Adams, 1990; Ehri, 1991; Rieben & Perfetti, 1991; Wagner & Torgesen, 1987). In particular, let's examine two straightforward predictions of the phonological awareness hypothesis.

First, in comparing groups of good and poor readers, the phonological awareness hypothesis predicts that students who have difficulty in reading tend to have difficulty on tests of phonological awareness. Bradley and Bryant (1978) measured the phonological awareness of younger good readers and older poor readers by asking them to identify which of four words lacked a sound contained in the other words (e.g., answering "rag" for the set "sun, sea, sock, rag," or answering "man" for the set "cot, hut, man, fit") and to produce a word that rhymed with a target word (e.g., saying "fun" for the target word "sun"). As predicted by the phonological awareness hypothesis, in spite of having had more exposure to reading, the older poor readers performed more poorly than the younger good readers on both measures of phonological awareness. Similarly, other researchers also found that children who have difficulty in learning to read in elementary school often lack skill in phonological awareness (Pennington, Groisser, & Welsh, 1993; Stanovich, 1991). Although these results suggest that lack of phonological awareness is related to reading difficulties, group comparisons such as these do not allow us to tell whether phonological awareness has a causal relation with reading achivement. For this reason longitudinal studies are useful in determining whether a child's phonogical awareness at an early age is related to his or her reading achievement at a later age.

Second, in longitudinal studies the phonological awareness hypothesis predicts that a child's level of phonological awareness at an early age is related to his or her level of reading performance in primary grades. For example, Bradley and Bryant (1985) tested four- and five-year-olds on phonological awareness tasks and retested them three years later on a standardized test of reading achievement. The correlation was strong ($r = .5$) providing support for the phonological awareness hypothesis.

In a more focused study, Juel, Griffin, and Gough (1986) tested students at several points during their first and second grade school years on phonological awareness (as exemplified in Table 2–2) and reading skills (such as pronouncing a printed word and writing a spoken word). Phonological awareness correlated strongly with children's ability to pronounce printed words at the end of the first grade ($r = .8$) and at the end of the second grade ($r = .5$), and phonological awareness correlated strongly with children's ability to write spoken words in the end of the first grade ($r = .8$) and at the end of the second grade ($r = .6$). Even after the effects of intelligence were statistically removed from the analysis, phonological awareness strongly influenced year-end performance on basic reading skills.

In a review of longitudinal studies, Wagner and Torgesen (1987) found 20 instances in which measures of phonological awareness at an early age correlated strongly with later reading achievement, even when the effects of general cognitive ability were taken into account. They concluded that "phonological awareness and reading are related independent of general cognitive ability" (p. 202). Of course, many factors other that phonological awareness may be related to a child's reading level, but this research demonstrates that phonological awareness may be one important contributing factor.

Although these results are consistent with the phonological awareness hypothesis, you might ask whether they prove it. These results seem to be consistent with several possible relations between phonological awareness and reading skill: (1) phonological awareness might cause reading skill (i.e., as claimed by the phonological awareness hypothesis); (2) reading skill might cause phonological awareness; and (3) both phonological awareness and reading skill might be caused by a third factor (such as general intelligence). A useful way of distinguishing among these three possibilities is to conduct a training study in which prereaders who are equated on basic characteristics are taught phonological awareness skills and later tested on their level of reading achievement. This approach is taken in the next section.

IMPLICATIONS FOR INSTRUCTION: PHONOLOGICAL AWARENESS TRAINING

If the phonological awareness hypothesis is correct, then teaching students how to recognize phonemes will improve their ability to learn to read. In addition to providing an important theoretical test of the hypothesis, training studies offer practical implications for early reading instruction. Based on the kinds of results reported in the previous section, Juel, Griffin, and Gough (1986) argue for the practical need to provide instruction in phonological awareness:

> These findings suggest the need for oral phonemic awareness training for entering–first grade children with poor phonemic awareness. Without special training, children with poor phonemic awareness appear disadvantaged in learning to read and write. . . . [S]uch children are frequently minority children. It may be that training in oral phonemic awareness should be a routine precursor to reading instruction. (p. 249)

Does phonological awareness training help students learn to read? To answer this question, Bradley and Bryant (1983, 1985, 1991) provided phonological awareness training to five- and six-year-olds through 40 10-minute sessions spread over a two-year period (phoneme-trained group). The training involved recognizing phonemes in words presented as pictures or as spoken words. For example, in some sessions, the child was shown a picture of a bus and asked to select the picture of a word starting with the same sound in a set of pictures. In other sessions, the child was given a set of pictures and asked to select the one that started with a different sound than the others. In yet other sessions, the child was given a large array of pictures and asked to classify them based on shared sounds while stating which sound each group had in common. In sessions involving spoken words, the child was asked to determine whether two spoken words rhymed, whether two spoken words began with the same sound, which of several spoken words ended in a sound different from the others, and so on. In contrast, a control group received 40 lessons involving the same words, but in which the task was to categorize words based on semantic category (such as grouping pictures of a cat, bat, and rat together because they are all animals). By the end of the training period, the phoneme-trained group scored almost one year ahead of the control group on a standardized test of reading performance. Importantly, the advantage of the phoneme-trained students persisted so that five years later the phoneme-trained group still scored higher than the control group on reading performance.

In a shorter-term study, some kindergarteners received instruction in phonological awareness during 28 20-minute sessions over a 7-week period in the winter (phoneme-trained group), whereas an equivalent group received no intervention beyond regular classroom instruction in reading (control group). For example, phoneme-trained students were taught to repeat a word spoken by the teacher and then say each phoneme in the word. Other activities were like those used by Bradley and Bryant (1983, 1985) as well as letter-naming tasks.

The left two columns in Table 2–3 show that the training seems to have a strong effect on children's phonological awareness: Although both phoneme-trained and control students scored at the same level on a pretest of phonological awareness, the phoneme-trained group showed a

TABLE 2–3		Phonological Awareness		Word Reading	Word Spelling
Percentage correct on four tests for phoneme-trained and control students	**Group**	**Pretest**	**Posttest**	**Posttest**	**Posttest**
	Phoneme-trained	40%	72%	52%	46%
	Control	40%	45%	10%	25%

Adapted from Bradley and Bryant (1983)

large improvement on a posttest, whereas the control group improved only slightly. More importantly, the right two columns of Table 2–3 show that the training had a positive effect on children's reading skills: On a word-reading posttest administered after the training, phoneme-trained students were able to correctly pronounce printed words containing two or three phonemes much better than did the control students. In addition, on a word-spelling posttest, phoneme-trained students performed much better on phonetic spelling of spoken words than did control students. Finally, according to a standardized reading test administered at the end of the school year, 35% of the phoneme-trained group could be classified as readers compared to only 7% of the control group.

These results, like those of other training studies (Cunningham, 1990; Lundberg, Frost, & Peterson, 1988), provide evidence that explicit instruction in phonological awareness can facilitate early reading skill. Indeed, there is reason to suspect that the benefits of phonological awareness in young children extend beyond initial learning of basic reading skills. For example, Stanovich (1986) has shown how teachers may be initiating "a causal chain of escalating negative side effects" (p. 364) if they fail to provide phonological awareness instruction to beginning readers with poor phonological skills. The negative effects begin when students with poor phonological skills have more difficulty in learning to read words, thus limiting the amount of text they are exposed to, which in turns reduces opportunities to develop automaticity in decoding. Without automated decoding skills, students must pay attention to the process of decoding words rather than to comprehending the meaning of what they are reading. The consequence is a more limited vocabulary and knowledge base compared to those acquired by more skilled readers. Research on phonological training suggests that it may be possible to break this chain before it starts.

Although phonological awareness does not develop naturally in some children, there is encouraging evidence that it can be taught. In reviewing research on phonological training, Spector (1995) concludes that "the research to date provides clear evidence that phonemic awareness training works" (p. 47). Based on this research base, Spector (1995) recommends engaging "children in activities that direct their attention to the sounds in words . . . at the preschool level" (p. 41). This includes teaching students both to segment (i.e., analyze words into their constituent sounds) and to blend (i.e., to combine sounds into words) in addition to offering instruction in letter-sound relations.

Goswami and Bryant (1992) provide a useful summary of the instructional implications of phonological awareness research:

> There can be little doubt that phonological awareness plays an important role in reading. The results of a large number of studies amply demonstrate a strong (and consistent) relationship between children's ability to disentangle and to assemble the sounds in words and their progress in learning to read. . . . There is also evidence that successful training in phonological awareness helps children learn to read. . . . [P]honological awareness is a powerful causal determinant of the speed and efficiency of learning to read. . . . However, it is only the first step. (p. 49)

The next step seems to be the development of cognitive processes for decoding words, which is examined in the next section.

DECODING

WHAT IS DECODING?

Decoding refers to the process of translating a printed word into a sound. This is a rather restricted process, for it involves being able to pronounce (or name) printed words rather than being able to explain what they mean. In this section, we explore the long-standing debate over how to teach decoding, some major research findings that are related to decoding, and instructional research on decoding training.

THE GREAT DEBATE

One of the great debates (Adams, 1990; Chall, 1967, 1983) in the teaching of reading concerns whether to use a *phonics* or a *whole-word* approach. The phonics (or *code-emphasis*) method involves teaching children to be able to produce sounds for letters or letter groups, and to blend those sounds together to form words. Adams (1990) notes that the central component in phonics instruction is "teaching of correspondences between letters or groups of letters and their pronunciations" (p. 50). For example, Table 2–1 lists forty-two basic sounds in spoken English and gives examples of letters that correspond to the sounds. Readers learn to associate the appropriate sound with the appropriate letter(s). Figure 2–6 shows a pic

FIGURE 2–6 Phonics instruction involves associating sounds with letters or letter groups

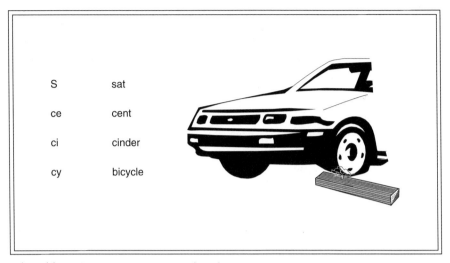

S	sat
ce	cent
ci	cinder
cy	bicycle

Adapted from Open Court Phonics Kit *(1979)*

ture of a flat tire (making the "sssss" sound) along with letters that can correspond to this sound.

In contrast, the whole-word method involves teaching children to "sight read" words, that is, to be able to pronounce a whole word as a single unit. For example, an early reading program may concentrate on introducing a few hundred words. Figure 2–7 shows some typical first words to be learned by beginning readers. Over time, new words are systematically added to the reader's repertoire. The whole-word approach is generally part of a *meaning-emphasis method,* in which determining the meaning of each word is a major goal.

FIGURE 2–7 Whole-word instruction involves associating word names with printed words

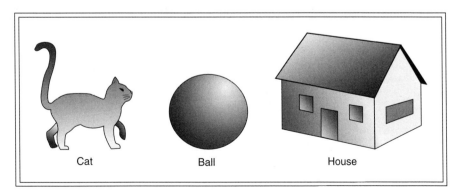

Cat   Ball   House

The history of reading research in the United States documents several swings between the phonics and whole-word approach (Adams, 1990; Singer, 1981). In the beginning, during the 1700s, the phonics method was emphasized. The standard textbook was *The New England Primer,* originally published in 1690. First, children learned the alphabet; then, they learned to read two-letter combinations (*ab, ac, ad, af,* and so on) and consonant-vowel syllables (*ba, da, ca,* and so on); next, children were asked to read words containing up to five syllables. Students were drilled on the correct pronunciation for each syllable and the correct spelling of words until they could spell and read short words by sight. Finally, children orally read sentences and stories and afterward answered comprehension questions.

The phonics tradition was heavily used through the early 1800s, when the dominant textbook was *The American Spelling Book.* Published in 1790, this book, like *The New England Primer,* progressed from alphabet to syllables to words. However, whereas *The New England Primer* focused on religious material, *The American Spelling Book* focused on national loyalty and traditions.

During the mid-nineteenth century, there was a swing to the whole-word method. The dominant textbooks were *McGuffey Readers,* which appeared between 1836 and 1844. They systematically introduced a new word by letting the student see the word, hear the word, see a picture or sentence referring to the word, and later spell the word (or break it into sounds). Unlike previous texts, *McGuffey Readers* were a graded series that allowed for children to be grouped by age and achievement.

By the 1880s emphasis had come to be placed on the reading of fine literature, and there was a return to the phonics method of instruction. The scientific alphabet was introduced in 1902; it consisted of forty-four phonemes along with forty-four corresponding symbols. Students learned to write sentences phonetically, using these symbols. Other techniques involved teaching students to sound out words before giving any hints with pictures or sentence context.

By the early 1900s scientific research in education was influencing reading instruction. In schools, silent reading rather than oral reading was stressed. For example, as an introductory lesson a teacher might write "Come here" on the blackboard; students would then carry out the commands that were written. Emphasis was also placed on getting the meaning out of stories; teachers would question children about their experiences before asking them to read a story. Students learned to recognize whole words before they learned how to break them into parts.

Since the end of World War II, the dominant reading textbooks in American schools have been basal readers. Like *McGuffey Readers,* the modern basal readers are an integrated and graded series of reading books and activities, with each successive book in the series requiring more sophisticated and difficult reading skills. Most basal readers employ aspects of both the whole-word and phonics approach, but according to many critics (Singer, 1981; Flesch, 1955), more attention is given to whole-word methods. For example, Flesch's (1955) famous book *Why Johnny Can't Read and What You Can Do About It* called for a shift back to the phonics method of instruction.

Deciding which method is best for teaching beginning reading has become "the most politicized topic in the field of education" (Adams, 1990, p. 13). Fortunately, the debate is informed by a large and fairly consistent research base. In her classic book *Learning to Read: The Great Debate,* Challs (1967) reviewed the research literature and concluded that children should learn the relation between sounds and letters before they learn to read for content and meaning. In a more recent review of research, Adams (1990) came to the same conclusion: "programs that include some explicit, systematic phonic instruction tend to produce better word reading skills than those that do not" (p. 93). Although today's reading programs attempt to balance phonics and whole-word approaches, the preponderance of research shows that children need to develop fast and automatic word decoding processes before they can become proficient in reading comprehension. In other words, children must first learn to read (code emphasis) before they can successfully read to learn (meaning emphasis).

As you can see, there have been several swings in American reading instruction between a "phonics method" that progresses from letters to syllables to words to sentences versus a "whole word method" that progresses from meaningful context to words to parts. In a recent review of research on beginning reading instruction, Adams (1990) observed that the "great debate" goes on. What does research have to say about how people read and how to conduct beginning reading instruction? The next section explores research on three important aspects of the great debate about decoding—automaticity effects, involving how people learn to decipher symbols; word superiority effects, involving how people identify letters, and pronunciation strategy effects, involving how people put letters together to make words.

RESEARCH ON DECODING

AUTOMATICITY EFFECTS. As a historical introduction to the great debate, consider the following scene. The story begins in the fall of 1895. The place is the Western Union telegraph office in Brookville, Indiana. The characters are an 18-year-old young man named Will Reynolds and a 17-year-old woman named Eydth Balsley. Both have come to learn to become telegraph operators, under the tutelage of the telegraph office's operator, Mr. Balsley. They are bright and eager learners, so by June of 1896, both can send and receive ordinary business letters over the main line. More importantly, during this period both have agreed to be tested once a week on how fast they can send and receive telegraph messages. In doing so, Will and Edyth enter the annals of educational psychology history by becoming participants in what is today widely recognized as the first major psychological study of skill learning (Bryan & Harter, 1897).

To measure their receiving speed, the tester gave them a message in Morse code at a certain rate for a two-minute period; the student's task was to listen to the incoming dots and dashes and write down the message in words. If the student failed to decipher the code correctly, the task was repeated at a slower rate. If the student succeeded, a faster rate was tried. Figure 2–8 shows the number of letters per minute that Will and Eydth could correctly receive on each of the weekly tests from the day they started until they mastered the basics. This is a learning curve, in which the *x*-axis indicates the amount of practice and the *y*-axis shows the level of learning.

Bryan and Harter (1897) noted in Will's and Edyth's deciphering skill both quantitative and qualitative changes. These quantitative and qualitative changes constitute an *automaticity effect,* that is an ability to carry out a task without having to pay attention to each step. First, as you can see in the learning curves, over the course of training both students improved greatly in the speed with which they could decode incoming messages. It took them about six months of practice before they could handle messages coming in at the slowest main line rate (71 letters per minute), but within nine months they could receive 100 words per minute and were on a tra-

FIGURE 2–8 How many letters per minute could Eydth and Will receive during their first 36 weeks of learning?

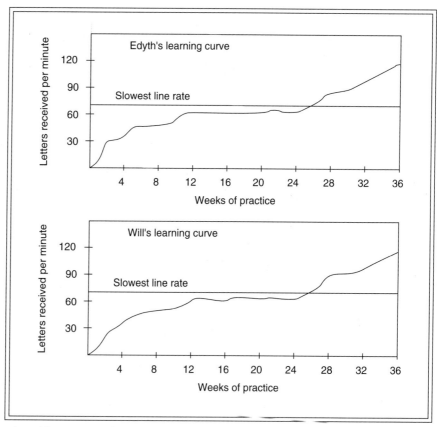

Adapted from Bryan and Harter (1897)

jectory of getting faster every week. The increasing speed of the students is evidence that components of their decoding skill were becoming automated, that is, that their conscious attention was not required.

Second, in addition there was also a qualitative change in which the students first translated the code on a letter-by-letter basis, then word by word, and finally phrase-by-phrase. According to Bryan and Harter (1897), this qualitative shift is reflected in the observation that both students reached a plateau in the middle of their training—their learning curves became somewhat flat between the 16th and 20th weeks. Bryan and Harter interpreted this pattern as evidence of stages in skill learning: the increase in speed from the first week to the 16th week reflects a phase of increasing skill at decoding individual letters and even short words, the plateau represents a phase of consolidation of letter-decoding skill so that it becomes automatic, and the increase in speed from the 24th week onward represents a shift of focus to decoding by words and phrases. By observing operators as they progressed from novices to experts, Bryan and Harter found that at first they decoded messages letter-by-letter, then after more practice, they began to decode word-by-word, and eventually were able to decode phrase-by-phrase, so that their writing was 6 to 12 words behind the flow of the incoming code. The plateau represents a period in which a component skill—letter-by-letter decoding—has reached its highest speed but is still not completely automatic; once it becomes automatized, it can be used as a component in learning higher-order skills such as decoding words and phrases. Importantly, when novices decoded letter-by-letter, they reported being unaware of the meaning of the message, whereas expert operators who listened to an entire phrase before writing it down stated that they were aware of the meaning of the message.

What can this nineteenth-century study of telegraph operators tell us about how today's children learn to read? When the famous educational psychologist E. L. Thorndike (1913) examined Bryan and Harter's classic study of skill learning, he was struck by the possibility that "in learning to read (first year primary) . . . one's progress is analogous to that of the student of telegraphy" (p. 100). The crucial event in learning to decipher code—whether it is printed words or the sounds of the Morse code—is the development of automaticity of low-level skills. Accordingly, it is crucial that students develop the ability to recognize the relation between a letter (or letter group) and its sound rapidly and automatically, that is, phonological deciphering must become effortless. This goal is accomplished through practice.

Consistent with this view of the development of automaticity of basic skills, many authors have proposed that students who must consciously monitor their decoding process have less attentional capacity for making inferences and otherwise trying to comprehend the passage (Adams, 1990; Chall, 1967; Perfetti & Lesgold, 1979). In order to investigate this idea, Perfetti and Hogaboam (1975) selected third- and fifth-graders who either scored low in standardized tests of reading comprehension (below the thirtieth percentile) or scored high in reading comprehension (above the sixtieth percentile). Reading comprehension involves being able to answer meaningful questions about a passage that you have just read. Subjects were asked to participate in a word-pronunciation task: A word was presented on a screen and the subject's job was to say the word as soon as he or she knew what it was. This task requires decoding, but not comprehension.

Some of the words were very familiar; as Figure 2–9 shows, skilled and less skilled readers did not differ greatly in their pronunciation times for familiar words. Other words were unfamiliar to the readers; as Figure 2–9 shows, the less skilled readers averaged 1 second longer than the skilled readers. One explanation may be that skilled readers are more familiar with the "unfamiliar" words, perhaps because they spend more time reading more difficult texts. However, Figure 2–9 also shows that the less skilled readers required an average of over 1 second more than the skilled readers to pronounce pseudowords (i.e., nonsense words that could be pronounced). Apparently, skilled readers employ fast and automatic decoding processes, even for words that have no meaning, whereas less skilled readers have great difficulty in decoding words that are not part of their sight-reading vocabulary. These results are consistent with the idea that well-practiced decoding skills allow the reader to use his or her attentional

FIGURE 2–9 Mean pronunciation time for highly and less skilled readers

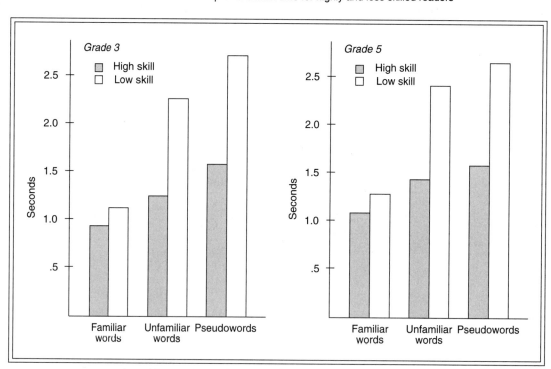

Adapted from Perfetti and Hogaboam (1975)

resources to comprehend the passage. In fact, fluent readers may be so well practiced in decoding that they are unaware of the rules of pronunciation (Calfee, Chapman, & Venezky, 1972). Apparently, learning efficient decoding skills is a prerequisite for learning efficient comprehension skills.

WORD SUPERIORITY EFFECTS. One way to provide more detailed information concerning the great debate over decoding is to determine how skilled readers, such as normal adults, read letters in words. For example, we might ask: Do people read each letter and put these parts together to form a word, as would be suggested by a phonics approach to reading? Alternatively, do people read the whole word first and then recognize each letter?

The second alternative may sound odd, because common sense seems to tell us that you must recognize the parts before you recognize the whole. However, some early research may surprise you. For example, Cattell (1886) found that letters can be perceived more accurately when they are part of a word than when they are not. In experiments, if unrelated letters were flashed on the screen for very brief exposures, people could correctly perceive about three letters; however, if the letters formed simple three-letter words, subjects correctly perceived about six letters. This phenomenon—that people can read letters faster and more accurately when they are parts of words—has been called the *word superiority effect* (Baron, 1978; Kreiger, 1975; Reicher, 1969; Smith & Spoehr, 1974).

The word superiority effect is one of the oldest and best-established facts in experimental psychology. As an example of research on the phenomenon, let's consider an experiment by Johnston (1978, 1981). Subjects were asked to watch a screen, and to be ready to report on letters that were flashed on a screen. Table 2–4 shows that a word (such as "COIN"), a letter string (such as "CPDT"), or a letter (such as "C") was presented briefly (e.g., for 30 milliseconds); then a mask (such as "XXXXX") was flashed to blot out any afterimages; finally, subjects were asked to take a forced choice test concerning one of the letters (e.g., Was the first letter of the word "C" or "J"? or Was the letter that you saw a "C" or "J"?). Subjects were not told in advance which letter in a word or letter string would be

TABLE 2–4 The word superiority effect	Treatment	Example of Stimulus	Mask	Forced Choice Test		Proportion Correct
	Word	COIN	XXXXX	COIN	JOIN	.845
	Letter string	CPDT	XXXXX	CPDT	JPDT	.686
	Single letter	C	XXXXX	C	J	.710

Adapted from Johnston (1981)

the one they would be tested on. As Table 2–4 indicates, subjects more accurately recognized letters when they were parts of words (such as the "C" in "COIN") than when they were presented singly (such as "C" alone) or in nonsense strings. In Johnston's experiment, the word superiority effect represents a difference of about 13 percentage points in accuracy.

The word superiority effect has been used as a rationale for teaching reading by the whole-word method (Singer, 1981), since it seems to imply that readers perceive words more easily than individual letters. However, you need to be suspicious of this conclusion. The word superiority effect is not a theory; it is just a well-established empirical fact. What is needed is a theory of how people read and how they learn to read. Educational practice should be based on our understanding of the reading process (i.e., a unified theory of reading) rather than single facts.

Johnston (1981) has suggested three different ways to interpret the word superiority effect. Theory 1 says that the visual shape of the word provides information that is not present for single letters. However, in contrast to this theory, the word superiority effect still is obtained when the word is presented all in capital letters (such as "COIN"), in alternating letters (such as "CoIn" or "cOiN"), or with irregular spacing (such as "CO IN"). Theory 2 argues that the word provides cues about what the letters can be; for example, if you know that the last three letters of a four-letter word are "NOB," you can limit your hypotheses concerning the first letter to "S" and "K." However, in contrast to this theory, words that constrain the possible first letters to one of three letters (such as "-RIP") do not provide better word superiority effects than words that constrain the possible first letter to one of nine possible letters (such as "-ATE"). Theory 3 states that the word allows for better retention through the mask. However, this theory is inadequate because it cannot explain why the code for a word should be easier to remember than the code for a letter. In short, Johnston (1981) concludes that all of the popular theories for the word superiority effect should be rejected.

What causes the word superiority effect? Johnston and his colleague (1981; Johnston & McClelland, 1980) offer a theory based on the idea that a word is analyzed on several levels. When a word such as "COIN" is presented, the reader begins to form and test hypotheses about the word on each of the following levels:

Feature detectors, which determine whether the lines of the letters are curved or straight and the orientation of lines for each position.
Letter detectors, which determine the letter that is present at each position, based partly on information from the feature detectors.
Word detectors, which determine the word that is present, based partly on information from the letter detectors.

However, as soon as the mask is presented, the feature and letter detectors are erased. Thus the only level of analysis that survives the mask is the word level. If the stimulus is a letter or a letter string, no word-level analysis can take place, and thus the mask is more likely to damage performance.

Thus Johnston and his colleague seem to be able to explain the word superiority effect by assuming that readers analyze words by their parts; if this theory is correct, the word superiority effect does not suggest that the whole-word method of instruction is better than the phonics method for beginning readers.

PRONUNCIATION STRATEGY EFFECTS. As another source of research information, let's return for a moment to the pronunciation task shown in Figure 2–2. Baron (1977) presented pronounceable nonsense words like these to adults, who were asked to pronounce each one and to tell how they decided on the pronunciation.

The results indicated that Baron's subjects tended to use three distinct pronunciation strategies. With the similarity strategy, they pronounced a nonsense word so that it sounded exactly the same as a familiar real word. For example, "BLUD" was pronounced "blood." With the analogy strategy, subjects pronounced the nonsense word so that it partially rhymed with a real word. For example, "ROTION" was pronounced to rhyme with "motion." With the corresponding strategy, subjects used phonetic rules to sound out each part of the word and then blended the sounds together. For example, "SHUD" was pronounced as "sh" for "SH," "ah" for "U," and "d" for "D," yielding "sh-ah-d."

In Baron's study, the most commonly used strategy was the corresponding strategy, in which the word was sounded out. This strategy corresponds to the phonics method of reading instruction in which students learn the relation between letters and sounds. In contrast, the similarity strategy corresponds somewhat to the whole-word method of reading instruction. Finally, the analogy approach seems to involve a compromise that deals with sounds of word parts (phonics) and whole words. An analysis of subjects' errors in pronunciation tended to favor the analogy strategy as the most effective.

To test the merits of the analogy strategy, Baron (1977) provided explicit training to some subjects in how to use the analogy strategy to pronounce nonsense words. Subjects given such analogy strategy training showed a large improvement in pronunciation performance, with errors dropping from 9 to 4%. Baron also has shown that training in the analogy strategy can be applied successfully to children as young as four years old. For example, students can be taught to pronounce three-letter words ending in "IN" and "AX," such as "TIN" and "TAX," or "PIN" and "WAX," by using rhymes.

There is increasing evidence that beginning readers who have not yet fully mastered phonological decoding are able to read words by analogy (Goswami, 1986; Goswami & Bryant, 1990). In one study, beginning readers received a sheet with a clue word on top, such as "beak," followed by other words and nonwords such as "bean," "beal," "peak," "neak," "lake," and "pake." The teacher pronounced the clue word and then asked the child to read aloud the other words on the sheet. Children performed better in reading words that rhymed with the target, such as "peak" and "neak," than words that shared some word parts, such as "bean" and "beal," or that shared no sounds with "beak," such as "lake" and "pake." In a follow-up study, Ehri and Robbins (1992) provided additional evidence that "reading unfamiliar words by analogy to known words . . . can be executed by beginners more readily than reading unfamiliar words by phonologically recoding the words" (p. 22).

A first step in building automaticity in English letter-sound combinations is to learn the 42 major sounds in English (as summarized in Table 2–1) and the 26 letters of the alphabet. Next, a student must learn the rules by which letters are related to sounds, but unfortunately the rules relating letters to sounds are far from regular (Clymer, 1967). For example, Clymer (1967) generated a list of 45 rules, including those selected for Table 2–5, but most had many exceptions. What is the best way to learn phonological decoding in a language such as English? One promising answer to this question grows out of early work on skill learning, which indicates that the path to automatic decoding includes practice.

IMPLICATIONS FOR INSTRUCTION: AUTOMATICITY TRAINING

The major implication of the research cited above is that readers must become automatic in recognizing letters and sounding out letter groups. In short, a main focus of reading instruction during the first few years of school should be to help students develop decoding skills that are automatic (i.e., that do not require extensive conscious effort by the reader). This section focuses on how to provide training for decoding automaticity.

TABLE 2–5

Selected phonics rules for vowels and consonants

Rule	Example	Exception	Percentage Consistent
When there are two vowels, one of which is the final *e*, the first vowel is long and the *e* is silent.	bone	done	63%
When a word has only one vowel, the vowel sound is short.	hid	kind	57%
When there are two vowels side by side, the long sound of the first one is heard, and the second is silent.	bead	chief	45%
When two of the same consonants are side by side, only one is heard.	carry	suggest	99%
Ch is usually pronounced as it is in *chair*.	catch	machine	95%
When *g* precedes *i* or *e*, it sounds like *j* in *jump*.	engine	give	64%

Adapted from Clymer (1963)

Stanovich (1980) has summarized research on decoding by noting that good readers differ from poor readers mainly in their rapid context-free word recognition. The limited capacity of the memory system requires that if some processes demand a great deal of attention, there will not be attention available for other processes. For example, LaBerge and Samuels (1974) have proposed that fluent readers are able to decode text automatically, which means that they have attention available for comprehension processes. In contrast, beginning readers' attention must be devoted mainly to decoding, leaving relatively little processing capacity available for comprehension processing. Perfetti and Hogaboam (1975) summarize this idea as follows: "To the extent that decoding is a mainly automatic process, it does not make great demands on the readers' higher comprehension processes" (p. 466).

LaBerge and Samuels (1974) have proposed three stages in the development of automaticity:

1. **Nonaccurate stage,** in which the reader makes errors in word recognition.
2. **Accuracy stage,** in which the reader can recognize words correctly but must use great attention to do so.
3. **Automatic stage,** in which the reader can recognize words correctly without requiring attention.

How can we teach students to gain automaticity in decoding? Samuels (1979) has suggested a technique called the *method of repeated readings.* According to this technique, a student reads a short, easy passage over and over again until a satisfactory level of fluency is reached. This procedure is repeated for another passage, and so on. Figure 2–10 shows the changes in reading and word-recognition rate as a student read five different passages using the method of repeated readings. Two findings are particularly interesting. First, for each passage, the fluency improves greatly with repetition. Second, fluency tends to improve from one passage to the next, even though the words are different.

What is the best way to increase word recognition automaticity? Samuels (1967) has proposed the *focal attention hypothesis,* which holds that visual attention should be focused on the printed word rather than the context. Thus word-recognition training that relies on context such as pictures and sentences is seen as distracting the reader from focusing on the printed word. For example, Ehri and Roberts (1979) asked first-graders to learn to read sixteen words using flash cards. For some students, each card contained just one word; for others, each card contained a target word within the context of a sentence. As expected, students in the word-only condition could sight-read the words faster (averaging 10.9 seconds) than could students in the context condition (averaging 15.7 seconds). Students in the word-only condition, as compared to the context condition, remembered more about the orthographic characteristics of the words, such as the correct spelling, but less of the semantic characteristics of the words needed to generate a sentence. Similarly, Nemko (1984) asked first-graders to learn to

FIGURE 2–10 Improving decoding fluency by repeated readings

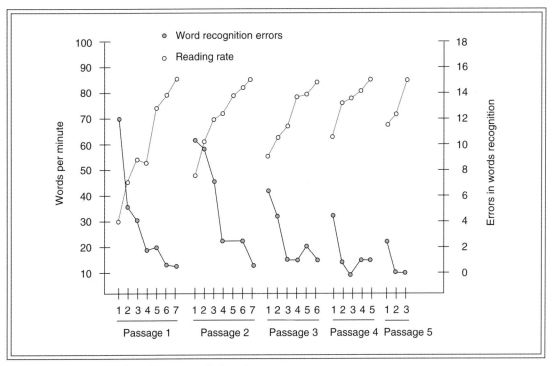

Adapted from Samuels (1979)

read sixteen words using flash cards, with each word presented either individually or in the context of a sentence. The test involved reading each word either individually or within a sentence. The best performance was for students who learned and were tested with individual words.

Samuels (1979) argues that as readers become more fluent, their comprehension will improve, for "as less attention is required for decoding, more attention becomes available for comprehension" (p. 405). Unfortunately, there has not been universal support for the idea that training in decoding automaticity will improve reading comprehension. Fleisher, Jenkins, and Pany (1979) gave decoding training to poor readers in the fourth and fifth grades. First, students in the trained group practiced by rapidly reading single words from flash cards, while students in the control group received no training. Then, all students took a criterion test in which they were asked to read a randomly ordered list of the words that the trained group had practiced reading. Students in the trained group reached a level of automaticity in which they made nearly no errors and read at least 90 words per minute; in contrast, the control students read at half the rate and made many more errors. Next, all students read two passages containing the practice words and took a twelve-item comprehension test. Although the trained group read the passage faster than the control group (91 words per minute versus 61 words per minute, respectively), there were no significant differences between the groups in comprehension test performance. A reasonable conclusion to draw from this study is that automatic decoding is a necessary but not sufficient condition for improved comprehension. Rapid decoding skill may help to reduce the bottleneck (or demands on memory processes), but a skilled reader also needs to know how to use comprehension strategies.

In a recent review, Dowhower (1994) concluded "because of the strong evidence of the effectiveness of repeated reading . . . this procedure should be integrated into the fabric of daily literacy instruction" (p. 343). Based on current research, Dowhower argued that students benefit from unassisted repeated-reading procedures in which they read and reread aloud on their own, and from assisted repeated-reading procedures in which they read and reread along with a teacher. If both methods are used, Dowhower suggests beginning with the assisted procedure and subsequently introducing the unassisted procedure for each passage. Blum and Koskinen (1991) have developed a modified version of repeated reading in which children work in pairs as they take turns reading 50-word passages three times to each other. The ultimate goal of the method of repeated readings and other forms of automaticity training is for children to be able to decode words without having to pay conscious attention to the decoding process.

ACCESSING WORD MEANING

WHAT IS MEANING ACCESS?

How does a person read a word? The preceding sections showed how word reading involves being able to recognize sound units and blend them together. However, blending sounds may be only half of the story. Readers also make use of their knowledge of semantics (i.e., word meaning) and syntax (i.e., grammatical rules about parts of speech) in trying to understand words found in text. The search for word meaning can be called *meaning access*. This section explores basic research relevant to meaning access (including context effects and vocabulary effects) and instructional studies aimed at improving the process.

RESEARCH ON MEANING ACCESS

CONTEXT EFFECTS. Context effects are the impact of the context of a word within a sentence on the speed and accuracy of word recognition. Tulving and Gold (1963) reported a landmark study concerning the role of sentence context on word meaning. In the experiment, a word was flashed on the screen and the subjects were asked to read the word aloud. Before the word was flashed, subjects were given a cue such as, "The actress received praise for being an outstanding _____." As you can see, this cue provides what Tulving and Gold called an *appropriate context* for the target word "performer," but an *inappropriate context* for the target word "potato." The length of the cue given before the target word was either zero (i.e., no cue), one, two, four, or eight words. Longer cues, presumably, provide a stronger context for the target word.

Figure 2–11 summarizes the results of the experiment. The researchers measured the amount of time that a word had to be presented for a subject to be able to read it. When the target word was presented after an appropriate context, subjects were able to read it even when the duration of the flash was short. But when the target word was presented after an inappropriate context, it had to be presented for a longer time. As shown in Figure 2–11, the time needed to read a word that followed a long, appropriate cue was about half as much as the time needed to read a word that followed a long, inappropriate cue. Compared to having no cue, inappropriate contexts tended to inhibit the subject's ability to read a word, whereas appropriate contexts tended to facilitate that ability.

FIGURE 2–11 Time to read a word in an appropriate versus inappropriate sentence context

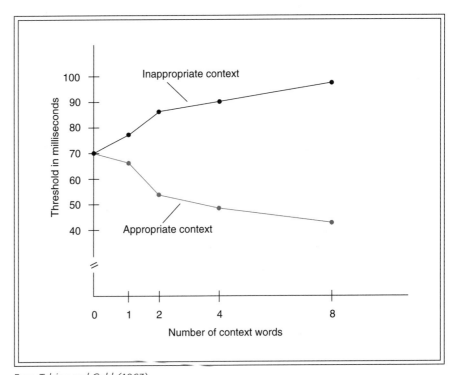

From Tulving and Gold (1963)

These results demonstrate the role of the reader's knowledge of meaning and syntax in word reading. One explanation is that the context provides syntactic cues (i.e., cues about what part of speech should occur) and semantic cues (i.e., cues about the possible meanings of the word). These cues allow the reader to generate specific hypotheses even before the target word is presented. If the hypotheses are correct, less reading time will be required; if the hypotheses are incorrect, more time will be required to generate and test new hypotheses.

West and Stanovich (1978) extended the Tulving and Gold research method to younger readers. For example, fourth-graders, sixth-graders, and adults were asked to read words that were presented on a screen. Some target words were preceded by a sentence context that was not congruent with the word, some target words were preceded by a sentence context that was not congruent, and others were preceded only by "the." West and Stanovich measured the amount of time between presentation of the target word and the subject's pronunciation of the word. Figure 2–12 shows that for all age groups, performance was better for words in congruous

FIGURE 2–12 Average time to pronounce a word in a congruous or noncongruous context or preceded only by "the"

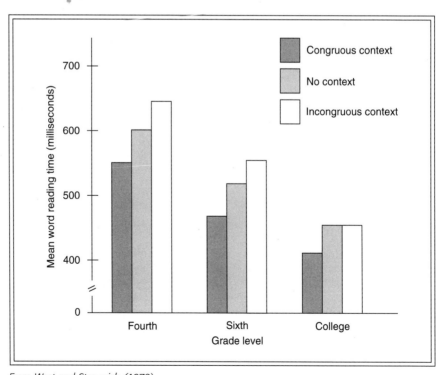

From West and Stanovich (1978)

sentences; however, the effects of context appear to weaken for older subjects. Apparently, adults are less reliant on context than children. One possibility is that adults search for word meaning in an automatic way, while children are more conscious of the context.

In a review of research comparing good and poor readers, Spoehr and Schuberth (1981) found that poor readers were more influenced by context cues than good readers. For example, in the West and Stanovich study, poorer readers showed a greater context effect than good readers. Similarly, Schvaneveldt, Ackerman, and Semlear (1977) found a developmental trend similar to that obtained by West and Stanovich in which younger readers showed a greater context effect than older readers. These results are consistent with the idea that use of context cues becomes automatic in good readers, while it is more time-consuming and conscious in poorer or younger readers.

IMPLICATIONS FOR INSTRUCTION: VOCABULARY TRAINING

The foregoing results show that good readers are more efficient than less skilled readers in finding a word's meaning from memory. Let's suppose that improvement in the speed of meaning access (i.e., the time needed to retrieve a word's meaning from long-term memory) is a skill that can be taught. Vocabulary training is a popular technique for increasing the efficiency of readers' meaning-access processes (Pressley, 1990).

VOCABULARY TRAINING. Not surprisingly, children who have better vocabularies (i.e., knowledge of the meanings of more words) perform better on reading comprehension tests (Anderson & Freebody, 1981). Similarly, changing unfamiliar words in a passage to more familiar synonyms increases children's reading comprehension (Marks, Doctorow & Wittrock, 1974), and word recognition is easier when words are embedded in a familiar rather than unfamiliar context (Wittrock, Marks, & Doctorow, 1975). The explanation for these results is that when the words in a passage are unfamiliar, students must focus their attention on the process of meaning access; in contrast, when the words are familiar, students can access their meaning automatically and use their attention to comprehend the passage.

A straightforward implication of these findings is that reading comprehension will be enhanced if students are given vocabulary training. However, analyses of school reading materials in grades three to nine found that as many as 88,000 distinct word meanings are required, and the average school student acquires about 3000 to 5000 words per year (Nagy & Anderson, 1984; Nagy & Herman, 1984; Nagy, Herman, & Anderson, 1985). According to Nagy and his colleagues, the direct instruction of vocabulary words would not be able to produce such large vocabulary growth in students. Instead, the bulk of new vocabulary words must be learned from context—that is, from reading or listening to or producing prose. Thus exercises such as silent sustained reading, in which students read books for a certain period of time on a regular basis, may serve as vocabulary training exercises.

In spite of these warnings concerning the limitations of direct vocabulary instruction, there have been numerous studies aimed at teaching vocabulary to young readers. Many of these studies are successful in teaching vocabulary as measured by multiple-choice tests, but not in greatly influencing readers' comprehension (Nagy & Herman, 1985; Pearson & Gallagher, 1983). One reason for the failure of some vocabulary training programs is that much printed material in schools can be understood with a vocabulary of only 4000 words. Training in new words reaches a point of diminishing returns, since most words outside of this basic core of 4000 words occur very rarely in school materials. For example, Nagy and Anderson (1984) found that most of these words in school materials occur less than one per million. Learning the meaning of words that occur with such low frequency is unlikely to have a substantial effect on comprehension.

Vocabulary training programs that are successful in enhancing comprehension tend to be those that help the reader to embed each word within a rich set of experiences and knowledge and that involve test passages containing the just-learned vocabulary words (Kameenui, Carnine, & Freschi, 1982). For example, in a series of studies, fourth-, fifth-, and sixth-graders read a passage and then answered test questions about the passage. Some of the subjects received a passage that contained difficult vocabulary words, while others received a passage where easier synonyms were substituted. The following example is a portion of the passage with the difficult words in italics and the easier synonyms in parentheses:

> Joe and Ann went to school in Portland. They were *antagonists* (enemies). They saw each other often. They had lots of *altercations* (fights). At the end of high school, Ann *maligned* (said bad things about) Joe. Then Ann moved away. Joe stayed in Portland. He got a job as a *bailiff* (worked for a judge). One day Joe was working, and he saw Ann. Ann did not see Joe. Ann looked *apprehensive* (afraid). She was being *incarcerated* (under arrest).

The test included literal questions such as:

> Joe and Ann saw each other _____ in school.
> (a) never
> (b) not much
> (c) frequently
> (d) often

In addition, the test included inference questions such as:

> Joe works in a _____.
> (a) school
> (b) hospital
> (c) courthouse
> (d) university

Figure 2–13 shows the percentage of correct answers given by students reading the difficult and easy vocabulary versions of the passage on literal and inferential questions. Those who read the easy version performed slightly better on literal questions and much better on inference questions. Apparently, a reader who understands the words has more opportunity to make meaningful inferences about the story.

The most interesting aspect of the study, however, involved an attempt to train some readers in the meanings of the six difficult vocabulary words before they read the passage. The training involved extensive discussions about each word, such as the following dialogue for altercations.

The experimenter placed an index card containing one vocabulary word and its meaning on the desk in front of the subject.

EXPERIMENTER: This word is "altercations." What word is this?
CHILD: "Altercations."
EXPERIMENTER: Correct, "altercations." What does "altercations" mean?
      [The experimenter points to the meaning given on card.]
CHILD: "Fights."

FIGURE 2–13 Percentage correct on literal and inferential questions for three vocabulary treatment groups

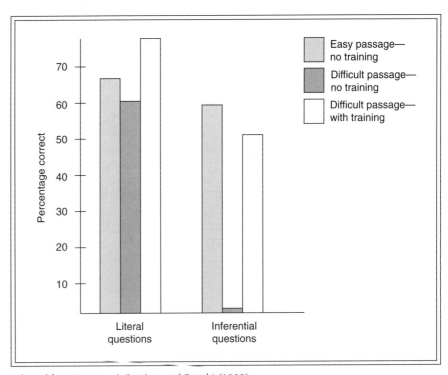

Adapted from Kameenui, Carnine, and Freschi (1982)

EXPERIMENTER: Yes, "altercations" means "fights." Listen, do you have altercations with your teacher? [Child responds.] Do you have altercations with a tree? [Child responds.] So what does "altercations" mean?

CHILD: "Fights."

The new vocabulary word is then integrated with the next one. For example, after the experimenter has gone through the same process for "antagonists," the experimenter asks: "Listen, do you have any antagonists? [Child responds.] Do you have any altercations with your antagonists? [Child responds.]"

Does vocabulary training improve reading comprehension? As Figure 2–13 indicates, students who were given vocabulary training before reading the difficult vocabulary version of the passage tended to excel in answering both literal and inference questions. You should note, however, that the training was for words that were specifically required for the passage and that the training forced the reader to connect the vocabulary words with the reader's prior knowledge and experience.

Beck and her colleagues (Beck, Perfetti, & McKeown, 1982; McKeown, Beck, Omanson, & Perfetti, 1983) have also developed techniques for helping readers to embed words within their own experiences. Their extensive vocabulary training has been successful in increasing readers' comprehension of texts that contain the just-learned words. Again, success seems to be tied to knowledge-based training and tests that involve the specifically taught words (Stahl & Fairbanks, 1986).

SENTENCE INTEGRATION

WHAT IS SENTENCE INTEGRATION?

The previous sections have shown that reading a word involves both decoding and accessing meaning. However, reading a text also involves fitting the words together into a coherent sentence structure. This process could be called *sentence integration,* and one way of investigating this process is to observe readers' eyes as they read a passage.

RESEARCH ON SENTENCE INTEGRATION

EYE MOVEMENTS DURING READING. Let me ask you to introspect about what your eyes are doing as you read the words in this paragraph. Does reading seem to involve a smooth and continuous flow of information from the page into your eyes? Does it seem that your eyes move smoothly across the page, taking in information that is analyzed by your brain? If so, your description corresponds to what has been called a "buffer model" of reading—the idea that your eyes smoothly scan each line from left to right, placing information into a short-term buffer so that it can be continuously analyzed.

Although this description of reading may be consistent with the common-sense experiences of skilled readers, it has been subjected to rigorous experimental tests by researchers. One technique that can provide some information is to observe a reader's eye movements during reading. In the late 1800s, researchers discovered that readers' eyes tend to move in discontinuous jumps rather than in a smooth, continuous flow. You can confirm this observation by carefully watching someone's eyes as the person reads from a book or computer screen.

Research conducted during the last 20 years (Crowder & Wagner, 1992; Rayner & Pollatsek, 1989; Rayner & Sereno, 1994) provides clear and consistent evidence of the following aspects of eye movements during reading:

Fixations: A reader's eyes typically focus on a point in the text for an average of 200 to 250 milliseconds.

Fixation span: The fixation span of an eye focused on text is about six to eight letters. When the eyes are fixated on some point in the text, the center of the reader's field of vision (which is used for word identification) extends about seven letter positions to the right of this point. Thus, in normal reading a person can identify one medium-sized word or perhaps two short words in a single fixation. In addition, a reader may have some reduced acuity for about four letter positions to the left and up to fifteen letter positions to the right of the fixation point on the line of text being read. Although some useful information can be extracted to help guide the reading process, this additional information is not used for word identification.

Saccades: The eyes rapidly jump to another point in the text, with the jump (or saccade) lasting about 15 to 30 milliseconds; no information can be acquired during the jump. Most of the time, readers move to the next important word in the text, but about 10% to 15% of eye movements are regressions (i.e., when readers look back to reread part of the text).

Saccade lengths: For readers of English, the eyes move from left to right across the page (or return to the beginning of the next lower line) at a rate averaging eight letter positions (or about one and a half words) per move.

The fact that the eyes move in a pattern of fixations and saccades tends to conflict with readers' reports that the information seems to flow smoothly. This experience of smooth processing might result if the eyes moved at a regular rate (i.e., if all fixations averaged about the same time) and at a regular distance (i.e., if all saccade lengths averaged about the same number of spaces). However, many researchers (Crowder & Wagner, 1992; McConkie, 1976; Rayner & Sereno, 1994) have documented that there is great variance within a reader in both the duration of the fixation (ranging from less than 100 milliseconds for simple words to more than 1 second for words at the ends of sentences) and saccade length (ranging from one to fifteen letters, depending on the shape of surrounding words). Thus readers do not sweep their eyes across the page at regular intervals and for regular distances; instead, eye movements seem to be controlled partially by the text.

HOW MUCH IS SEEN IN ONE FIXATION? How can the text control the eye fixations and movements until the reader knows what he or she is reading? In other words, how can you know where to move your eyes until you have looked to see what is ahead? To investigate this question, McConkie and Rayner (1975) asked high school students to read a passage on a computer screen. The computer determined where the reader was fixating on the screen; the computer did not alter the area around the fixation point (called the "window"), but did alter the rest of the text.

On each fixation, the size of the window was 13, 17, 21, 25, 31, 37, 45, or 100 letter positions; this means that if a person was reading the line shown in Figure 2–14 with a window of 17 letters, all the letters would be correct for the 8 letter positions before and the 8 after the fixation point. However, beyond this window, each word would be changed to nonsense letters or *X*s. For some readers, the spaces between words were filled with either other letters or *X*s, whereas for other readers the spaces were retained. (Figure 2–14 shows examples for fixation on "d" in "diagnosis.")

Figure 2–15 shows the median saccade length and average reading time for each window size. As you can see, when the window is artificially restricted, the saccade length drops from about eight letter spaces to six letter spaces, and the reading rate falls. In addition, filling spaces between words with letters also tended to reduce the saccade length, with window

FIGURE 2–14

Examples of the reading task used by McConkie and Rayner

Original Text
Graphology means personality diagnosis from handwriting. This is a

Window Size of 17 with Peripheral Text Filled
Hbfxwysyvoctifdlexiblonality diagnosiscabytewfdnehbemedveee clfw

Window Size of 17 with Peripheral Text Spaced
Hbfxwysyvo tifdl xiblonality diagnosis abyt wfdn hbemedv. Awcl el f

Adapted from McConkie and Rayner (1975)

FIGURE 2–15 Median length of forward saccades and median reading rates for eight windows

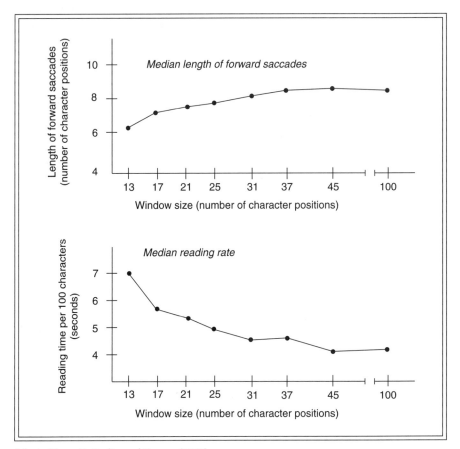

Adapted from McConkie and Rayner (1975)

sizes up to 25. In a subsequent study, Rayner, Well, and Pollastek (1980) found that readers are affected only by the size of the window to the right of the fixation point; for example, similar results are obtained for a window of eight letters on either side of the fixation point and for one of eight letters to the right of the fixation point only. These findings suggest that readers focus on about six to eight letters at a time and can look ahead approximately fifteen letters to determine the appropriate length of the next saccade.

WHERE DO READERS' EYES FIXATE? As another example of eye movement research, consider the passage shown in Figure 2–16. Carpenter and Just (1981) asked a college student to read this passage while a computer monitored where and how long the reader's eyes fixated on the text. In Figure 2–16, numbers are given above places in the line on which the eyes fixated; the numbers in parentheses indicate the order of fixa-

FIGURE 2–16

A reader's eye
fixations while
reading a
passage on
radioisotopes

The sequence of fixations within each sentence is indicated by the successively numbered fixations above the word being fixated. The duration of each fixation (in milliseconds) is shown immediately below the fixation number.

```
(4)     (11)
286     466
(1)     (2)     (3)  (5)          (6)     (7)          (8)               (9)
166     200     167  299          217     268          317               399
Radioisotopes  have  long  been  valuable  tools  in  scientific  and  medical
```

```
                              (16)
                              183
   (10)              (12)(13)      (14)(15)          (17)      (18) (19) (20)
   463               317  250      367 416           333       183  450  650
research.  Now,  however,  four  nonradioactive  isotopes  are  being  produced.
```

```
         (24)                      (28)
         366                       183
(21)     (22)   (23)   (25)  (26)      (27)   (29)  (30)  (31)(32)(33)
250      200    367    400   216        233   317   283   100  683  150
They are called "icons"—four isotopes of carbon, oxygen, nitrogen, and sulfur.
```

From Carpenter and Just (1981)

tions, and the numbers below them indicate the length of the fixations in milliseconds.

What do Carpenter and Just's observations tell us about the reading process? First, the results demonstrate that fixation points are neither randomly nor evenly selected. For example, almost all content words are fixated, while blank spaces between sentences are not heavily fixated. There is also great variability in the length of the jumps from one fixation point to the next, with some saccades spanning just three letters (such as from the twelfth to the thirteenth fixation) and others spanning about ten letters (such as from the twenty-first to the twenty-second fixation).

Second, the findings show that each fixation is not treated equally. For example, there is great variability in the duration of fixations, which range from 100 to 683 milliseconds. Unfamiliar words, such as "radioisotopes" and "icons," are fixated for much more time than familiar words. Similarly, other researchers have found that reading a uncommon word, such as "steward," takes an average of 30 to 90 millseconds longer than reading a common word, such as "student," even when both are placed within otherwise identical sentences (Rayner & Duffy, 1986). These results are inconsistent with the buffer theory (i.e., the idea that the eye moves at a relatively constant rate, taking in information that is analyzed later). Instead, these results suggest that eye movements are guided, in part, by the difficulty of the text.

A third major discovery is that readers seem to be thinking about what they read during the reading process. For example, in Figure 2–16 fixation durations are generally much longer at the end of a sentence, such as for "medical research" in the first sentence and "being produced" in the second. This result suggests that readers may be trying to integrate the information at sentence or major clause boundaries. Since the fixation seems to be much longer than is required to perceive the word, the long fixations at sentence (and clause) boundaries imply that additional cognitive processing is occurring. Carpenter and Just (1981) called this activity *sentence wrap-up,* and suggest that it includes searching for referents, building relations among clauses, drawing inferences, and resolving inconsistencies.

Just and Carpenter (1978) provided an example of how eye fixations may be related to reader's integration of information. In their study, subjects read two-sentence passages. One text was as follows:

> It was dark and stormy the night the millionaire was murdered.
> The killer left no clues for the police to trace.

Other readers received a slightly different passage:

> It was dark and stormy the night the millionaire died.
> The killer left no clues for the police to trace.

As you can see, the noun "killer" in the second sentence is the agent for the verb "murdered" or "died" in the first sentence. In reading the second sentence, the reader must make the inference that the killer is responsible for the death of the millionaire. Just and Carpenter found that readers paused an average of 500 milliseconds longer for the second sentence in the second passage than in the first. The two main places that required extended fixation times were the word "killer" and the word "trace" at the end of the sentence.

As another example of how readers adjust their reading rates to meet the demands of the text, consider the following two sentences:

Al is a doctor.
Bill is a doctor, too.

In this case, the two sentences are somewhat independent, so that the information in the first sentence is not needed to help you make sense of the second. However, now read the following two sentences:

Al is a surgeon.
Bill is a doctor, too.

To comprehend the second sentence, you need to make a logical inference based on your knowledge that all surgeons are doctors; namely, you need to infer that Al is a doctor. Singer, Revlin, and Halldorson (1990) found that the time needed to read the second sentence was about 500 milliseconds greater when such an inference was required than when no inference was required. These results show that the reader's integration of information can be observed through careful observation of eye fixations and reading times.

IMPLICATIONS FOR INSTRUCTION: SPEED READING

The research described in this section has implications for speed reading programs, which generally attempt to teach students how to increase their fixation span (i.e., how many letters they see in one fixation), to decrease their fixation duration (i.e., how long their eyes remain fixated), and to decrease the number of their fixations or increase their saccade length (i.e., to skim across or down a page). Many speed reading programs claim to be able to increase a person's reading speed without decreasing comprehension. Crowder and Wagner (1992) observed that the following techniques are often used to accomplish these goals:

1. The student is taught to eliminate subvocal speech so that less time is spent on each fixation.
2. The student is encouraged to chunk words visually into meaningful units so that more information can be processed during each fixation.
3. The student is taught to use the index finger as a guide that moves down the page so that fewer fixations will be made.
4. The student is taught to read more actively by making inferences during reading.

How does the eye movement research square with these practices and claims? Unfortunately, the research on eye movements would lead us to be cautious in accepting the claims of speed reading advocates. First, the foregoing research shows that pauses in reading (e.g., long fixations at the end of phrases or sentences) may be related to the reader's integration of the information in the phrase or sentence. Thus teaching students to reduce their fixation time could disrupt the integration process. Second, the research also shows that a reader can usually take in only one or two words per fixation, so increasing the saccade length (or decreasing the number of fixations) means that some words may never be seen.

How fast can the visual system work? According to research on eye movements humans can clearly see no more than two words per fixation and can fixate no more than four times per second, yielding a maximum possible reading rate of about 480 words per minute (wpm). In an admittedly generous analysis, Crowder and Wagner (1992) set the upper limit at 900 wpm by estimating that readers have access to three words per fixation and can fixate five times per second. Thus, there are physiological constraints on the reading rate, with estimates ranging from 480 to 900 wpm. Interestingly, the average reading rate for college students falls well within even the lower of these estimates, at about 300 wpm (Crowder & Wagner, 1992).

Can some people read much faster than 900 wpm? To answer this question, Carver (1985) carefully tested exceptionally fast readers, such as graduates of speed reading programs who were tauted as having reading rates above 20,000 wpm. In addition, Carver tested college students who performed at the top of the class on reading tests and students who earned perfect scores on the reading sections of the Scholastic Aptitude Test. After three days of well-controlled testing, the results were in: Average rates ranged from 250 to 450 wpm, corresponding to the estimates based on eye movement research.

Can people learn to read faster than 900 wpm? To evaluate the effectiveness of a typical speed reading program, consider the following scenario. A school district decides to hire a speed reading company to improve students' reading rates. The company agrees to provide approximately fifty hours of instruction and practice, and guarantees that at least 75% of the students will quintuple their reading rates and increase their comprehension by 10%. Do you think the program will succeed? A program just like the one described was carried out in a school district in southern California (Crowder, 1982). Students were given reading speed and comprehension tests before and after instruction. The average reading rate rose from 155 wpm before instruction to 657 wpm after instruction, while comprehension scores fell slightly from 35 to 33% correct.

Should you be happy with these results? Crowder (1982) pointed out that the company failed to reach its goal, since only 13% of the students quintupled their reading rates and increased their comprehension by 10%. In addition, Crowder noted that there was no comparison group, so we do not know how much improvement there would have been over the course of the year if students had not received speed reading instruction. In fact, most standardized tests show that students gain in comprehension each year. Finally, Crowder stated that the reading speed test given after training was easier than the test given before training; thus any gains claimed by the speed reading company cannot be accepted as valid.

In summary, this example shows why you should critically examine any claims about speed reading. The good news is that adults with low reading rates (e.g., 100 to 200 wpm) may be able to increase their rates (e.g., closer to the average of 300 wpm for college students) without losing comprehension. The bad news is that readers are unlikely to be able to increase their reading rates beyond 900 wpm without serious loses in comprehension. For example, Carver (1971) has shown that speed reading courses that teach people to move their eyes faster often do not help people to comprehend more text. Apparently, readers need some pauses to make inferences, access meanings of unusual words, and integrate the information into a coherent message. The positive features of speed reading training are that students may learn how to skim material effectively, and some students may become more automatic in their decoding skills. The negative features are that when the rate of reading is pushed beyond the physical limits of how fast the eye can move, the reader is forced to skip some material and to spend less time integrating the material, which results in less comprehension.

CONCLUSION

A great deal of cognitive processing occurs during the quarter of a second that a reader's eye looks at a word on the printed page. This chapter has explored four related processes: recognizing phonemes, decoding words, accessing word meaning, and integrating sentences.

Research on reading is notable for several reasons. First, it represents a very old area in psychology that is currently experiencing a welcome revival. Second, there is an extremely large and rapidly growing literature on reading. Third, there are many different approaches to the study of reading, ranging from pronunciation tasks to eye movement tasks, and many different theoretical approaches.

Basic research on phonological awareness shows that students need to be able to segment a spoken language into its sound units. Phonological awareness appears to be a readiness skill for reading, so some students who have not acquired it by the primary grades may benefit from direct instruction in how to recognize phonemes.

Some of the basic findings concerning decoding have implications for the decision about whether to use a whole-word or phonics approach in reading instruction. First, there is an automaticity effect in which skilled learners can perform a task without paying attention to what they are doing. Second, there is a word superiority effect in which skilled readers can recognize letters in words more easily than individual letters. Third, skilled readers possess and use pronunciation strategies for combining letters or letter groups into words. The research suggests that skilled readers have automated the processes involved in word decoding, including the use of word context to identify letter sounds and of pronunciation strategies to combine letters. As children's decoding processes become more automatic, they have more attentional capacity to use for comprehending the material. The current consensus of reading researchers is that the best way to help children acquire automatic decoding processes is to rely on the phonics approach.

Some of the research findings concerning meaning access have implications for vocabulary training. Beginning or younger readers tend to rely on the context of the other words in a sentence to recognize the meaning of a word; in contrast, older or more skilled readers are able to access word meaning directly. In order to help children become more automatic in their use of sentence context and in understanding unusual words, students can benefit from vocabulary training. Other forms of direct training include encouraging children to engage in silent sustained reading regularly and providing an environment where children hear spoken language. The ultimate goal of such instruction is to help students automate their meaning accessing processes, so that more attention can be devoted to sentence integration and other comprehension processes.

Some of the research findings concerning sentence integration have implications for speed reading training. First, reading involves eye movements, with each fixation requiring a certain amount of time, during which the reader can take in only a small amount of text. Second, long fixations (or pauses) often occur at the end of a phrase or sentence, suggesting that the reader needs time to integrate the material. Speed reading programs that reduce the fixation time may also reduce the time for integration; similarly, speed reading programs that reduce the number of fixations per page may reduce the amount of information that a reader takes in. Thus while speed reading training may help students learn how to skim, it may also result in poorer comprehension.

In summary, the implications of psychological research on reading are still far from complete; however, based on the current state of our understanding, instruction in reading should: (1) insure that beginning readers possess phonological awareness; (2) emphasize phonics for beginning readers as well as meaning approaches for developing readers; (3) develop automatic word reading skills through practice; and (4) promote increased reading speed only when a reader does not lose comprehension or when skimming is the goal of reading.

SUGGESTED READINGS

Adams, M. J. (1990). *Beginning to read.* Cambridge, MA: MIT Press. (An award-winning review of research on reading and its relevance to reading instruction.)

Crowder, R. G., & Wagner, R. K. (1992). *The psychology of reading: An introduction* (2nd ed). New York: Oxford University Press. (An excellent textbook that summarizes psychological research on the reading process.)

Gough, P. B., Ehri, L. C., & Treiman, R. (Eds.). (1992). *Reading acquisition.* Hillsdale, NJ: Erlbaum. (A thoughtful overview of research and theory on how children learn to read.)

CHAPTER Reading Comprehension

This chapter examines techniques for improving students' comprehension of text. Three kinds of knowledge needed for effective reading comprehension are content knowledge, which includes having and using prior knowledge; strategic knowledge, which includes making inferences during reading and using prose structure to determine important information; and metacognitive knowledge, which includes monitoring whether one comprehends the material. In particular, this chapter investigates the reading comprehension processes of skilled readers and the degree to which these processes can be taught. Finally, it examines reading programs that attempt to teach one or more of these kinds of knowledge.

EFFORT AFTER MEANING

Let me ask you to read the passage in Figure 3–1. After you have read over the passage one time, please put it aside and write down all you can remember.

THE WAR OF THE GHOSTS

One night two young men from Egulac went down to the river to hunt seals, and while they were there it became foggy and calm. Then they heard war-cries, and they thought: "Maybe this is a war-party." They escaped to the shore, and hid behind a log. Now canoes came up, and they heard the noise of paddles, and they saw one canoe coming up to them. There were five men in the canoe, and they said:

"What do you think? We wish to take you along. We are going up the river to make war on the people."

One of the young men said: "I have no arrows."

"Arrows are in the canoe," they said.

"I will not go along. I might be killed. My relatives do not know where I have gone. But you," he said, turning to the other, "may go with them."

So one of the young men went, but the other returned home.

And the warriors went on up the river to a town on the other side of Kalama. The people came down to the water, and they began to fight, and many were killed. But presently the young man heard one of the warriors say: "Quick, let us go home, that Indian has been hit." Now he thought: "Oh, they are ghosts." He did not feel sick, but they said he had been shot.

So the canoes went back to Egulac, and the young man went ashore to his house, and made a fire. And he told everybody and said: "Behold I accompanied the ghosts, and we went to fight. Many of our fellows were killed, and many of those who attacked us were killed. They said I was hit, and I did not feel sick."

He told it all, and then he became quiet. When the sun rose he fell down. Something black came out of his mouth. His face became contorted. The people jumped up and cried.

He was dead.

From Bartlett (1932)

This passage was used by Bartlett (1932) in his famous research on how people learn and remember meaningful prose. Bartlett asked British college students to read a folk story from a North American Indian culture, so his readers did not have much prior experience with the ideas in the passage. In Bartlett's study, first one person read the passage twice and then 15 minutes later wrote down all he could remember; the version that the first person had written was then read by a second person, who wrote down all he could remember; this version was in turn passed on to the next person; and so on. By the time the story was read and recalled by the last person, it had changed greatly, as shown in Figure 3-2. If you are like the subjects in Bartlett's study, here are some of the changes you made in your recall:

Leveling or flattening: You left out many of the details, such as proper names (e.g., Egulac, Kalama). You lost the verbatim writing style of the writer and instead remembered the general points or gist of parts of the story.

Sharpening: You emphasized a few distinctive details, such as the fact that one Indian was not able to go to fight because he had an old mother at home.

Rationalization: You made the passage more compact, more coherent, and more consistent with your expectations. For example, if you viewed the passage as a story about a fishing trip or a naval battle, you would be less likely to remember references to spirits and ghosts.

As you can see, the main point of this demonstration is that people's memories do not work like computers' memories. We do not tend to remember information perfectly in verbatim form. We remember some things, but not necessarily in the form they were presented. We often add other elements that were not given, and we try to organize our memories in a way that makes sense.

According to Bartlett, when we read a meaningful prose passage we are not passively putting the information into our minds; instead, we are actively trying to understand the passage. Bartlett referred to this active comprehension process as "effort after meaning." In reading a text, humans must assimilate the new information to existing knowledge—or to what Bartlett called "schemas." What a person learns from reading a text does not correspond directly to what is presented, but rather to a combination of what is presented and the reader's schema to which it is assimilated. The reader changes the new information to fit his or her existing concepts, and in the process, details are lost and the knowledge becomes more coherent for that person. For "The War of the Ghosts" passage, for example, most readers lacked the appropriate schema concerning spirits. Since learning involves assimilating new material to existing concepts, the readers were at a loss. According to Bartlett (1932), "without some general setting or label as we have repeatedly seen, no material can be assimilated or remembered" (p. 172). Because mystical concepts were not a major

FIGURE 3-2

What readers remember from "The War of the Ghosts"

VERSION REPRODUCED BY THE FIRST SUBJECT

THE WAR OF THE GHOSTS

There were two young Indians who lived in Egulac, and they went down to the sea to hunt for seals. And where they were hunting it was very foggy and very calm. In a little while they heard cries, and they came out of the water and went to hide behind a log. Then they heard the sound of paddles, and they saw five canoes. One canoe came toward them, and there were five men within, who cried to the two Indians, and said: "Come with us up this river, and make war on the people there."

But one of the Indians replied: "We have no arrows."

"There are arrows in the canoe."

"But I might be killed, and my people have need of me. You have no parents," he said to the other, "you can go with them if you wish it so; I shall stay here."

So one of the Indians went, but the other stayed behind and went home. And the canoes went on up the river to the other side of Kalama, and fought the people there. Many of the people were killed, and many of those from the canoes also.

Then one of the warriors called to the young Indian and said: "Go back to the canoe, for you are wounded by an arrow." But the Indian wondered, for he felt not sick.

And when many had fallen on either side they went back to the canoes, and down the river again, and so the young Indian came back to Egulac.

factor in the readers' culture, these aspects of the story were not well remembered; as a result, the passage was changed into a more common "war story."

Bartlett also proposed that recalling a story involves an active "process of construction" rather than straightforward retrieval. During recall, we use a general schema—such as a war story—to help generate details that fit with it. Memory is not detailed but rather is schematic, that is, based on general impressions. Although recall produces specific details that seem to be correct, many are, in fact, wrong.

Bartlett's work, although done more than sixty-five years ago, is concerned with many of the same issues raised by modern cognitive psychologists. Of particular interest is Bartlett's view of the reader as actively engaged in an "effort after meaning", that is, in an effort to make sense out of the text by relating it to his or her existing knowledge.

FIGURE 3–2

(continued)

Then he told them how there had been a battle, and how many fell and how the warriors had said he was wounded, and yet he felt not sick. So he told them all the tale, and he became weak. It was near daybreak when he became weak; and when the sun rose he fell down. And he gave a cry, and as he opened his mouth a black thing rushed from it. Then they ran to pick him up, wondering. But when they spoke he answered not.

He was dead.

VERSION REPRODUCED BY THE TENTH SUBJECT

THE WAR OF THE GHOSTS

Two Indians were out fishing for seals in the Bay of Manpapan, when along came five other Indians in a war-canoe. They were going fighting.

"Come with us," said the five to the two, "and fight."

"I cannot come," was the answer of the one, "for I have an old mother at home who is dependent upon me." The other said he could not come, because he had no arms. "That is no difficulty," the others replied, "for we have plenty in the canoe with us"; so he got into the canoe and went with them.

In a fight soon afterwards this Indian received a mortal wound. Finding that his hour was coming, he cried out that he was about to die. "Nonsense," said one of the others, "you will not die." But he did.

From Bartlett (1932)

SCHEMA THEORY

WHAT IS A SCHEMA?

Bartlett was one of the first psychologists to address the question of how people learn from meaningful prose. Bartlett's main theoretical concept was the *schema*—a person's existing knowledge that is used both to assimilate new information and to generate recall of information. For example, in reading "The War of the Ghosts," you must construct an appropriate schema (such as a war story), assimilate facts from the passage to the schema (such as being mortally wounded), and then use the schema to construct a recalled version that includes inferences consistent with the theme.

What is a schema? In a sense, answering this question is a major goal of modern cognitive psychology. Although each theorist offers a slightly different interpretation of what a schema is, a general definition would contain the following points (Mayer, 1992):

General: A schema may be used in a wide variety of situations as a framework for understanding incoming information.

Knowledge: A schema exists in memory as something that a person knows.

Structure: A schema is organized around a theme.

Comprehension: A schema contains "slots" that are filled by specific information in the text.

Thus a schema is a reader's general knowledge structure that serves to select and organize incoming information into an integrated, meaningful framework.

SCHEMAS FOR NARRATIVE PROSE. Several authors have proposed *story grammars* that readers might use to understand narrative prose, that is, text that tells a story (Mandler & Johnson, 1977; Rumelhart, 1975; Thorndike, 1977). For example, Mandler and Johnson (1977) have suggested that most folk stories can be divided into two main parts: *story = setting + episode(s).* An episode in turn can be split into two parts: *episode = beginning + development.* The development of an episode contains two parts: *development = response + ending.* A response can consist of two simple parts: *response = simple reaction + action,* or it can be more complex: *response = complex reaction + goal path.* A goal path is composed of two parts: *goal path = attempt + outcome.* Figure 3–3 shows how "The War of the Ghosts" can be broken into a setting and five episodes according to Mandler and Johnson's story grammar. Episode 1 is followed by Episode 2, which is followed by Episode 5; Episodes 3 and 4 are subepisodes connected to Episode 2. Within each episode, there is usually a beginning event followed by some reaction that results in an outcome or ending.

When a reader is given a story to read or listen to, the reader will have expectations that the story will have a structure, such as is indicated in Mandler and Johnson's story grammar. For example, readers expect that there will be episodes in which some beginning event is followed by attempts to respond to it that result in an ending. Graesser (1980), Gernsbacher (1990), and others have pointed out that younger readers often lack appropriate schemas to understand prose. For example, Whaley (1981) found that third-graders are far less able than sixth-graders to predict what will come next in a story. Presumably, younger readers are not as aware of story grammars as older readers. Thus learning to read involves learning to fill in each general part of the structure (such as the beginning, action, and ending of each episode) with specifics from the story.

FIGURE 3–3

Analysis of "The War of the Ghosts" using story grammar

Setting	1	One night two young men from Egulac went down to the river to hunt seals,
	2	and while they were there it became foggy and calm.

Episode 1

Beginning	3	Then they heard war-cries,
Complex reaction	4	and they thought: "Maybe this is a war-party."
Attempt	5	They escaped to the shore,
	6	and hid behind a log.
	7	Now canoes came up,
Ending	8	and they heard the noise of paddles,
	9	and then saw one canoe coming up to them.

Episode 2

Setting	10	There were five men in the canoe,
Beginning	11	and they said: "What do you think? We wish to take you along.
	12	We are going up the river to make war on the people."
Attempt	13	One of the young men said: "I have no arrows."
Outcome	14	"Arrows are in the canoe," they said.
	15	"I will not go along.
Attempt	16	I might be killed.
	17	My relatives do not know where I have gone.
	18	But you," he said, turning to the other, "may go with them."
Outcome	19	So one of the young men went,
	20	but the other returned home.
Ending	21	And the warriors went on up the river to a town on the other side of Kalama.

Episode 3

Beginning	22	The people came down to the water,
	23	and they began to fight,
	24	and many were killed.
	25	But presently the young man heard one of the warriors say: "Quick, let us go home; that Indian has been hit."

(continued)

FIGURE 3-3

(continued)

Simple reaction	26	Now he thought: "Oh, they are ghosts."
	27	He did not feel sick,
Action	28	but they said he had been shot.
Ending	29	So the canoes went back to Egulac,

Episode 4

Beginning	30	and the young man went ashore to his house, and made a fire.
	31	And he told everybody and said: "Behold I accompanied the ghosts, and we went to fight.
	32	Many of our fellows were killed,
Action	33	and many of those who attacked us were killed.
	34	They said I was hit,
	35	and I did not feel sick."
	36	He told it all,
Ending	37	and then he became quiet.

Episode 5

Beginning	38	When the sun rose he fell down.
	39	Something black came out of his mouth.
	40	His face became contorted.
Action	41	The people jumped up and cried.
Ending	42	He was dead.

From Mandler and Johnson (1977)

WHAT SKILLS ARE NEEDED FOR READING COMPREHENSION?

This chapter is concerned with the process of reading comprehension and in particular with understanding the skills that underlie a reader's "effort after meaning." What are these skills? In a review of five major basal reading series, Rosenshine (1980) found that all emphasized the following eight skills: (1) locating details; (2) identifying the main idea; (3) recognizing the sequence of events; (4) developing conclusions; (5) recognizing cause-and-effect relationships; (6) understanding words in context; (7) making interpretations; and (8) drawing inferences from the text. However, Rosenshine found no evidence that all basal series taught these skills in the same order and sequence. Similarly, Pearson and Fielding (1991) noted that reading comprehension instruction often teaches students how to activate background knowledge, to use text structure, or to summarize text. Brown and Palinscar (1989; Palinscar & Brown, 1984) idenified four major reading comprehension skills: (1) generating questions that are answered by the text; (2) identifying words that need to be clarified; (3) summarizing text; and (4) predicting what will come next in a text. Although these skills have long been part of reading comprehension programs taught to millions of students, we are just beginning to understand how these skills are related to the process of reading comprehension.

In this chapter, we explore three kinds of knowledge suggested by Brown, Campione, and Day (1981) that a reader might use in the process of "effort after meaning":

Content knowledge refers to information about the subject domain of the passage. This is discussed in the section below, "Using Prior Knowledge."

Strategic knowledge refers to the reader's collection of procedures for learning more effectively. These are discussed in the sections "Using Prose Structure" and "Making Inferences."

Metacognitive knowledge refers to the reader's awareness of her own cognitive processes and whether she is successfully meeting the demands of the task. These skills include comprehension monitoring, which is explored in the section "Using Metacognitive Knowledge."

In particular, we focus on the cognitive processes of using prior knowledge, using prose structure, making inferences, and using metacognitive knowledge.

USING PRIOR KNOWLEDGE

WHAT IS THE READER'S PERSPECTIVE?

One of the most persistent findings in the literature on adult prose learning is that people's prior knowledge about the topic of a passage influences what they remember from that passage. The reader's perspective includes the prior knowledge that the reader uses to understand the passage. What is remembered seems to depend both on what is presented in the passage and on what perspective the reader brings to the reading task.

RESEARCH ON DIFFERENCES IN READERS' PRIOR KNOWLEDGE

DIFFERENCES IN THE AMOUNT OF PRIOR KNOWLEDGE. As an example of the role of prior knowledge, consider the passage shown in the top of Figure 3–4. Bransford and Johnson (1972) asked college students to read this passage, to rate its comprehensibility (1 is low and 7 is high), and

FIGURE 3–4

The "Washing Clothes" passage

THE PASSAGE

The procedure is actually quite simple. First you arrange items into different groups. Of course one pile may be sufficient, depending on how much there is to do. If you have to go somewhere else due to lack of facilities, that is the next step; otherwise, you are pretty well set. It is important not to overdo things. That is, it is better to do too few things at once than too many. In the short run this may not seem important, but complications can easily arise. A mistake can be expensive as well. At first, the whole procedure will seem complicated. Soon, however, it will become just another facet of life. It is difficult to foresee any end to the necessity for this task in the immediate future, but then, one never can tell. After the procedure is completed, one arranges the materials into different groups again. Then they can be put into their appropriate places. Eventually they will be used once more, and the whole cycle will then have to be repeated. However, that is part of life.

Comprehension and Recall Scores for the Passage

	No Topic	Topic After	Topic Before	Maximum Score
Comprehension ratings	2.29	2.12	4.50	7.00
Number of idea units recalled	2.82	2.65	5.83	18.00

From Bransford and Johnson (1972)

to recall it. Some students were given a title ("Washing Clothes") for the passage before they read the passage, other students were given the title after they had read the passage, and still others were given no title at all. The table at the bottom of Figure 3–4 shows the performance of the three groups on the recall and comprehension rating tasks. The group that had the title before reading had a much higher comprehension score and recalled about twice as much as the other groups. Apparently, giving students the title of the passage allowed them to relate the new information to their prior knowledge about washing clothes; providing the title after reading or not at all left the reader without a way of meaningfully relating the new information to prior knowledge during reading.

Figure 3–5 presents another passage for you to read. Suppose I asked you to read the passage from the perspective of a potential home buyer. Alternatively, suppose I asked you to read it from the perspective of a burglar. Would what you remembered from the passage be influenced by your

FIGURE 3–5

"The House" passage

The two boys ran until they came to the driveway. "See, I told you today was good for skipping school," said Mark. "Mom is never home on Thursday," he added. Tall hedges hid the house from the road so the pair strolled across the finely landscaped yard. "I never knew your place was so big," said Pete. "Yeah, but it's nicer now than it used to be since Dad had the new stone siding put on and added the fireplace."

There were front and back doors and a side door which led to the garage, which was empty except for three parked 10-speed bikes. They went in the side door, Mark explaining that it was always open in case his younger sisters got home earlier than their mother.

Pete wanted to see the house, so Mark started with the living room. It, like the rest of the downstairs, was newly painted. Mark turned on the stereo, the noise of which worried Pete. "Don't worry, the nearest house is a quarter of a mile away," Mark shouted. Pete felt more comfortable observing that no houses could be seen in any direction beyond the huge yard.

The dining room, with all the china, silver, and cut glass, was no place to play so the boys moved into the kitchen, where they made sandwiches. Mark said they wouldn't go to the basement because it had been damp and musty ever since the new plumbing had been installed.

"This is where my Dad keeps his famous paintings and his coin collection," Mark said as they peered into the den. Mark bragged that he could get spending money whenever he needed it since he'd discovered that his Dad kept a lot in the desk drawer.

There were three upstairs bedrooms. Mark showed Pete his mother's closet, which was filled with furs, and the locked box which held her jewels. His sisters' room was uninteresting except for the color TV, which Mark carried to his room. Mark bragged that the bathroom in the hall was his since one had been added to his sisters' room for their use. The big highlight in his room, though, was a leak in the ceiling where the old roof had finally rotted.

From Pichert and Anderson (1977)

perspective—home buyer versus burglar—while reading the passage? Pichert and Anderson (1977) asked students to read the house passage from the perspective of a potential home buyer or burglar or with no perspective instructions. Students' recall of details from the passage was greatly influenced by their perspective while reading. For example, details such as where the father keeps the coin collection were better recalled by the subjects who had read with the burglar perspective. Again, these results show that what is learned from reading depends on both the passage and the reader's perspective.

Similar results have been obtained in studies using younger readers. Pearson, Hansen, and Gordon (1979) asked second-graders to read a modified basal passage on spiders. Although all of the children were classified as good readers based on their scores on standardized reading comprehension tests, half of the students knew a lot about spiders and half did not. After reading the spider passage, the children answered text-explicit questions that dealt with information specifically presented in the passage, such as, "What does Webby bite insects with?" and text-implicit questions that required inferences, such as "What part of Webby's body is nearly the same as part of a snake's body?" Figure 3–6 shows that the high-knowledge readers scored almost three times better than the low-knowledge readers on questions requiring inference and about 25% better on questions requiring retention of facts. These results are consistent with the idea that good reading skill is not the sole determinant of what is learned from reading a passage. In addition, the knowledge that the reader brings to the reading situation seems to influence heavily the reader's ability to make inferences about the material.

Marr and Gormley (1982) also found evidence that prior knowledge tends to enhance readers' inference-making performance more than simple retention of facts. Fourth graders were asked to read either familiar or unfamiliar passages, and then asked to retell the story and to answer some questions. Examples are given in Figure 3–7. Responses were scored as "textual" if they referred to material in the text and as "scriptal" if they involved inferences. As you can see in Figure 3–7, the differences between the familiar and unfamiliar texts were not great for textual responses on the retelling and question-answering tasks; however, the familiar texts generated considerably more scriptal responses as compared to the unfamiliar

FIGURE 3–6 Effects of background knowledge on reading comprehension and retention

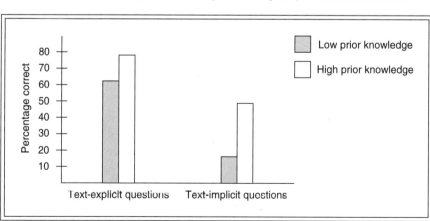

Adapted from Pearson, Hanson and Gordon (1979)

FIGURE 3-7

Effects of
familiar and
unfamiliar
passages on
reading
comprehension
and retention

A FAMILIAR SPORTS PASSAGE

Baseball is a summer game. Usually it is played outdoors on a field. Baseball is a team sport that has nine players. A baseball has a rubber center that is covered with both string and leather. The pitcher winds up and throws the baseball to the batter. Then the batter tries to hit the ball out of the baseball field. A run is made each time a baseball batter hits the ball, runs all three bases, and touches home plate. A game is won by the team scoring the most runs. This game is an exciting sport.

AN UNFAMILIAR SPORTS PASSAGE

Curling is a winter game. Usually it is played indoors on the ice. Curling is a team sport that has four players. A curling stone is a round rock that has a handle on the top. The curler slides the stone down the ice toward colored circles. The team captain or skip stands at the end with these circles. A point is scored each time the curling stone is thrown, aimed toward the skip, and stops on a colored circle. A game is won by the team scoring the most points. This game is an unusual sport.

NUMBER OF TEXTUAL AND SCRIPTAL RESPONSES ON TWO TESTS

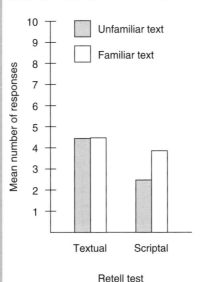

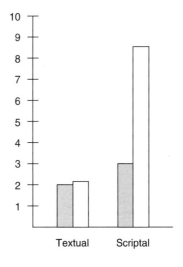

Retell test

Question-answering test

Adapted from Marr and Gormley (1982)

text for both retell and question-answering tasks. Again, it appears that prior knowledge has its strongest effects on helping readers make useful inferences rather than on simply retaining facts.

DIFFERENCES IN THE KINDS OF PRIOR KNOWLEDGE. In a better controlled study, Lipson (1983) varied the background knowledge of readers who were all given the same passages to read. The subjects were Jewish and Catholic students in grades four, five, and six. All were classified as good readers, but they differed in their knowledge of Jewish and Catholic ceremonies. The passages included one entitled, "Bar Mitzvah" and one entitled, "First Communion." Students were asked to read and recall the material in the passages. As expected, the Jewish students read the Bar Mitzvah passage faster than the Catholic students, while the Catholic students read the First Communion passage faster than the Jewish students. Figure 3–8 summarizes the number of pieces of information correctly recalled (text-explicit recall), the number of correct inferences (inference recall), and the number of errors (error recall). As you can see, readers recalled more text-explicit information, made more inferences, and made fewer errors on passages for which they possessed a large amount of prior knowledge than on passages for which they did not.

IMPLICATIONS FOR INSTRUCTION: PROVIDING PRIOR KNOWLEDGE

The main theme of this section of the chapter is that readers of all ages seem to use their prior knowledge to help them understand what they are reading. The foregoing examples demonstrate that a passage may be diffi-

FIGURE 3–8 How different perspectives affect what is remembered from the same passage

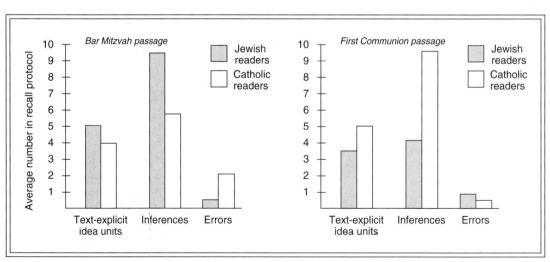

Adapted from Lipson (1983)

cult to comprehend when the reader lacks an appropriate perspective or has a perspective that is different from that of the writer. Overall, research on the role of prior knowledge in reading comprehension has consistently "demonstrated strong effects of knowledge on comprehension" (Roller, 1990, p. 83). In summary, reading comprehension depends partly on the content knowledge that the reader brings to the task.

For example, consider what happens when elementary school students read a text on events leading to the Revolutionary War from their textbook on American history. For example, Beck, McKeown, Sinatra, and Loxterman (1991) examined a textbook lesson that began with the following sentence: "In 1763 Britain and the colonies ended a seven-year war with the French and Indians" (p. 257). What prior knowledge does a fourth- or fifth-grade student need to make sense of this statement? Some of the things they need to know are that about 250 years ago both Britain and France claimed the same land, that the land was in North America, just west of the 13 American colonies; that the Americans colonies belonged to Britain, so the colonists fought on the same side as Britain; that many Indians fought on the same side as the French; and that the war that resulted was called the French and Indian War because Britain; and the American colonies were fighting against the French and Indians.

Do students come to such a reading task with appropriate prior knowledge? To answer this question, McKeown and Beck (1990) interviewed elementary school children before they took a course in American history. Although their textbooks assumed that the readers possessed adequate background knowledge, McKeown and Beck found that the students had only a small part of the needed background knowledge and that this knowledge was not well interconnected.

To examine the role of providing background knowledge in aiding comprehension, Beck et al. (1991) rewrote the passage on the French and Indian War to contain appropriate background knowledge. For example, the original first sentence in the text was replaced with the following seven sentences:

> About 250 years ago, Britain and France both claimed to own some of the same land, here, in North America. This land was just west of where the 13 colonies were. In 1756, Britain and France went to war to see who would get control of this land. Because the 13 American colonies belonged to Britain, the colonists fought on the same side as Britain. Many Indians fought on the same side as France. Because we were fighting against the French and Indians, the war has come to be known as the French and Indian War. The war ended in 1763. (Beck et al., 1991, p. 257)

As you can see, the first sentence is thus intended "to activate a conflict schema in the reader's mind" (Beck et al., 1991, p. 257), so the reader can understand that the motive for the war was that two parties wanted to possess the same object. Activating this schema can help the reader see how the pieces of information fit together. The first and second sentences also set the time and place for the conflict episode in a way that is familiar to the reader. The third sentence explicitly shows how the war was a result of the conflict introduced in the first sentence. The next sentences explain who fought on which side and why, and how the war got its peculiar name.

The next sentences in the original text were (p. 258): "As a result of this war France was driven out of North America. Britain would now rule Canada and other lands that had belonged to France" (Beck et al., 1991, p. 258). According to Beck et al. (1991), the problem with this text is that it begins by talking about the loser and uses the unfamiliar wording "driven out of North America." To activate appropriate prior knowledge, they revised the passage as follows: "Britain won the war. Now Britain had control of North America, including Canada. The French had to leave North America" (Beck et al., 1991, p. 259). This wording is intended to activate an important slot in the child's conflict schema, namely the "winner." The children can use their knowledge about winning a conflict to understand that Britain won control of North America and that France had to give up control of North America.

Beck et al. (1991) asked fourth- and fifth-grade students to read either the original or revised versions of four American history lessons, including one on the French and Indian War. When they were asked to recall the information in the lessons, students who had read the original lesson remembered 44% of the key facts in the original lesson, whereas students who had read the revised lesson remembered 58%. On an open-ended question-answering test covering the material in the original lesson, students who had read the original lesson had 30% correct, whereas those who had read the revised lesson had 49% correct.

In a follow-up study using the same text, McKeown, Beck, Sinatra, and Loxterman (1992) found that students who had read some background information (e.g., material emphasizing the idea of Britain as the owner of the colonies) were better able to remember and answer questions about the original passage than were students who had not received the background information. Taken together, these results provide strong evidence that students learn better when they can use their background knowledge to understand a text. An important educational implication is that the teacher should play a central role in helping students use appropriate background knowledge for making sense out of text. However, Beck and McKeown (1994) pointed out that "many teachers need assistance, because, at the elementary level, few have the background in subject matter that allows them to easily take stock of the texts and provide students with the kind of enhanced information they need" (p. 254).

The implications of these findings for instruction include making sure that reading material is appropriate for the interests and experience of the child. This recommendation is particularly important when children are reading either far above or below their grade level. For example, a student who reads books intended for children who are three or four years older may be able to decode each sentence, but may lack the necessary prior knowledge to appreciate the theme of the material. Similarly, a student who is reading books intended for children three or four years younger may be bored with the immature theme of the material.

A related implication is that reading should be integrated with other subject areas. For example, if a topic such as the Maya Indians in Mexico is covered in social studies, then it might be appropriate to read a folk story about the life of Mayan children. The material learned in the social studies unit could provide the prior knowledge students need to appreciate the folk story.

Finally, classroom discussion and activity can also provide the prior knowledge readers need for comprehending a passage. This kind of pre-reading activity can help to turn unfamiliar passages into familiar ones.

USING PROSE STRUCTURE

DOES THE READER REMEMBER IMPORTANT INFORMATION?

Another persistent finding in the literature on adult learning from prose is that important information from a passage is remembered better than unimportant information (Johnson, 1970; Gernsbacher, 1994; Mayer, 1992; Meyer & McConkie, 1973; Meyer, 1975; Kintsch, 1976). This suggests that skilled readers know about the macrostructure of the passage—that is, about how the passage may be broken down into ideas and how the ideas may be related in a hierarchical outline.

As an example, suppose that we broke a typical story passage into idea units—sentences or phrases that convey one event or action. Then suppose that we asked some skilled adult readers to point out one-fourth of the idea units as the least important (rated 1), one-fourth as the second least important (rated 2), one-fourth as the second most important (rated 3), and one-fourth as the most important (rated 4). Now, let's ask some other skilled adult readers to read this story in its normal form and then recall the information. Do you think that they will show a preference for recalling the important information over the unimportant information? Figure 3–9 summarizes the results of just such a study carried out by Brown and Smiley (1978). As shown, the recall of important information is much better than the recall of unimportant information. This pattern, obtained in many studies, can be called a *levels effect,* because the level of importance of an idea unit influences its probability of being recalled.

RESEARCH ON DIFFERENCES IN CHILDREN'S USE OF PROSE STRUCTURE

AGE-RELATED DIFFERENCES IN THE USE OF PROSE STRUCTURE. There is some evidence that more able and older readers have a better awareness of the structure of passages that they read as compared to less able or younger readers. Awareness of structure would be reflected in recognizing and paying attention to information that is important to the theme of the passage. For example, Brown and Smiley (1977) conducted a study

FIGURE 3–9 Percentage recalled by skilled readers for four levels of importance

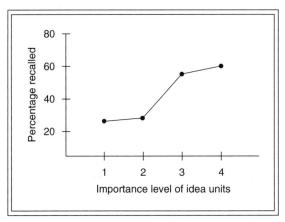

Adapted from Brown and Smiley (1978)

using the short stories called "The Dragon's Tears" and "How to Fool a Cat." First, they broke the story down into idea units and asked a group of skilled adult readers to identify one-quarter of the idea units as least important (rated 1), one-quarter as second least important (rated 2), one-quarter as second most important (rated 3), and one-quarter as most important (rated 4). Then, Brown and Smiley asked third-graders, fifth-graders, seventh-graders, and college students to rate the importance of each idea unit, using a procedure similar to that just described. Figure 3–10 gives the average rating for each category by age group. As you can see, the third- and fifth-graders were not able to recognize which of the idea units are important and which are unimportant; they tended to rate the most important idea units about the same as the least important ones. However, seventh-graders and to a greater extent college students displayed an awareness of the relative importance of idea units; they tended to give high ratings to important idea units and low ratings to unimportant ones. In follow-up studies, older readers were better able to summarize text—such as identifying the important points—than were younger readers (Brown & Day, 1983).

ABILITY-RELATED DIFFERENCES IN THE USE OF PROSE STRUCTURE. Meyer (1975) has devised a technique for determining whether readers use the *top-level structure* of a passage, which is a sort of skeleton outline of the main topics. Use of this top-level structure would be indicated if students recall the main superordinate ideas before they recall the subordinate ideas. If more mature readers are more sensitive to top-level structure, their recall protocols should be organized around this structure and recall should be enhanced mainly for the superordinate rather than the subordinate information in a passage.

Taylor (1980) asked good fourth-grade readers, poor sixth-grade readers, and good sixth-grade readers to read and recall a short passage. As

FIGURE 3–10 Average importance ratings for text given by students at four age levels

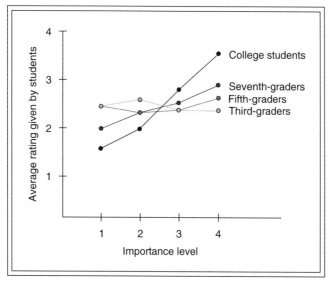

Adapted from Brown and Smiley (1977)

expected, on delayed recall, 59% of the good sixth-grade readers used top-level structure in recalling the material compared to only 18% of the poor sixth-grade readers and 12% of the good fourth-grade readers. If skilled readers focus more on top-level structure, we would expect them to excel particularly in the recall of superordinate ideas. As expected, on delayed recall, the good readers in the sixth grade recalled about 75% more of the superordinate information than the poor readers in the sixth grade, but only 30% more of the subordinate information than the poor readers. These results are summarized in Figure 3–11.

AGE-RELATED DIFFERENCES IN SENSITIVITY TO TOPIC SHIFTS. If skilled readers are more sensitive to prose structure, we would expect them to pay more attention to topic sentences. Gernsbacher (1990) has shown how reading a text involves a process of structure building in which "the goal of comprehension is to build a coherent mental representation or structure of the information being comprehended" (p. 1). Gernsbacher argues that the first step in building a structure is to lay a foundation, a process that presumably takes time. To study this process, skilled readers were asked to read a passage that was presented one sentence at a time on a computer monitor. When readers finished reading a sentence, they pressed a button to see the next sentence. In a series of research studies, Gernsbacher found that skilled readers spent more time reading the initial sentence in a passage than subsequent sentences. According to Gerns-bacher (1990), "comprehenders slow down on the initial sentences of paragraphs because they use those initial sentences to lay a foundation for mental structures representing paragraphs" (p. 5).

FIGURE 3–11 Recall of superordinate and subordinate information by three groups

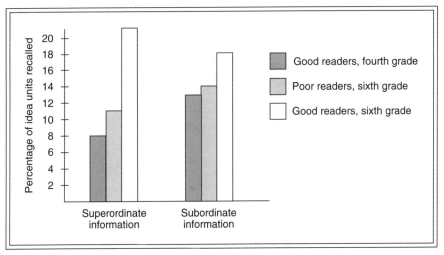

Adapted from Taylor (1980)

For example, consider the story shown in left portion of Table 3–1. According to a structural analysis by Haberlandt (1984), the story consists of a statement of the setting followed by two episodes and an ending. An episode consists of a beginning, reaction, goal, attempt, and outcome. These components are labeled in the second column in the table. If students use the first sentence of a episode to lay the foundation for representing the episode, we would expect their reading time to be longer for the first sentence than for the other sentences in the episode. The right-hand column of the table shows the mean reading times by skilled readers for each sentence in the two episodes. Consistent with the predictions of structure-building theory, the first sentence took much more time to read than the other sentences.

Interestingly, when the story shifts from the first episode to the second, the readers' reading time increases. This increase indicates that the readers are sensitive to the topic shift, as skilled readers are aware of text structure. In a recent review, Hyona (1994) found consistent evidence for a "topic-shift effect" in which skilled readers devote "increased processing time for the sentence that introduces a new topic in the text" or in which "sentences located at episode boundaries are allocated more reading time than within-episode sentences" (p. 77).

Are skilled adult readers more sensitive than children to topic shifts? To examine this question, Hyona (1994) asked fifth-graders and adults to read a story, "Life at the Market Square," that was presented one sentence at a time on a computer monitor. The reader was told to read each sentence, pressing a button to go on to the next, and to be prepared for a test on the

TABLE 3–1	Sentence	Type	Reading Time (Seconds)
How much time does it take to read each sentence in a story?	Mike and Dave Thompson lived in Florida.	Setting	
	They lived across from an orange grove.		
	There was a river between their house and the grove.		
	One Saturday they had nothing to do.	Beginning	3.1
	They were quite bored.	Reaction	2.3
	They decided to get some oranges from the grove.	Goal	2.1
	They took their canoe and paddled across the river.	Attempt	2.2
	They picked a crate full of oranges.	Outcome	2.1
	While they were paddling home the canoe began to sink.	Beginning	2.6
	Mike and Dave realized that they were in great trouble.	Reaction	2.1
	They had to prevent the canoe from sinking further.	Goal	1.8
	They threw the oranges out of the canoe.	Attempt	2.1
	Finally the canoe stopped sinking.	Outcome	2.5
	Now all the oranges were gone.		
	Their adventure had failed after all.	End	2.4

Adapted from Haberlandt (1984)

passage. A portion of the story is presented in Figure 3–12, with the topic-shift sentences underlined. The results showed that both adults and children devoted more time to topic-shift sentences than to other sentences, but that adults showed a stronger topic-shift effect than did children, especially when more difficult expository texts were used. Apparently, children are most able to build coherent structures when they are reading relatively easy stories.

IMPLICATIONS FOR INSTRUCTION: SUMMARIZATION TRAINING

What can be done to help readers learn to pay attention to the top-level structure (or superordinate information) in a passage? Brown and Smiley (1978) provide some evidence concerning the potential trainability of structure-based reading strategies. For example, fifth-, seventh-/eighth-, and eleventh-/twelfth-graders were asked to read along as the experi-

FIGURE 3–12

Portion of
"Life at the
Market
Square"

What is happening at the market square? You can join me to get a feeling of life at the square on a typical autumn day.

I buy an ice cream at a stand and go sit on a bench. Peach ice cream—yum, yum. I enjoy my ice cream while watching the people at the square. The square is full of life. There are shouting salesmen, crying kids, fighting drunkards, couples in love, grim-looking elderly ladies, and crazy pigeons.

There comes a strong smell of vomit from somewhere. Two drunkards have fallen asleep on the ground. One of them is surrounded by vomit. I begin to feel sick when watching them.

I go to a fish stand to look for some herring. The little stand is just in the middle of the square. The fish seller advertises his fish to me. I don't want to buy his fish, because they look old. On the ground, in front of the fish stand, there are scales of fish that stick to my shoes.

The pigeons seem to be having their meal. Besides me, there is a whole bunch of them rushing around. The pigeons are permanent customers of the market. In front of me, a pigeon couple fights for a herring that has fallen from the fish stand. Other pigeons join in the fight.

A man gets in front of a microphone. People at the square are clearly amazed. They start to gather around the man. The place is getting crowded.

Adapted from Hyona (1994)

menter read a short story such as "The Dragon's Tears" or "How to Fool a Cat." Then subjects were asked to recall the passage, with the results summarized by the solid line in Figure 3–13. The results shown in Figure 3–13 indicate that there was a level effect for each age group in which students performed better on recall of more important idea units than on less important idea units. After the first recall test, students were given a five-minute study period and told to undertake any activity that would improve recall. Paper, pens, and a copy of the passage (in primary type) were available. Then, a second recall test was administered, with the results summarized by the dotted line in Figure 3–13. The results show that the extra study time did not have much of an effect on the younger students but did improve the performance of the older students, particularly on recall of the more important idea units. Apparently, the older students knew to use the study time in order to focus on important information, while the younger students did not spontaneously use this strategy.

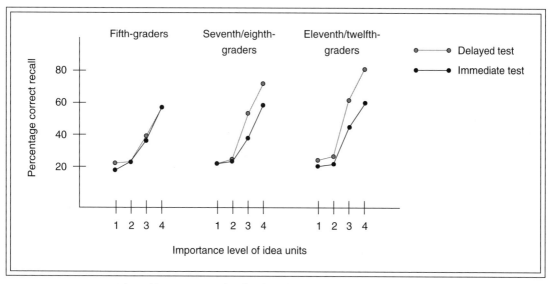

Adapted from Brown and Smiley (1978)

Can the younger students be induced to apply helpful study strategies even if they would not use them spontaneously? To investigate this question, Brown and Smiley (1978) continued the experiment for a second day. The procedure was identical except that during the five-minute study interval students who did not show evidence of actively studying were prompted to engage in study activities such as underlining. Figure 3–14 shows the recall patterns for fifth-graders who underlined spontaneously, fifth-graders who were induced by the experimenter to underline, and fifth-graders who could not be induced to underline during the five-minute study period. Again, the solid line is the recall performance on the first test and the dotted line is the recall performance on the second test after the five-minute study period. As can be seen, the students who spontaneously underlined without having to be instructed to do so seem to have focused on important information; this is indicated by the improvement in recall of important idea units but not of other information. In contrast, inducing students to underline did not focus their attention on important information, as is indicated by the improvement in recall of unimportant information only. Similar results were obtained for the seventh- and eighth-graders. Apparently, younger readers need practice in effective techniques for recognizing and using the hierarchical organization of a passage.

In a direct training study, Taylor and Beach (1984) taught seventh-graders to use a hierarchical summary procedure for reading social studies texts. For each training passage, the student made a skeleton outline consisting of a thesis statement for the entire passage at the top of the page and a statement of the main idea of each section as indicated by

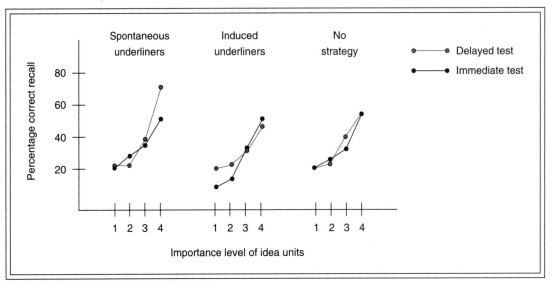

Adapted from Brown and Smiley (1978)

headings. Then the student generated two or three important supporting details for each main idea statement, and wrote superordinate topic headings in the left margin to connect to sections of the text. Figure 3–15 gives an example of a hierarchical summary of a three-page social studies text containing one heading and six subheadings. The trained students received seven one-hour training sessions, while the control students received no training. To test the effectiveness of the hierarchical summary procedure, students in both groups were given pretests and posttests that involved reading passages and then recalling and answering questions about them. As expected, the trained students showed greater pretest-to-posttest gains in recall and in answering questions than the control group.

What techniques do skilled readers use for summarizing a text, and can these skills be taught to less skilled readers? By analyzing skilled reading processes, Brown and Day (1983) identified the following principles of text summarization: deleting irrelevant information, deleting redundant information, substituting a superordinate term for a list of items, substituting a subordinate term for a series of events, selecting a topic sentence, and inventing a topic sentence if none is given. Over the course of 12 30-minute sessions, Bean and Steenwyk (1984) taught sixth-grade students to use these principles to summarize a series of paragraphs. In contrast, a control group was told to find the main ideas but was given no explicit instruction. On a subsequent test of summarizing a paragraph, the summarization-trained group obtained a much better score than the control group (17.6 versus 11.0, respectively). Importantly, on a subsequent test of

FIGURE 3–15

A hierarchical
summary for a
three-page
social studies
text

I. *Johnson developed many programs to fight injustice and poverty.*

A. *Lyndon Johnson became President of the U.S. after Kennedy was assassinated.*

hard worker, tried to carry out some of Kennedy's programs

Civil Rights

B. *Johnson fought for civil-rights law.*

purpose: to protect blacks from discrimination in hotels and restaurants, blacks had not been allowed in some hotels or restaurants in the South

C. *Johnson persuaded Congress to pass a law ensuring all people the right to vote.*

protected black people's right to vote, literacy tests now illegal

D. *Johnson started a "war on poverty."*

job training, education for poor people, plans for a "Great Society"

Great Society programs

E. *Johnson persuaded Congress to develop a Medicare program.*

for people at least 65 years old, hospital bills paid, doctor's bills paid in part

F. *Johnson persuaded Congress to pass a law giving money to schools.*

purpose: to improve education of children from poor families, $1 billion in aid to schools

From Taylor and Beach (1984)

reading comprehension, the summarization-trained students scored 62% correct, whereas the control group scored 47% correct. These results provide additional evidence that summarization skills can be taught and that learning them improves students' reading comprehension.

MAKING INFERENCES

WHAT IS INFERENCE-MAKING?

The process of comprehending text often requires the reader to make inferences. For example, consider the sentence "Our neighbor unlocked the door." An inference you might make is that the instrument used to unlock the door was a key (Paris & Lindauer, 1976). As another example, consider the sentence "She slammed the door shut on her hand." An inference you might make is that she hurt her finger (Paris, Lindauer, & Cox, 1977).

Overall, inference-making is so important to reading comprehension that "the ability to draw inferences is a cornerstone of reading competence" (Winne, Graham, & Prock, 1993, p. 53). For example, Weaver and Kintsch (1991) estimate that as many as a dozen implicit inferences may be required to understand every explicit statement in a passage fully. Yet, an important educational issue is that young readers are notoriously poor at making inferences during reading (Oakhill & Yuill, 1996).

RESEARCH ON THE DEVELOPMENT OF CHILDREN'S INFERENCE-MAKING

Paris and his colleagues (Myers & Paris, 1978; Paris & Lindauer, 1976; Paris et al., 1977; Paris & Upton, 1976) have found evidence of a developmental trend in which younger readers are less likely to make inferences during reading than older readers. For example, kindergartners, second-graders, and fourth-graders listened to eight sentences. The sentences each suggested an implicit inference about the instrument used to carry out the action mentioned in the sentence. For example, "Our neighbor unlocked the door" implies that the instrument is a key. Students were given a cued recall test in which for each sentence the experimenter gave either an explicit cue—the subject, verb, or object of the sentence—or an implicit cue—the instrument. For example, an explicit cue for the preceding sentence is "neighbor," "unlocked," or "door," whereas an implicit cue is "key." Figure 3–16 shows the percentage of correctly recalled sentences when the cue was explicit versus implicit for each age group. For the kindergartners, performance was much better with the explicit cue, but for the second- and fourth-graders implicit cues were just about as useful as explicit ones. Apparently, the younger children do not spontaneously go beyond the information given to make and use inferences as well as the older children. Paris et al. (1977) obtained a similar developmental trend using inferences about consequences such as the "door slamming" sentence given earlier.

In a related series of studies, Paris and Upton (1976) examined developmental changes in children's inference-making for short paragraphs. Students in each grade K–5 listened to six stories, including the following:

> Chris waited until he was alone in the house. The only sound he heard was his father chopping wood in the barn. Then he pushed the red chair over to the sink, which was fill of dishes. Standing on the edge of the sink, he could just barely reach the heavy jar. The jar was behind the sugar and he stretched until his fingers could lift the lid. Just as he reached inside, the door swung open and there was his little sister.

FIGURE 3–16 Age-related differences in children's use of inference

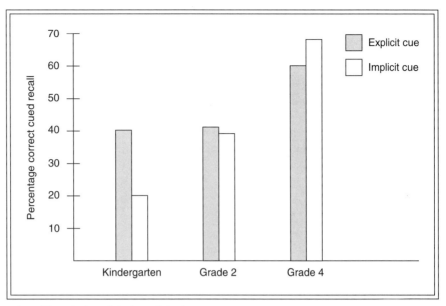

Adapted from Paris and Lindauer (1976)

Students were asked eight questions about each passage. Half of the questions concerned verbatim memory, such as "Was the jar heavy?" or "Was the chair brown?" The other half concerned inferences, such as "Was Chris's father using an ax?" or "Was Chris caught in the act of doing something he was not supposed to do?" Performance on both verbatim and inferential questions improved with age, but there was a larger increase in inference performance. In addition, ability to make inferences was highly correlated with overall amount recalled. These results suggest that as children develop, they become more able to make inferences that give meaning to their reading of the passage.

IMPLICATIONS FOR INSTRUCTION: INFERENCE TRAINING

Inference training is a central feature of most basal reading programs (Pressley, 1990; Rosenshine, 1980) and of many traditional reading programs. However, until recently there has been little empirical research concerning the effectiveness of inference training. For example, Hansen (1981) developed a five-week classroom program for second-graders. Some students were given practice in answering inference questions for each of several practice passages; other students used the same practice passages in class but followed the normal instructional program. On a posttest, all students read new passages and answered some literal and inference questions about the passages. The question-trained group performed 12% better than the control group on literal questions and 26% better on inference questions. However, a group that received training in the use of prereading strategies, such as trying to predict what would happen or relating the story to one's own experiences, did not show strong posttest advantages over the control group. Apparently, an effective way to teach students how to answer inference questions is to give them direct instruction and practice in answering inference questions.

In a follow-up study, Hansen and Pearson (1983) provided five weeks of inference training to poor and good fourth-grade readers. The training included prereading strategies such as discussing the reader's own experiences and making predictions about the story. For example, the script for prereading strategies was as follows:

TEACHER: What is it that we have been doing before we discuss each story?

DESIRED RESPONSE: We talk about our lives and we predict what will happen in the stories.

TEACHER: Why do we make these comparisons?

DESIRED RESPONSE: These comparisons will help us understand the stories.

TEACHER: Last week I asked you to think about a social studies lesson on Japan. Today, pretend that you are reading a science article about conservation. What might you be thinking about while you are reading the article?

DESIRED RESPONSE: [Students relate personal experiences with conservation and explain how the experiences would be related to the text.] For example, students talked about how their families heat with wood to conserve oil and stated that they wanted to find out how the Japanese conserve oil.

Training for a story on a man who is embarrassed by his appearance focused on understanding the main ideas:

TEACHER: Sometimes people are embarrassed by their personal appearance. Tell us about a time you were embarrassed about the way you looked.

TYPICAL RESPONSES: I got a short haircut. I wore short pants. I'm too short.

TEACHER: In the next story there is an old man who is embarrassed about the way he looks. What do you think is the thing that embarrasses him?

TYPICAL RESPONSES: Ragged clothes. Cane. Gray hair. Wrinkles.

These prereading scripts led to discussions that lasted approximately 20 minutes. Then students read the passage independently. Students in the control group did not engage in the prereading activities. After reading the story, the class was asked to discuss ten questions. For the trained group, all the questions required inferences. For example, in a discussion of a basal version of *Charlotte's Web*, the teacher asked, "What kind of person do you think Templeton [the rat] would be if he were human?" The control group discussion involved questions using the ratio of four literal questions for each inference question. This ratio corresponds to the normal pattern of reading discussions. Following the training program, students were tested by asking them to read a passage appropriate for their reading level and to answer both literal and inference questions. Figure 3–17 shows that the training seems to have had no effect on the good readers, presumably because they already possessed good inference strategies. However, Figure 3–17 also indicates that the training greatly enhanced the performance of the poor readers on both inference and literal questions.

Does inference training affect students' reading comprehension performance? To help answer this question Yuill and Oakhill (1988; Oakhill & Yuill, 1996) provided seven thirty-minute training sessions to seven- and eight-year-olds who had scored either low or high on a test of reading comprehension. In the training, students read short stories, performed several inference-inducing tasks with them, and then received feedback

FIGURE 3–17 Effects of inference training on poor and good readers

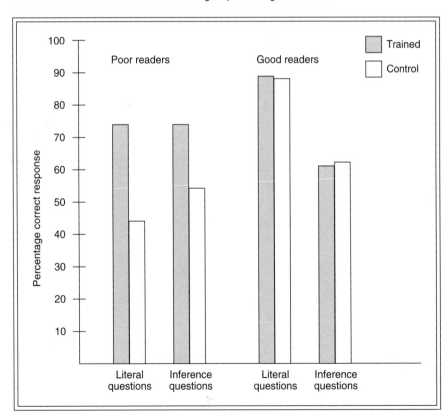

Adapted from Hansen and Pearson (1983)

and discussed their answers. One task was to generate questions based on a short passage, such as shown in Figure 3–18. Some possible questions that students could generate for this story are "Where was Lucy?," "Why was she there?," and "Why couldn't she move?" A second task was to identify words in the story that suggested what a character was like, where the story takes place, and the like. In a third task, part of the text was covered, and students were asked to guess at what was missing.

Students were given a reading comprehension test before and after the training period. For those who had done poorly on the pretest, scores increased greatly for the trained group but not for a control group that received practice in decoding. For those who had done well on the pretest, the trained group did not show large gains, nor did it gain more than the control group. Overall, these results show that inference training has a strong effect on students who scored low in reading comprehension, suggesting that the ability to make inferences is a key component in skilled comprehension.

Although many students develop reading comprehension competence in elementary school, some do not. These students are often labeled as "learning disabled" and receive special pull-out instruction during the academic year. Will inference training help these young readers? Winne et al. (1993) tackled this question by providing nine sessions of inference training to a group of students in grades four through six who had poor comprehension skills. During the sessions, students worked individually with an adult tutor on answering inference questions about short texts.

For example, in one session the tutor read the summer camping passage in Figure 3–19 and then asked the student to answer a series of questions aimed at promoting inference making, such as those in the bottom

---

FIGURE 3–18

An inference-training exercise based on generating a question

Read this text:
Lucy saw the ground below her. It seemed very far away. She heard the cat and tried to move, but she realized it was unsafe. What could she do? Then she saw her father walking toward the house. She called loudly to him. Father looked up and saw Lucy; then he ran toward the tree.

Write some questions that can be answered by the text:
1. _____
2. _____
3. _____

Adapted from Oukhill and Yuill (1996)

FIGURE 3-19

An inference-
training
exercise based
on answering
questions

Read this passage:

It was summer at last! John and Peter were going camping. They wanted to find a really good campsite this year. Last summer they were almost two kilometers from the store and ice cream stand.

Both the boys loved camping. John had been a Boy Scout for five years. Peter and his mother had camped in the woods every summer when he was younger. This year, the boys decided that their campsite should be near water.

When they arrived at the campground, the park ranger told them that only two campsites were left. "One site is close to a Dairy Queen store," he said. "There are many beautiful wild flowers nearby. The other site is by a small pond. It is a peaceful camping spot away from other campers. However, there are lots of insects there."

Answer these questions:

1. Where did the boys camp?
   (Answering this question requires making an inference, namely, that the boys camped near a pond.)
2. Why?
   (Answering this question requires remembering a rule—"their campsite should be near some water"—and a critical fact—"the other site . . . by a small pond" was the only available site near water.)
3. What did John and Peter want to find?
   (The answer is "a really good campsite." The reader must notice that this is the problem statement, that is, the main problem in the story.)
4. What sort of a campsite had the boys decided they wanted this year?
   (The answer is one "near some water." The reader must note that this is a rule, that is, a major constraint in the story.)
5. What campsites did the ranger give the boys to choose from?
   (The answer is "one site is close to a Dairy Queen" and "the other site is by a small pond." The reader must determine that these are the important relevant facts in the story.)
6. What was wrong with the campsite by the pond?
   (Although the answer is that "there are lots of insects there," the reader must also realize that this information is not relevant to the boys' decision.)

Adapted from Winne, Graham, and Prock (1993)

of Figure 3–19. The correct answer to the first question is that the boys camped near the pond; this can be derived by noting that "the boys decided that their campsite should be near some water" and that only one of the available sites was near water. After each answer, some students received feedback on the correct answer and were shown where in the text it was found (abbreviated feedback group), whereas others received the same feedback along with explanations of how the answer could be derived from the relevant portion of the text (explanatory feedback group). As expected, students in the explanatory feedback group showed more improvement in their inference-making than did those in the abbreviated feedback group. The results suggest that students with poor comprehension skills need practice not only in inference-making but also in explaining how the inferences are made.

USING METACOGNITIVE KNOWLEDGE

WHAT IS METACOGNITIVE KNOWLEDGE?

Metacognition is knowledge and awareness of one's own cognitive processes. Brown et al. (1981) have pointed out that although metacognitive skills are particularly difficult to teach to readers, they are crucial for effective reading. For example, one kind of metacognitive knowledge related to reading is *comprehension monitoring,* which we focus on in this section.

RESEARCH ON DIFFERENCES IN METACOGNITIVE KNOWLEDGE

COMPREHENSION MONITORING. Comprehension monitoring is an awareness of whether you understand what you are reading. In essence, a reader with good comprehension monitoring skills is continually asking, "Does this make sense?" For example, Markman (1979) read three short essays to third-, fifth-, and sixth-graders. Each story contained either an explicit or an implicit inconsistency as shown in italic in Figure 3–20. For example, the inconsistency in the fish essay is that there is not enough light at the bottom of the ocean to see colors and that fish see the color of their food at the bottom of the ocean. The experimenter told the students that she was trying to write a children's book and that she needed them to serve as consultants. The children were asked to assess the understandability of the essays and to suggest ways of making them easier to understand. After reading the story twice, the experimenter prompted the students to point out any inconsistencies. The first seven prompts for the passages in Figure 3–20 were:

FIGURE 3–20

Do young
readers
recognize
inconsistency
in prose
passages?

*A PASSAGE WITH AN EXPLICIT
INCONSISTENCY*

Many different kinds of fish live in the ocean. Some fish have heads that make them look like alligators, and some fish have heads that make them look like cats. Fish live in different parts of the ocean. Some fish live near the surface of the water, but some fish live way down at the bottom of the ocean. *Fish must have light in order to see. There is absolutely no light at the bottom of the ocean. It is pitch black down there. When it is that dark the fish cannot see anything. They cannot even see colors. Some fish that live at the bottom of the ocean can see the color of their food; that is how they know what to eat.*

*A PASSAGE WITH AN IMPLICIT
INCONSISTENCY*

Many different kinds of fish live in the ocean. Some fish have heads that make them look like alligators, and some fish have heads that make them look like cats. Fish live in different parts of the ocean. Some fish live near the surface of the water, but some fish live way down at the bottom of the ocean. *There is absolutely no light at the bottom of the ocean. Some fish that live at the bottom of the ocean know their food by its color. They will only eat red fungus.*

*PERCENTAGE OF CHILDREN WHO
RECOGNIZED INCONSISTENCIES IN AT
LEAST TWO OF THREE PASSAGES*

Grade Level	Explicit Condition	Implicit Condition
Grade 3	50%	0%
Grade 5	60%	10%
Grade 6	60%	0%

Adapted from Markman (1979)

1. Read the essay.
2. Reread the essay.
3. That's it. That's the information about fishes.
4. What do you think?
5. Do you have any questions?
6. Did I forget to tell you anything?
7. Did everything make sense?

Did the children respond to these prompts by referring to the inconsistency in the passage? Figure 3–20 lists the percentage of students at each grade level who recognized the inconsistencies in at least two out of three essays. As you can see, about half the students found the explicit inconsistencies in at least two essays, while almost none found the implicit inconsistencies. Apparently, it is very difficult for students to recognize spontaneously that the text they are reading is incomprehensible, especially when inconsistencies are implicit.

CAN CHILDREN BE INDUCED TO MONITOR THEIR COMPREHENSION? To test this question, Markman (1979) conducted a follow-up study on third- and sixth-graders using the same task described above. However, this time half the children were told, "There is something tricky about each of the essays. Something which does not make any sense. Something which is confusing. I would like you to try and spot the problem with each essay, and tell me what it was that did not make any sense." These instructions did not greatly influence the ability of the third-graders to find either implicit or explicit inconsistencies, but it did greatly improve the ability of the sixth-graders to find both. Apparently, the older children are capable of comprehension monitoring but do not engage in this activity spontaneously.

Myers and Paris (1978) interviewed second- and sixth-graders concerning their metacognitive knowledge about reading. Some of the questions focused on comprehension monitoring, such as "Do you ever have to go back to the beginning of a paragraph or story to figure out what a sentence means? Why?" About 60% of the sixth-graders were able to explain why they reread (e.g., to get context cues); in comparison, less than 10% of the second graders were able to explain why they reread. Apparently, younger readers are less aware of the role of comprehension monitoring in reading.

These results suggest that skilled readers are able to focus on inconsistencies in text. To examine this idea, Baker and Anderson (1982) asked college students to read short expository passages, some of which contained inconsistencies. The passages were presented on a computer terminal screen with only one sentence on the screen at a time. The reader pressed the "Next" button to see the next sentence, the "Back" button to see the previous sentence, and the "Lab" button to start over at the beginning of the passage. The results indicate that readers spent much more time reading a sentence that conflicted with previously presented information compared to reading the same sentence in a consistent passage. In addition, skilled readers were far more likely to look back to an inconsistent sentence than to the same sentence when it was in a consistent passage. These results suggest that comprehension monitoring is a characteristic of skilled readers.

WHY DO CHILDREN FAIL TO RECOGNIZE INCONSISTENCIES IN A PASSAGE? There are two major explanations for why children fail to detect inconsistencies in passages. According to a representational theory, students fail to adequately represent and retain the two inconsistent statements in their working memory. According to a processing theory, students adequately represent the two conflicting statements in working memory but fail to compare them adequately. To test these two theories, Vosniadou, Pearson, and Rogers (1988) asked first-, third-, and fifth-graders to listen to (or read) stories, such as the one partially shown in Figure 3–21. As you can see, the stories had contradictions, such as the sentence in Figure 3–21 stating that "when you pour spaghetti and water into a strainer, the water passes through the holes and the spaghetti stays in the

FIGURE 3–21

How recall affects detection of inconsistencies in stories

Read this story, then recall it, and point out what does not make sense in the story:

First Georgette filled a pot with water and put it on the stove. She turned on the flame and soon the water was boiling, so she put a boxful of spaghetti into the water. The water boiled again, and Georgette watched it until the spaghetti got soft and looked like it was done. Now she had to think of a way to take the spaghetti out of the water.

Then she remembered that her father had used a strainer to separate spaghetti from water. When you pour spaghetti and water into a strainer, the water passes through the holes and the spaghetti stays in the strainer.

So Georgette looked in the kitchen cabinets and found a strainer. She put the strainer over a bowl. She then poured the spaghetti and water into the strainer. As she did this, the spaghetti passed through the holes in the strainer into the bowl and the water stayed in the strainer. Georgette was glad that the water and spaghetti were separated. She placed the bowl of spaghetti on the counter.

INCONSISTENT STATEMENTS:

1. When you pour spaghetti and water into a strainer, the water passes through the holes and the spaghetti stays in the strainer.
2. As she did this, the spaghetti passed through the holes in the strainer into the bowl and the water stayed in the strainer.

PERCENTAGE OF INCONSISTENCIES RECOGNIZED AND INCONSISTENT STATEMENTS RECALLED BY FOUR GROUPS:

Group	Recognize Inconsistencies	Recall Inconsistencies
Grade 1 (listen)	35%	35%
Grade 3 (listen)	47%	65%
Grade 3 (read)	27%	51%
Grade 5 (read)	63%	74%

Adapted from Vosniadou, Pearson, and Rogers (1988)

strainer," and another sentence stating that when Georgette poured the spaghetti and water into the strainer, "the spaghetti passed through the holes of the strainer into the bowl and the water stayed in the strainer." The children were told:

> Listen very carefully to each story because there is something wrong with each one of them, something wrong with the way the author wrote them, something that doesn't make sense. We would like you to listen very carefully to each story and then tell the story back to us and also tell us what it is that does not make any sense. (Vosniadou et al., 1988, p. 30)

Then, each child was asked to recall the story, to say what about it did not make sense, and to justify the answer.

The left panel of the table in Figure 3–21 shows that there was a developmental trend in which younger readers tended to miss the inconsistencies, whereas older readers were more likely to catch them. In addition, third-graders were more likely to notice the inconsistencies when they listened to the story than when they read it themselves, presumably because they had less attentional capacity available when they had to do the reading. The right panel of the table shows that there was a developmental trend in which younger readers were less successful in remembering the conflicting statements than were older students. The recall data show that younger readers' difficulties in detecting inconsistencies occurred mainly because younger readers were more likely than the older readers to forget the inconsistent information. Vosniadou et al. (1988) concluded that "greater attention should be paid to how children's mental representations of text affect inconsistency detection and comprehension monitoring" (p. 36). According to this view, an important factor in comprehension monitoring is the prior knowledge of the reader, because inconsistent statements are more easily represented (and therefore compared) when they are familiar to the reader.

IMPLICATIONS FOR INSTRUCTION: COMPREHENSION MONITORING TRAINING

Can children learn to be more effective comprehension monitors? In a classic study, Markman and Gorin (1981) provided encouraging evidence that students more accurately detect inconsistencies in text when they are given minimal instruction in how to do so. Eight- and ten-year-olds listened to a series of short stories that either did or did not contain inconsistencies, and after each indicated whether it was easy to understand or there was some problem in understanding it. For example, the following story has an inconsistency between the second and final sentences:

> Corn can be served in many ways. I've never met anyone who didn't consider corn, in one form or another, one of their favorite

foods. Corn can be steamed and served with melted butter; mixed with flour and egg to make a bread; or made into popcorn for a favorite snack. The people I know don't enjoy eating corn very much. (p. 322)

Some of the students (instructed group) received brief examples of how to detect inconsistencies, such as the following:

For example, suppose you heard, "John loves to ski" and later you heard, "John hates to ski." Those two sentences do not make sense together. Any time two parts of an essay do not make sense together, that would be confusing. Suppose one part of an essay said, "Suzie is a tiny baby," then another part said "Suzie is big enough to walk to school." It would be confusing to have two sentences that do not make sense together. (p. 322)

Other students did not receive these examples (control group).

Figure 3–22 shows the percentages of 8- and 10-year-old students in each group who correctly detected inconsistencies. Those who had

FIGURE 3–22 Percentage of inconsistencies detected by four groups

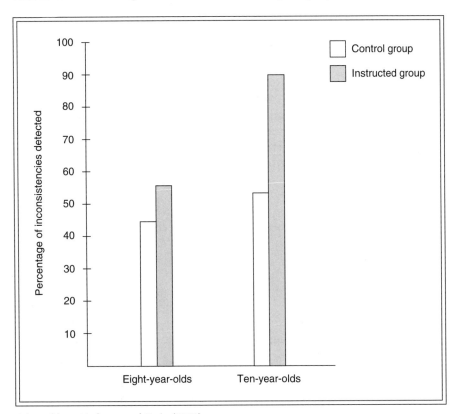

Adapted from Markman and Gorin (1981)

received instructions on how to detect inconsistencies performed better than did those who had not. The instructions were particularly helpful for the 10-year-olds, suggesting that they had known the strategy for detecting inconsistencies but had not been fully aware that they should use it in this task before instruction. Markman and Gorin (1981) concluded that "when children are given examples of what types of problems to look for, they are capable of adjusting their standard of evaluation" (p. 325).

In an important extension of this study, Elliot-Faust and Pressley (1986) asked third-graders to listen to four stories, two of which contained inconsistencies such as the following:

> The sea horse is a fascinating fish. Sea horses are found in oceans and seas. Sea horses are very small. Sea horses grow to be twelve centimeters long. The sea horse's head looks like a tiny horse's head. The sea horse has a small body and a long tail. When the sea horse swims it looks like it's standing on its tail. It moves through the water by moving its fins on its head and back. The sea horse is not a very fast swimmer. It makes jerky movements as it swims. The sea horse moves slowly through the water. The sea horse escapes enemy fish by swimming quickly away. That is how the sea horse keeps from being eaten by other fish. That's the story about sea horses. (p. 28)

After listening to each story the students were asked, "Did the story make sense?" If they answered no, the experimenter asked, "Why?" and "What part didn't make sense?" In this example, the correct answer is to point out the contradiction between "the sea horse is not a very fast swimmer" and "the sea horse escapes enemy fish by swimming quickly away."

Some students were given examples of inconsistent sentences (instructed group), while others received no training (control group), as in the Markman and Gorin (1981) study. In addition, some students (strategy group) received the same training as the instructed group as well as explicit training in how to use comprehension monitoring strategies for detecting contradictions between sentences. The strategy training included practice in controlling one's use of comprehension monitoring strategies by asking questions such as "What is my plan?," "Am I using my plan?," and "How did I do?" As in the Markman and Gorin study, the instructed group detected more inconsistencies (73%) than the control group (37%). In addition, the strategy group detected more inconsistencies (91%) than either of these groups. These results demonstrate that extended strategy training can greatly improve the comprehension-monitoring skills of young readers.

What can be done to help students develop appropriate metacognitive skills? Based on research on children's comprehension monitoring, Markman (1985) makes the following suggestions:

1. Children should read a "variety of well-organized, tight passages" that involve "simple logical, causal, and temporal relations." (p. 288) Unfortunately, textbooks written for young children often are unstructured, with many paragraphs consisting of lists of descriptive sentences. Thus, they do not offer children practice in determining whether the material makes sense, because the text has often been rewritten to minimize logical, causal, or temporal structure. In addition, children should be asked to predict the next logical event or the actions of a character, to infer the order of events in a causal sequence, to guess the cause of an event, or to infer the motives of a character.
2. Children should be given a set of general questions to ask themselves as they read, such as "Do I understand?," "What is the main point?," "What else do I know that is related?" Self-testing has been successfully used in improving the reading comprehension of educable retarded children (Brown, Campione, & Barclay, 1979).
3. Children should be exposed to teachers who model appropriate comprehension-monitoring techniques.
4. Children should practice evaluating explanations of a passage, such as choosing which of several possible explanations makes the most sense.
5. Children should practice detecting inconsistencies or other problems in text.

In summary, children often fail to use appropriate comprehension monitoring and related skills, even though they are capable of doing so. Instruction in using metacognitive knowledge may improve their comprehension performance. Clearly, research is needed to help determine how to apply these recommendations to the needs of individual children.

BUILDING A READING COMPREHENSION PROGRAM THAT WORKS

The research on reading comprehension presented in this chapter demonstrates that progress is being made in identifying the strategies that successful readers use and in teaching these strategies to beginning readers. In particular, this chapter has focused on four active cognitive processes in reading that can be taught:

Integrating: Using one's prior knowledge to make sense out of text.
Organizing: Identifying important ideas and the relationships among them.

Elaborating: Making necessary inferences while reading.

Monitoring: Evaluating one's comprehension and adjusting one's reading strategy.

During the past twenty years, accumulating research evidence has shown that it is possible to help students learn component skills such as how to write a summary of a passage, how to predict what will come next, how to clarify a sentence, how to generate questions, and how to detect inconsistencies (Pearson & Fielding, 1991). These findings are consistent with Bartlett's (1932) vision of reading comprehension as an active search for meaning.

The task for any effective reading program is to incorporate successful techniques into an integrated reading program for classroom use. As we have seen in this chapter, there is a large body of scientific research on how readers use their prior knowledge, make judgments of importance, draw inferences, and monitor their comprehension process. Since school reading comprehension instruction is shaped by a few major basal reader series (Chall & Squire, 1991; Rosenshine, 1980), it would make sense for such programs to be coordinated with research on reading comprehension. An important trend for the future would be for reading programs to be developed in accord with the research on reading and for theories of reading instruction to be tested within the context of real school reading programs. This section briefly examines two programs that integrate several reading comprehension processes within the context of larger reading tasks—a traditional reading comprehension program that has a long history (SQ3R) and a more recent research-based reading comprension program (reciprocal teaching of reading comprehension skills).

SQ3R

Suppose we could find a well-established and long-lived program that is widely used in many schools to promote reading comprehension. SQ3R is a reading comprehension program that fits this definition. It was developed long before most of the research cited in this chapter was conducted, but seems consistent with the general theme that reading comprehension is an active process of making sense out of text.

Robinson (1941, 1961) suggested that learners be trained to use five steps in reading a new passage: survey, question, read, recite, and review (SQ3R). During the survey step, the reader skims the material to get an idea of what the passage is about. For example, in reading this chapter, you might read the beginning and concluding sentences and headings of each section. During the question step, the reader formulates a question for each subheading or unit of the passage. For example, for this section of the text you might ask, "What are the procedures of SQ3R?" In the read step, the student reads the passage with the goal of answering the question for each subheading or part of the passage. In the recite step, the student answers each question in his or her own words. In the review step, the student practices recalling as much information as possible from each section of the passage. A revised version, PQ4R, adds a reflect step in which readers try to think of examples and relate material to prior knowledge (Thomas & Robinson, 1972).

Adams, Carnine, and Gersten (1982) pointed out that since its inception SQ3R has been "widely reported in textbooks and teacher training manuals as being empirically based, though in fact the research literature does not support the claims" (p. 31). For example, Adams, Carnine, and Gersten (1982) were able to locate only six studies evaluating the effectiveness of SQ3R, but five had serious methodological flaws and the sixth did not use school-aged subjects. Similarly, Shepard (1978) has argued that some students fail to use this system because it appears to be too time-consuming. In a more recent review, Pressley and McCormick (1995) noted that "although recommended in many study skills courses, [SQ3R] does not have a track record of exceptional effectiveness" (p. 374).

Adams et al. (1982) developed a four-day training program similar to SQ3R, but with each step based on the current reading comprehension research. Direct instruction was provided in each of the five skills listed above, using sample passages in social studies. Unlike previous studies, the subjects were elementary school children (fifth-graders) who possessed adequate decoding skills but poor study skills. To assess the effectiveness of the training program, students were asked to read a passage and then to retell it and answer some factual questions about it. Students who were given the training scored 47% correct on the questions compared to only 28% correct by students who were not trained. The trained group also remembered more of the important information than the control group, but the difference failed to reach statistical significance. Apparently, students can be taught to read in ways that will enhance their ability to answer factual questions. However, more research is needed to understand when, why, where, and for whom SQ3R affects reading comprehension.

RECIPROCAL TEACHING OF READING COMPREHENSION SKILLS

How can we put some of the key reading comprehension skills together into a powerful reading program that will work in school classrooms? Many scholars have recognized that since school learning takes place within a social context, reading comprehension should be taught as a collaborative activity. One way of accomplishing this goal is by *reciprocal teaching*—an instructional technique in which students and teacher take turns leading a dialogue about strategies for how to study some material

(Palinscar & Brown, 1984; Brown & Palinscar, 1989). Reciprocal teaching takes place in a cooperative learning group consisting of a teacher and one or more students. The goal of each instructional episode is for the group to study a passage using a variety of reading comprehension strategies. Teacher and students take turns as discussion leaders, although the teacher provides comments, feedback, and hints as needed.

For example, suppose that the goal of a unit in a seventh-grade English course is to help students improve their reading comprehension skills. In particular, suppose that we want students to learn to use four widely acclaimed reading comprehension strategies: (1) *questioning,* in which a student generates an appropriate question for a passage; (2) *clarifying,* in which a student detects and corrects any potential comprehension difficulties such as definitions of unfamiliar words; (3) *summarizing,* in which a student produces a concise summary for a passage; and (4) *predicting,* in which a student suggests what will occur in subsequent text. In typical classroom practice, the teacher may model each of these strategies for the students (modeling method), or may describe each strategy and ask the students to apply them in workbook exercises (direct instruction method). By contrast, in reciprocal teaching the students get a chance to teach these strategies to the group. In short, the teacher and student reciprocate—the one who was instructed takes the role of teacher, and the one who instructed takes the role of student.

In reciprocal teaching, we begin with a teacher and a group of students who jointly are trying to make sense out of a paragraph, such as the text about crows in Figure 3–23. The participants engage in a structured discussion in which the discussion leader models the cognitive strategies of questioning, clarifying, summarizing, and predicting. At first, the teacher leads the discussion by generating a question about the text, summarizing the text, clarifying any comprehension problems, and making predictions about subsequent text. When disagreements arise, all participants reread the text and discuss options until consensus is reached. The teacher eventually turns over the job of discussion leader to the students, such as Chantal (identified as "S1" in Figure 3–23). When a student leads the discussion, the teacher periodically provides guidance on exercising cognitive strategies, such as how to ask appropriate questions or how to generate good summaries. The teacher prompts the student discussion leader, offers critiques, and generally provides support that enables the students to proceed. As the students become more proficient, the teacher reduces the amount of direction and feedback. The teaching dialogue in Figure 3–23 provides an example of reciprocal teaching in action.

Does reciprocal teaching work? To answer this question, Brown and Palinscar (1989) compared four groups of junior high school students who had reading problems. Students in the reciprocal teaching group took turns with the teacher in leading discussions about applying the four reading comprehension strategies; students in the modeling group observed the teacher as she modeled how to apply each of the four comprehension strategies to example paragraphs; students in the explicit

FIGURE 3–23

An example of reciprocal teaching

Text from Which Students Are Working:

Crows have another gift. They are great mimics. They can learn to talk and imitate animal sounds. Some have been known to learn 100 words, and even whole phrases. They can imitate the squeak of a chicken, the whine of a dog, or the meow of a cat.

Games have a certain fascination to crows. In a game of hide-and-seek, a crow hides in the hollow of a tree and then sounds a distress caw. The others rush to the spot, look around, then flap away. This may be done over and over, after which the young crow pops out of its hiding place and caws gleefully. Far from being annoyed at this, the flock bursts into loud cawing themselves. They seem to like the trick that has been played on them.

T: Chantel, you're our teacher, right? Why don't you summarize first? Remember, just tell me the most important parts.

S1: Crows have a hundred words they can learn by imitation. They can imitate chickens, the whine of a dog, and cats.

T: Okay. We can shorten that summary a bit.

S2: You could say they can imitate other animals.

T: Oh! Good one! There's a list there, Chantel, did you notice that? It says they can imitate the squawk of a chicken, the whine of a dog, or the meow of a cat; and you could call that "animal sounds." Can you ask us a question?

S1: Ain't no questions in here.

S3: The words [sic] that need to be clarified are [sic] "mimics".

S4: That means imitate, right?

T: Right. How did you figure that out, Shirley?

S4: The paragraph.

T: Show us how somebody could figure out what "mimic" means.

S5: They are great mimics. They can learn to talk and imitate animal sounds.

T: Yes, so the next sentence tells you what it means. Very good, anything else need to be clarified?

All: No.

T: What about that question we need to ask? (pause) What is the second paragraph about, Chantel?

S1: The games they play.

S3: They do things like people do.

S4: What kinds of games do crows play?

S3: Hide and seek. Over and over again.

T: You know what, Larry? That was a real good comparison. One excellent question could be, "How are crows like people?"

(continued)

FIGURE 3–23

(continued)

S4:   They play hide and seek.

T: Good. Any other questions there?

S2:   How come the crows don't get annoyed?

S5:   What does annoyed mean?

T: Irritated, bothered.

S5:   Because they like it, they have fun. If I had a crow, I'd tell him he was it and see what he'd do.

T: Let's summarize now and have some predictions.

S1:   This was about how they play around in games.

T: Good for you. That's it. Predictions anyone?

S2:   Maybe more tricks they play.

S4:   Other games.

T: Maybe. So far, they have told us several ways that crows are very smart; they can communicate with one another, they can imitate many sounds, and they play games. Maybe we will read about another way in which they are smart. Who will be the next teacher?

From Palinscar (1986)

teaching group listened to the teacher's description of each strategy and completed paper-and-pencil exercises; and students in the control group received no information about the four strategies. All students received 12 sessions of group instruction along with regular tests of reading comprehension. Figure 3–24 shows the average scores of each group on a pretest and posttest of reading comprehension. As you can see, all groups began with between 40% and 50% correct on the pretest; however, the reciprocal teaching group showed the largest gain. In a similar study, the reciprocal teaching students showed a twenty-month pretest to posttest gain on a standardized test of reading comprehension, whereas the control group showed a one-month gain (Palinscar & Brown, 1984). In addition, Brown and Palinscar (1989) reported that the improvements of the reciprocal teaching group were still strong when the students were tested two or six months later.

Why does reciprocal teaching work? The procedure combines several powerful techniques involving the what, where, and who of learning. First, what is learned are cognitive strategies for reading comprehension rather than specific facts and procedures; that is, the instruction focuses on how to learn rather than on what to learn. Second, the learning of the cognitive strategies occurs within real reading comprehension tasks, instead of having each strategy taught in isolation. The goal is not to learn the strategies per se, but to learn them in order to understand the

FIGURE 3-24 Pretest to posttest gains in reading comprehension for four groups

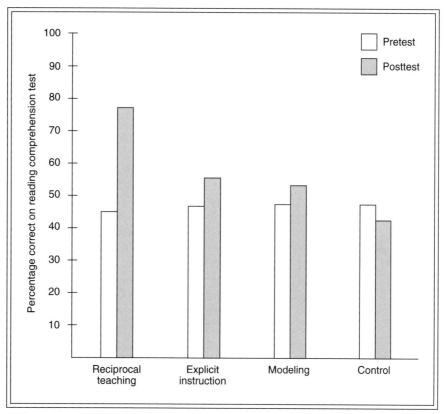

Adapted from Palinscar and Brown (1984)

passages. Third, students learn as apprentices within a cooperative group that is working together on a task. The teacher serves as a critic and helper who provides feedback and basic information as needed; in short, the teacher provides *expert scaffolding* within a group that is jointly working on a task. The most unique aspect of reciprocal teaching is that the student assumes the role of the teacher and learns by teaching; in other words, the student learns to assume an important role within a social context.

Research on reciprocal teaching offers a promising suggestion for the development of reading comprehension programs: Students can develop into competent readers when instruction focuses on an interrelated collection of learning-specific cognitive processes set within the context of working together on authentic reading tasks. However, in a recent review Rosenshine, Meister and Chapman (1996) found that students' reading comprehension skills could be improved equally well by reciprocal teaching and skill-based approaches.

CONCLUSION

This chapter has briefly explored the processes by which a reader comes to understand a passage, that is, the processes of reading comprehension. We began by examining Bartlett's (1932) concept of "effort after meaning," the view that reading involves trying to make sense out of what is presented. Then, we explored three kinds of knowledge that are related to reading comprehension: content knowledge, such as prior knowledge; strategic knowledge, such as using prose structure and making inferences; and metacognitive knowledge, such as comprehension monitoring.

First, this chapter presented examples of the well-documented evidence concerning prior knowledge. For both adults and children, a reader who has appropriate background knowledge comprehends a passage differently than one who lacks such knowledge. In particular, a reader with rich background knowledge is more likely to make inferences that give coherence to the passage.

Second, this chapter presented examples of the well-documented evidence concerning prose structure. For adults and older children, readers are more likely to remember important information than unimportant information from a passage. However, younger readers are less likely to be able to distinguish between important and unimportant information in the text and are less likely to spend their study time focusing on the important information.

Third, this chapter examined examples of research concerning inference making during reading. Younger readers are much less likely than older readers to make inferences spontaneously. Although answering inference questions can be taught, the general effects of inference training on reading comprehension are not yet clear.

Fourth, this chapter examined the research on metacognitive processes such as comprehension monitoring. Again, there is some evidence that younger readers are less likely than older readers to monitor their performance or to alter their reading strategy for different task.

For each of these cognitive processes in reading comprehension, we explored exemplary research studies in which students could be taught to use the process.

Finally, the chapter examined two reading programs that teach a collection of comprehension skills—a traditional one with a long record of use (SQ3R) and a modern one built on a solid research base (reciprocal teaching of reading comprehension). While this chapter cannot provide many definitive conclusions, it does point to the crucial contribution of the reader's existing knowledge—content, strategic, and metacognitive—in the reading process. Given the emerging research base on teaching reading comprehension processes, it may soon be possible to build an integrated reading comprehension program that develops students' content, strategic, and metacognitive knowledge for reading.

SUGGESTED READINGS

Barr, R., Kamil, M. L., Mosenthal, P., & Pearson, P. D. (Eds.). (1991). *Handbook of reading research* (Vol. 2). New York: Longman. (A collection of papers by leading researchers on reading.)

Bartlett, F. C. (1932). *Remembering.* London: Cambridge University Press. (Presents work that was the forerunner of modern cognitive research on learning from prose.)

Cesare, C., & Oakhill, J. (Eds.). (1996). *Reading comprehension difficulties.* Mahwah, NJ: Erlbaum. (A collection of papers aimed at understanding the cognitive processes underlying reading comprehension difficulties.)

CHAPTER 4 Writing

CHAPTER OUTLINE

T his chapter asks the question, What processes are involved in writing a composition? The answer to this question includes planning what to write, translating from the plan to words on the page, and reviewing what has been written. Students need training in each of these component processes in writing.

THE STORYTELLING PROBLEM

Read the story shown in Figure 4–1. Now, put the book aside and write the story in your own words. Assume that you are writing to a person who has never heard the story. Your task is not to recall the story verbatim, but rather to tell the main events in the story to someone else.

Figure 4–2 shows the main points of the story. Did your version of the story contain all or most of these points? Did you clearly introduce the lady and the fairy (rather than just referring to them as "she")? Could someone else read your story and understand it? Did your story present the events in the proper order?

This story is taken from an early study by Piaget (1926). In the study, a child between the ages of six and eight was asked to listen to the story and was given instructions like these:

> Are you good at telling stories? Very well then, we'll send your
> little friend out of the room, and while he is gone, we'll tell you a
> story. You must listen carefully. When you have listened to it all,
> we'll make your friend come back, and then you will tell him the
> same story. (pp. 96–97)

Some examples of the stories that children told are given in Figure 4–3. As you can see, the children make many mistakes in their retelling of the story. Some of their obvious problems are leaving out crucial pieces of information, such as the reason that the fairy attacked the lady; referring to characters by pronouns that lack clear referents; and ignoring the order of events. Piaget (1926) summarized the performance of his young story-tellers as follows: "The words spoken are not thought of from the point of view of the person spoken to" (p. 16). In other words, the children seemed to have trouble taking the listener's point of view, behaving as if the listener already knew the story (i.e., young children assume that everyone

FIGURE 4–1

Can you
retell this
story?

Once upon a time, there was a lady who was called Niobe, and who had twelve sons and twelve daughters. She met a fairy who had only one son and no daughter. Then the lady laughed at the fairy because the fairy only had one boy. Then the fairy was very angry and fastened the lady to a rock. The lady cried for ten years. In the end she turned into a rock, and her tears made a stream which still runs today.

From Piaget (1926)

FIGURE 4–2

The main points
in the story

1. Once there was a lady (or Niobe, etc.).
2. She had children (provided they outnumber those of the other character).
3. She met a fairy (or a girl, etc.).
4. This fairy had few children (or none, provided their number is inferior to the first lot).
5. The lady laughed at the fairy.
6. Because the fairy had so few children.
7. The fairy was angry.
8. The fairy fastened the lady to a rock (or a tree, etc.).
9. The lady cried.
10. She turned into a rock.
11. Her tears made a stream.
12. Which flows to this day.

From Piaget (1926)

else knows what they know). In contrast, adults are often able to adjust their stories for different audiences (i.e., adults can often take the listener's perspective into account).

In this chapter, we explore the nature of writing. What does Piaget's storytelling demonstration tell us about writing? His work suggests that one major aspect of speaking and writing is to influence an audience. In speaking, the audience is physically present, but in writing, the audience is not physically present. Thus the requirement of keeping the audience in one's mind as one writes is particularly difficult; adult writing often shows some of the egocentric characteristics and disorganization of Piaget's young storytellers. This demonstration suggests that writing is a skill that depends partly on the writer's ability to understand the perspective of the audience (i.e., of the potential readers).

What does a good writer need to know? In answer to this question, Applebee (1982) has identified three kinds of knowledge, each of which is exemplified in Piaget's storytelling study:

1. **Knowledge of language,** such as the grammatical rules of English.
2. **Knowledge of topic,** such as the specific information to be conveyed.
3. **Knowledge of audience,** such as the perspective of the potential readers.

The remainder of this chapter explores how writers use these bodies of knowledge in the writing process, and how the writing process can be improved through instruction.

FIGURE 4–3

How children told the story

Ri (age eight)
There was a lady once, she had twelve boys and twelve girls. She goes for a walk and she meets a fairy who had a boy and a girl and who didn't want to have twelve children. Twelve and twelve make twenty-four. She didn't want to have twenty-four children. She fastened N to a stone, she became a rock.

Gio (age eight)
Once upon a time there was a lady who had twelve boys and twelve girls, and then a fairy a boy and a girl. And then Niobe wanted to have some more sons. Then she was angry. She fastened her to a stone. He turned into a rock and then his tears made a stream which is still running today.

Met (age six)
The lady laughed at this fairy because she only had one boy. The lady had twelve sons and twelve daughters. One day she laughed at her. She was angry and she fastened her beside a stream. She cried for fifty months, and it made a great big stream.

Ce (age six)
There's a lady who was called Morel, and then she turned into a stream . . . then she had ten daughters and ten sons . . . and then after that the fairy fastened her to the bank of a stream and then she cried twenty months, and then after that she cried for twenty months and then her tears went into the stream, and then . . .

From Piaget (1926)

COGNITIVE PROCESSES IN WRITING

ANALYZING WRITING INTO THREE PROCESSES

Suppose that you were asked to write a short biographical story, such as an essay on how a water faucet works or a business letter. What cognitive processes would occur as you wrote? To examine this issue, Flower and Hayes (1981; Hayes & Flower, 1980; Hayes, 1996) gave writing assignments to people and asked them to describe what they were thinking as they carried out the assignment. This procedure is called *thinking aloud,* and the final transcript of everything that the writer says is called a *thinking aloud protocol.*

Based on their analysis of writers' thinking aloud protocols, Hayes and Flower (1980) identified three distinct processes in writing—planning, translating, and reviewing:

Planning involves searching for information from one's long-term memory, from the assignment, and from what has been written so far, and using this information to establish a plan for producing text. Three subprocesses in planning are generating, organizing, and goal setting. *Generating* involves retrieving information relevant to the writing task from one's long-term memory; for example, in writing an essay on the writing process, you might remember that the three major processes are planning, translating, and reviewing. *Organizing* involves selecting the most useful information that you have retrieved and structuring it into a writing plan; for example, in writing an essay on the writing process, you might devote one section to each of the three major processes in the order given earlier. *Goal-setting* involves establishing general criteria for guiding the execution of the writing plan; for example, you may decide that since your audience is unfamiliar with the material, your essay on the writing process should be kept simple and free of jargon. To be more consistent with newer taxonomies of planning (Kellogg, 1994), this chapter includes goal-setting under the planning subprocess of *evaluating* (i.e., determining the degree to which planned writing corresponds to the writer's goals).

Translating involves producing text that is consistent with the plan, that is, the act of putting words on the page. For example, the produced text should consist of legible, grammatically correct English sentences that convey the intended information in an effective way.

Reviewing involves improving the written text using the subprocesses of *reading* and *editing*. In reading, the writer detects problems in the text; in editing, the writer attempts to correct the problems. For example, if the first draft contains a sentence that is ungrammatical or that fails to convey the intended meaning the sentence will be rewritten as part of the reviewing process.

Figure 4–4 provides a simplified version of the general model of writing proposed by Hayes and Flower (1980). The three shaded rectangles represent the three major processes in writing. The two unshaded rectangles on the left represent the input into the writing process: the writing assignment (including an understanding of the topic and audience) and the writer's knowledge (including knowledge of the topic, the audience, and written English). The unshaded rectangle on the right represents the output (i.e., the text that is produced). The arrows indicate that the three writing processes interact rather than occur in a fixed order.

More recently, Hayes (1996) has offered a revised model that still contains three basic cognitive processes in writing. However, in his model

FIGURE 4–4 A model of the writing process

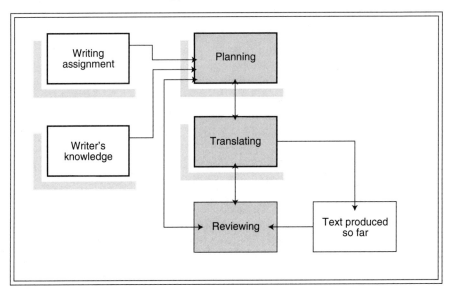

Adapted from Hayes and Flower (1980)

planning is subsumed into a broader process called *reflection,* "an activity that operates on internal representations to produce other internal representations" (Hayes, 1996, p. 13); translating is subsumed into a broader process called *text production,* "a function that takes internal representations . . . and produces written, spoken, or graphical output" (Hayes, 1996, p. 13); and reviewing is replaced by *text interpretation,* a process that "creates internal representations from linguistic and graphic inputs" (Hayes, 1996, p. 13). In addition, Hayes's revised model emphasizes the role of working memory in writing, includes visual and spatial representations in writing (such as graphs, tables, and pictures), and acknowledges the role of motivational and social factors in writing.

Similar analyses of the writing process have been proposed by other researchers. For example, Nold (1981) suggests three major processes: planning, transcribing (corresponding to translating), and reviewing. Similarly, Bruce, Collins, Rubin, and Gentner (1982) include the following steps in their model of writing: production of ideas (corresponding to planning), production of text (corresponding to translating), and editing (corresponding to reviewing). Gould (1980) lists four processes: planning, accessing additional information (corresponding to a part of planning), generating (corresponding to translating), and reviewing. In a recent review, Kellogg (1994) concluded that "writing involves four cognitive operations that play a role in all thinking tasks· collecting information, planning ideas, translating ideas into text . . . , and reviewing ideas and text" (p. 16). The first two processes would be considered part of planning in the Hayes and

Flower model, whereas the second two correspond to translating and reviewing, respectively. Apparently, there is some consensus that the major writing processes include planning, translating, and reviewing. Furthermore, all the analyses assume that there is a great deal of interaction among the processes, rather than each process occurring separately.

LOOKING AT STUDENT PROTOCOLS

As evidence to support their model of the writing process, Hayes and Flower (1980) presented an analysis of the thinking aloud protocol of a typical writer. The protocol contained fourteen pages covering 458 simple statements or comments made by the writer. The protocol could be divided into three sections. In the first section, consisting of the first 116 comments, the writer seemed to focus on the planning subprocess of generating information, with occasional interruptions to focus on reviewing. Some typical comments made during this section of the protocol were "And what I'll do now is simply jot down random thoughts . . ." and "Other things to think about in this random search are. . . ." In the second section, consisting of the next 154 comments, the writer concentrated on the planning subprocess of organizing the information, with occasional interruptions to focus on reviewing. Typical comments made during this section of the protocol included "Now I think it's time to go back and read over the material and elaborate on its organization." Finally, in the third section, containing the final 188 comments, the writer emphasized the process of translating, with occasional interruptions for generating and reviewing. Examples of typical comments were "Let's try and write something," or "Oh, no. We need more organizing." (p. 10)

Figure 4–5 shows the proportion of comments directed toward generating, organizing, translating, and reviewing for each section of the protocol. These data were derived using only major comments from two writers. As can be seen, the first section of the protocol is devoted mainly to generating ideas, the second mainly to organizing the ideas, and the third mainly to translating the writing plan into acceptable sentences. In addition, the reviewing process (consisting mainly of editing) seems to play a small part in each of the three sections of the protocol.

INSTRUCTIONAL THEMES

As can be seen in the foregoing analysis, the study of writing is in its early stages of development. However, even in this early work on writing, several implications for writing instruction have emerged.

PROCESS VERSUS PRODUCT. Much of the emphasis in writing instruction is typically on the final product, including spelling, punctuation, and grammar. An additional focus suggested by the cognitive analysis of writing is that writing instruction should also concentrate on the *process* of writing. In particular, the foregoing analysis suggests that most

FIGURE 4–5 What writers do during the writing process

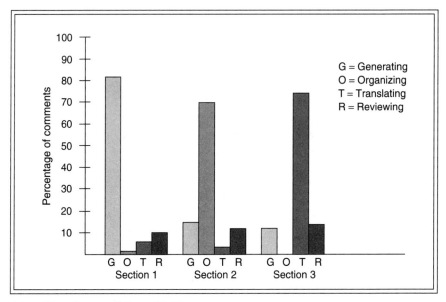

Adapted from Hayes and Flower (1980)

of the time and effort in writing is devoted to planning rather than to actually producing acceptable text. Steinberg (1980) summarizes this idea as follows: "teaching of writing focuses too much on product, on the written paper that the student submits, and not enough on process, on how to write" (p. 156).

PROBLEM-SOLVING VERSUS PROCEDURE APPLICATION. Much of the instruction in writing involves teaching procedures for producing sentences properly, such as "Never begin a sentence with 'because,'" or "Each paragraph should have a topic sentence, a summary sentence, and approximately three core sentences." In addition to using such procedures, a writer must also engage in an act of problem solving. For example, Kellogg (1996) shows that "in composing a written text, individuals . . . engage in a special form of thinking—the making of meaning—that may well define one of the most unique characteristics of our species" (p. 3). As in other types of problem solving, the writer must establish goals and work to achieve them. Thus instruction in writing may be viewed as instruction in problem solving. Flower and Hayes (1981) make this argument as follows: "writing is problem solving, and can be analyzed from a psychological view of problem-solving processes" (p. 40).

COMMUNICATION VERSUS COMPOSITION. Much of the instruction in writing involves learning to produce a composition that meets stylistic and grammatical requirements. Nystrand (1982a) points out there is an emphasis on "proper talk" and "standardized composition" rather than on writing in a way that influences the audience. In addition to teaching students how to write compositions that conform to "school English," students must learn to be sensitive to the idea that writing is an attempt to communicate with a reader. As Frase (1982, p. 130) points out, "effective writing is bringing one's own goals in line with the readers' constraints" (p. 130). Similarly, Nystrand (1982a) notes that writers need to develop a "notion of audience as person or persons whom . . . the writer hopes to influence" (p. 2).

KNOWLEDGE TRANSFORMING AND KNOWLEDGE TELLING. Bereiter and Scardamalia (1987) have distinguished between knowledge transforming, in which a writer selects and organizes ideas into a coherent message, and knowledge telling, in which a writer expresses ideas in the order they are thought of. In knowledge transforming, the writer modifies the knowledge he or she accesses in order to communicate with a reader, whereas in knowledge telling, the writer's goal is to present information to the reader. One of the main differences between knowledge transforming and knowledge telling lies in the role of planning in that knowledge transforming requires more planning than does knowledge telling. According to this analysis, a major goal of writing instruction is to help students progress from a knowledge-telling approach to a knowledge-transforming approach.

In the remainder of this chapter, we will examine each of the three major processes in writing—planning, translating, and reviewing—as well as the educational implications of work in these areas.

PLANNING

WHAT IS PLANNING?

As noted in the previous section, planning is a major process in writing. Planning includes generating information from memory, which Hayes and Flower (1980) call "generating"; evaluating that information with respect to criteria for writing, which Hayes and Flower (1980) call "goal-setting"; and organizing that information into a writing plan, which Hayes and Flower (1980) call "organizing."

RESEARCH ON PLANNING

HOW MUCH DO STUDENTS PLAN IN DICTATION? As an example of planning, let's suppose you were asked to dictate a one-page business letter. The dictation rate is potentially 200 words per minute (i.e., a person can speak comfortably at a rate of 200 words per minute). However, Gould (1980) reports that the normal dictation rate is approximately twenty-three words per minute. Similarly, suppose you were asked to write a one-page business letter. The writing rate is potentially forty words per minute, yet Gould (1980) reports that the normal writing rate for business letters is thirteen words per minute.

These results indicate that people produce text much more slowly than the limits imposed by the output device (writing or dictating). Why do people dictate (or write) at such slow rates? According to research summarized by Gould (1980), most of the speaking or writing time is devoted to planning. For example, by carefully recording pauses that are made during speaking or writing, Gould (1978a, 1978b, 1980) was able to determine that pauses accounted for approximately two-thirds of total composition time in both writing and speaking. These results are summarized in Figure 4–6.

WHEN DO STUDENTS PLAN IN WRITING? Interestingly, Gould's studies revealed that planning pauses occurred during the writing process (as *local planning*) rather than before it (as *global planning*), suggesting that writers rarely plan before they start writing. In a more focused study, Matsuhashi (1982, 1987) carefully observed the pauses made by high school students as they wrote essays. As in the Gould study, Matsuhashi found that planning time accounted for approximately one-half to two-thirds of the total writing time. In addition, Matsuhashi found that pauses occurred mainly at the borders between ideas (e.g., at the end of

FIGURE 4–6 How much planning time is used in writing or dictating a letter?

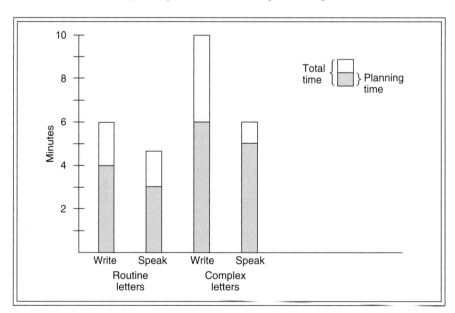

Adapted from Gould (1980)

sentences). Figure 4–7 shows the time spent by a high school student in writing an essay; the numbers after each word indicate the length of the pause (in seconds) that occurred before the writer moved on to the next word. As can be seen, the longest pauses are in line 4 (9.7 seconds before going on to a new clause), line 5 (16.6 seconds after the sentence), line 8 (13.3 seconds before the new paragraph), and line 11 (12.8 seconds after the sentence). During some of the longer pauses, the writer removed his pen from the paper and shifted position in his seat. Matsuhashi suggests that the pauses allowed the writer to organize the information and place it within the appropriate context.

HOW FAR AHEAD DO STUDENTS PLAN? Additional evidence concerning the planning process is reported by Scardamalia, Bereiter, and Goelman (1982). For example, in one study elementary school children were asked to write an essay. At various points during the writing process, the teacher would interrupt a student, asking what he or she was going to write. Usually students had the next five or six words in mind and had thought ahead to the end of the clause. Young children (in the primary

---

FIGURE 4–7

Pauses in
writing an
essay

1   Truly.⁶successful¹·¹person·⁵-to·⁸-person²·³communi-
2   ¹·⁸cation³·⁵is¹·⁹difficult¹·³because⁶·⁹people·⁶in·⁹general¹·¹are·⁹poor
3   ¹·⁰listeners. ⁷·⁰They¹·⁰would·⁷rather¹·⁴listen·⁵to·⁹themselves ¹·⁹speaking
4   ²·¹than·⁴someone·⁷else·⁵. ⁴·⁷It·⁹is·⁷my·⁷feeling¹·⁹that⁹·⁷this·⁸occurs
5   ¹·⁶because¹·¹of¹·²a·⁸basic²·⁷self-centeredness.¹⁶·⁶⁵·⁵people ⁴·⁸tend¹·²to
6   ¹·⁹be·⁶more·⁵interested·⁷in·⁷their·⁹own·⁷lives¹·⁵to¹·²bother¹·⁰ exposing
7   ¹·³themselves·⁷to·⁵how·⁷others·⁸live.
8   ¹³·³Communication¹·²is·⁷successful·⁸only·⁹when²·⁹there
9   ²·²is²·⁴"·⁵give·⁶and·⁸take"¹·¹between³·⁷the·⁷parties¹·¹. ³·⁷Each·⁷one
10   ¹·⁹should·⁹contribute¹·²equally²·¹,¹·⁰as·⁸well·⁷as²·⁰accepting·⁷the
11   ²·²contributions⁵·³of·⁶the·⁷others. ¹²·⁸The·⁶situation·⁷I¹·⁰have
12   ¹·⁸described⁶·⁶above³·²leads·⁶to·⁶poor·⁸communication¹·⁷,¹·⁰since
13   ¹·⁹everyone·⁸wants·⁹to·⁶"give"¹·²and·⁸no¹·⁰one·⁶wants·⁹to
14   ¹·²"take."

(Numbers after words indicate pause times, in seconds.)

From Matsuhashi (1982)

grades) tended to dictate to themselves, mouthing each word while writing. In contrast, older children (grade 4 and above) rarely vocalized during writing but did vocalize during pauses. Apparently, young children rely on external memory (i.e., self-dictation) in order to keep the next few words in their short-term memory, whereas older children behave as if a memory load of several words does not require external memory.

DO EXPERIENCED AND INEXPERIENCED WRITERS PLAN DIFFERENTLY? Experienced writers are more likely than inexperienced writers to generate, evaluate, and organize ideas before writing; that is, experienced writers engage in more global planning than do inexperienced writers. For example, Pianko (1979) found that few students—even at the high school and college levels—engage in any planning prior to writing a school assignment. In contrast, professional writers overwhelmingly report creating some sort of written outline before beginning a draft (Stotsky, 1990). When told to write a short story within a time limit ranging from 2.5 to 20 minutes, fifth-grade and tenth-grade students generally began writing immediately, whereas adults were more likely to engage in prewriting planning activities such as writing an outline (Zbrodoff, 1985). When given longer time limits for the assignment, adults, in contrast to elementary and high school students, spent more time planning and produced more detailed outlines (Zbrodoff, 1985). These results suggest that global planning is a hallmark of experienced writers.

Bereiter and Scardamalia (1987) analyzed the ideas generated by students at various ages, and identified three stages of planning activity. First, young children such as those entering elementary school have difficulty generating any ideas at all. Writers at this level have problems with even the most basic planning subprocess—generating ideas. Second, elementary school children (up to approximately 12 years old) engage in knowledge telling—expressing ideas as they are generated without evaluating or organizing them. Writers at this stage seem to have mastered one planning subprocess—generating ideas—but have not mastered others planning subprocesses, such as evaluating and organizing ideas. Third, older writers can engage in knowledge transforming—generating, evaluating, and organizing ideas before expressing them in order to communicate with the reader. This analysis shows how the ability to generate ideas is not enough, because students also need to learn how to evaluate and organize the ideas they have generated.

IMPLICATIONS FOR INSTRUCTION: PLANNING

In summary, this section has presented several important findings concerning the planning process: planning is a time-consuming process accounting for most of writing time, local planning seems to occur mainly at sentence and clause boundaries, local planning generally allows the writer to work on one clause or sentence at a time, and inexperienced writers often do not engage in global planning.

Although the ability to generate, evaluate, and organize ideas is central to the writing process, writing instruction does not normally teach students how to plan. The foregoing analysis of planning suggests that students may need instruction and practice in how to generate ideas, how to organize information, and how to evaluate whether that information fits into the organization.

A major finding of the research on planning is that students often fail to engage in global planning; that is, they fail to generate ideas, evaluate those ideas for relevance to the writing goals, and organize the relevant ideas before writing. If writers do not engage in these prewriting activities, they may have to try to generate, evaluate, and organize at the same time that they are engaged in translating. By trying to do two things at once—plan and translate—both processes might suffer, resulting in lower-quality essays. It follows that an important instructional intervention is to encourage students to engage in a range of planning subprocesses—including generating, evaluating, and organizing—before they begin to write.

For example, Kellogg (1994) investigated the hypothesis that asking students to plan before they write would result in better essays. College students were asked to write an essay on the pros and cons of professionals joining an "Anti-Greed" Club, based on the following instructions:

> Imagine that you are a successful professional. An "Anti-Greed" Club has been formed in your neighborhood. All the members of this club are professionals like you (attorneys, physicians, business executives, etc.) who earn over $50,000 per year. Each member pledges to give annual income over $50,000 to poor families in the community. The recipients and amount each receives are decided by chance—that is, by a drawing. Several members of your social club are considering joining the "Anti-Greed" Club and have asked your help in making an objective, rational decision. Write a paper giving the pros and cons of such a move as you see it. Be careful to give fair treatment to both sides of the issue, regardless of how you feel about it personally. (Kellogg, 1987, p. 262)

One group of students was not asked to engage in any prewriting activity (no-prewriting group) so that no planning processes were activated prior to writing. Another group was asked to write down as many ideas as possible without evaluating or organizing them (generating group), so that only the planning subprocess of generating was activated. Another group was asked to generate a list of relevant ideas (listing group), so that the planning subprocesses of generating and evaluating (or goal setting) were activated. Finally, a group was asked to produce an outline containing relevant ideas within a hierarchical structure (outlining group) so that the planning subprocesses of generating, evaluating (or goal setting), and organizing were activated.

How do prewriting activities affect what is written? Judges were asked to rate the quality of each essay on a 10-point scale. Figure 4–8 shows that

FIGURE 4–8 Quality of essays produced after four types of prewriting activities

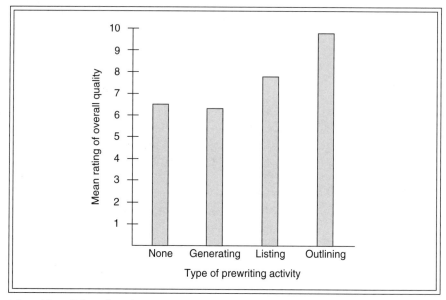

Adapted from Kellogg (1994)

the average quality ratings of the essays written by the no-prewriting group and the generating group were low, whereas the outlining group wrote the highest-quality essays. According to Kellogg (1994), students in the no-prewriting group and the generating group must try to engage in planning and translating processes at the same time. Given the constraints on how much can be processed in working memory at one time, the quality of their writing was affected. In contrast, when students engaged in intensive planning before writing, as those in the outlining group had done, memory resources could be used mainly for the translating processes during writing, thus allowing for better essays. Similarly, Kellogg (1988) found that students composed better business letters when they were forced to spend 10 minutes generating an outline before writing than when there was no prewriting activity. Kellogg's results are encouraging, because they show that it is possible to teach students to engage in productive planning processes before they begin to write.

Fostering planning skills in students includes helping students learn how to generate, evaluate, and organize ideas. First, training students in how to retrieve information is an important aspect of planning. Students need practice in how to search for needed information, including how to take (and use) notes from sources. A key finding in many writing studies is that students' knowledge of the domain is a crucial determinant of the quality of the writing (Voss & Bisanz, 1985). For example, Caccamise (1987) found that students generated far more ideas when writing about a familiar topic than when writing about an unfamiliar one. In short, students need to write about topics that they already know about or have researched. Second, students need practice in establishing goals and evaluating whether the ideas they generate meet their goals. This involves being able to write for a specific audience and for a specific purpose. Third, learning to organize ideas into a coherent structure is another important aspect of planning, which often involves being able to create and monitor outlines.

TRANSLATING

WHAT IS TRANSLATING?

The next component in the writing process is what Hayes and Flower (1980) call *translating*. This phase involves carrying out the writing plan by actually generating some written text. According to Hayes and Flower, translating is done interactively with planning; in other words, a writer generates a plan, translates a small part of it, then checks the next part of the plan, translates that part, and so on. Research described in the previous section suggests that people may translate about one phrase (or simple sentence) at a time.

CONSTRAINTS ON TRANSLATING. Suppose that you write by checking your overall writing plan, sentence by sentence. In other words, you check your plan for the first main idea and then try to translate it into a sentence. Then you check your plan for the next main idea and try to translate it into a sentence, and so on. As you move from your writing plan (i.e., your idea of what you want to say) to the production of prose (i.e., the sentence that you actually write), you are constrained by several factors. As listed by Nystrand (1982b), these constraining factors are:

Graphic: The sentences that you generate must be legible for the reader; they must use lettering, penmanship, layout, spacing, indentation, and spelling that are familiar to the reader.

Syntactic: The sentences that you generate must be based on the rules of written English; grammar, punctuation, and sentence organization must be appropriate for the reader.

Semantic: The sentences that you generate must convey the meaning to the reader that you intended; your assumptions about the information that a reader brings to the reading task must be appropriate.

Textual: The sentences that you generate must fit together into a cohesive paragraph and passage.

Contextual: The sentences that you generate must be written in the appropriate style (e.g., sarcasm or understatement).

Each of these types of constraints involves making sure that there is correspondence between your written words and the reader's understanding of them. Examples of writers' failures to follow the constraints on writer-reader communication are given in Figure 4–9. Nystrand (1982b) refers to these examples as *misconstraints* (i.e., cases in which the reader is either misled or misinterprets the writer's information).

RESEARCH ON TRANSLATING

REMOVING CONSTRAINTS ON TRANSLATING. The translation process may require a great deal of attentional capacity on the part of young writers, because so much of the translation process is not yet automatic to them. One solution to this problem is to ignore the normal constraints on writing, as the following writing from a six-year-old demonstrates:

> WONS A LITOL GIRL WOS WOKIG IN HR GARDIN INTIL SE GOT KOT BIY A ROBR AND TIN SE SKREMD AND TIN HR MON AND DAD KAM OUT AND HLPT HR OWT OV THE ROBRS HANDS AND TIN TAY KOLD THE POLES AND TIN THE POLES TOK KAR OV THE ROBR AN POT HIM IN THE GAOL (Read, 1981, pp. 106–107)

As can be seen, this young writer was able to tell a story without paying great attention to some of the basic rules of spelling, punctuation, gram-

FIGURE 4–9

Examples of five errors in writer-reader communication

Graphic Misconstraint
"now here" for "nowhere"

Syntactic Misconstraint
"Your still going to get where your going with a seatbelt on."

Semantic Misconstraint
"The law against drinking is for your own safety." (Written to adults whereas the law against drinking applies only to minors.)

Textual Misconstraint
"I think that the snowmobilers will get used to these new laws, and people will see the laws the government put out are for our protection." (The previous sentences have discussed only automobile seatbelts so the reader has not been prepared to consider snowmobiles.)

Contextual Misconstraint
Asking high school students to read the state laws on drunk driving.

Adapted from Nystrand (1982b)

mar, and the like. By freeing herself from the tedious constraints on writing, the young writer was able to produce a story.

Read (1981) suggests that "teachers and parents can look upon early writing in roughly the same way that they regard children's art, as an expression which is created with pleasure and which is not expected to be adult-like" (p. 114). In addition, Read provides evidence that the use of nonstandard spelling during writing does not adversely affect reading; for example, the little girl who wrote this story was able to sight-read words such as "girl" even though she wrote "GROL."

In most school writing tasks, the graphic and syntactic constraints (as well as others) are enforced. If the rules of spelling, grammar, and even penmanship are not yet automatic, this means that the writer's full attentional capacity must be devoted to the correct production of text rather than to organizational planning. For example, Scardamalia et al. (1982) propose that since the information-processing capacity of young writers is limited, and since the mechanical and syntactic aspects of writing are not automatic, an emphasis on correctly formed sentences results in poorer overall writing quality. The low-level aspects of writing (such as correct spelling, punctuation, and penmanship) interfere with higher-level planning.

To test this idea, Bereiter and Scardamalia (1987) asked fourth- and sixth-grade children to write an essay, dictate an essay at a normal rate, or dictate an essay at a slow rate. The dictation modes were used because they presumably freed the young writer from some of the mechanical and syntactic demands of translating. As predicted, the dictation modes resulted in about twice as many words being produced and in small increases in judged quality, as compared to writing. However, Gould (1980) notes that dictation does not tend to increase the quality of prose in adults. Apparently, the mechanical processes of handwriting, proper spelling, and punctuation are not automatic in young writers, but, for simple assignments, do eventually become automatic in adults. Thus the act of translating ideas into words may actually disrupt the flow of thinking in young writers.

POLISHED VERSUS UNPOLISHED FIRST DRAFTS. There is some potentially important evidence that the quality of adult writing is also hindered when attention must be focused on the mechanics of writing. For example, suppose that you were asked to write a formal business letter in order to persuade your teacher to use a future class period for either a film that is related to the course or for a library reading session. First, you will have 10 minutes to complete a preliminary draft. Then, after a 5-minute rest period, you will have 10 minutes to produce the final draft.

Suppose your goal is to produce a high-quality final draft, containing many persuasive arguments expressed in a coherent way. Would it be better to try to write a polished letter as your first draft—including proper sentence formation, punctuation, and spelling—or would it be better to try to concentrate only on generating arguments in the preliminary draft, with revisions for organization, sentence formation, and mechanics handled in the final draft?

Glynn, Britton, Muth, and Dogan (1982) investigated this question in a controlled experiment in which students were given writing assignments as just described. Some students were told to write a polished first draft:

> On this preliminary draft, you need to be concerned with content (i.e., the production of persuasive ideas), order (i.e., the logical sequence of these ideas), sentence formation (i.e., the incorporation of these ideas into sentences), and mechanics (i.e., compliance with punctuation and spelling rules). Communicate all the ideas that you think may be useful in persuading me to choose one alternative and not the other. More than one persuasive idea can be incorporated into each sentence. (p. 558)

Other students were told to write an unpolished first draft:

> On this preliminary draft you need to be concerned with content (i.e., the production of persuasive ideas). Communicate all the ideas that you think may be useful in persuading me to choose one alternative and not the other. Summarize each of these persuasive ideas using only three or four words, and write them in order. On this draft, do not attempt to work on order (i.e., the logical sequence of persuasive ideas), sentence formation (i.e., the incorporation of these ideas into sentences), or mechanics (i.e., compliance with punctuation and spelling rules). You will be permitted to work on order, sentence formation, and mechanics during the next draft. (pp. 558–559)

For the final draft, all students were told to "produce the best letter you can," including consideration of content, order, sentence formation, and mechanics.

Table 4–1 summarizes the differences between the final drafts produced by the two groups. Students who wrote unpolished first drafts tended to write final drafts containing more persuasive arguments, more arguments per sentence, and fewer mechanical errors, as compared to students who

TABLE 4–1 Differences in final drafts when preliminary drafts are polished versus unpolished	**Total Number of Arguments**	**Arguments per Sentence**	**Mechanical Errors per Sentence**
Polished preliminary draft	2.9	.38	.43
Unpolished preliminary draft	8.0	.85	.23

Adapted from Glynn, Britton, Muth, and Dogan (1982)

wrote a polished first draft. Subsequent experiments determined that this pattern was most strongly pronounced for students with average verbal ability as compared to students with low verbal ability. These results suggest that when good writers are forced to express early drafts in complete sentences, the quality of the final draft suffers. Apparently, the heavy load placed on attentional capacity limits the writers' ability to retrieve and organize information. By forcing ideas to be translated prematurely into polished sentences, without allowing time for planning, the result may be a final draft that lacks integrated content.

INDIVIDUAL DIFFERENCES IN TRANSLATING. Another approach to the study of the translation process involves comparing older and younger writers, or comparing more skilled and less skilled writers. For example, in one study (Scardamalia et al., 1982), fourth- and sixth-grade students were asked to write essays on topics such as, "Is it better to be an only child or to have brothers and sisters?," "Should boys and girls play sports together?," or "Should children be allowed to choose what subject they study in school?" When students finished their essays, they were given cues to keep working such as, "You're doing fine. Now I know it's a bit tough, but you can write some more about this."

The results indicated that the cues to keep writing encouraged both fourth- and sixth-graders to add about 50% more to their essays. However, the judged quality of the essays improved only for the fourth-graders. Apparently, the younger writers stopped writing before they were really finished, whereas the sixth-graders continued until they had written a good essay. One implication is that younger children may be using the conventions of oral speech (e.g., needing someone to tell them to go on) while older writers can tell themselves to continue producing text.

When young writers were asked to dictate their essays, the students produced longer essays than when they were asked to write them. However, cues to produce more text resulted in more words being produced but not in increased quality ratings for the essays. Apparently young writers stop too soon when they must physically produce the sentences; however, when they are encouraged to continue or when they are allowed to dictate, they produce more complete, coherent essays.

There is clear evidence that as children grow, the quality and quantity of their writing increase. For example, an analysis of a national child development study revealed that older children write longer and more complex sentences than younger children (Richardson, Calnan, Essen, & Lambert, 1975). In a typical research study, Bartlett and Scribner (1981) asked children in grades three to six to write a story based on the following: "A man leaves his house. His body is found the next morning." As expected, sixth-graders produced longer stories than third-graders (an average of 227 words versus 103 words, respectively); in addition, sixth-graders produced more complex referring expressions (e.g., pronouns) as compared to third-graders. Scardamalia, Bereiter and Goelman (1982) reported on a study in which fourth- and sixth-graders were asked to write essays. The experimenters measured the length of the longest "coherent string," that is, the longest string of words with no nonfunctional units (such as "you know") and no incoherent orderings. For fourth-graders the average was 4.1 words, and for sixth-graders the average was 6.3, suggesting that older writers produce longer coherent strings.

Scardamalia (1981) has compared different levels of sophistication in sentence production. For example, writers using a low level of sophistication state single facts without any integration, as in the following:

> In the state of Michigan the climate is cool. In the state of
> Michigan the fruit crop is apples. In the state of California, the
> climate is warm. In the state of California the fruit crop is oranges.

In contrast, writers using a high level of sophistication integrate all of the information into a coherent sentence, such as:

> In Michigan's cool climate they harvest apples, but with
> California's warm climate, oranges may be grown.

Scardamalia (1981) noted similar differences among levels of sophistication in the essays students wrote on the question "Should students be able to choose what things they study in school?" A low level of sophistication is exemplified in the following essay:

> Yes, I think we should. Because some subjects are hard like
> math. And because the teachers give us a page a day. I think the
> subjects that we should have is Reading. Because that is easyest
> one. I think we should't have math, science and social studies.
> Because in social studies and science we have to write up notes
> and do experiments. I think math is the worst subject. And I
> hate spelling to. Because in spelling there are so many words to
> write and they are all hard. And they waste my time. I think
> school shouldn't be to 3:45. I think it should be to 2:00. I think
> school is too long.

As can be seen, the writer simply expressed each idea that came into her head in the order that the ideas occurred to her. This type of writing is called *associative writing* by Bereiter (1980) and *writer-based prose* by Flower (1979).

In the following example from Scardamalia (1981), the writer used a high level of sophistication in the production of sentences (the spelling is original):

> Chose is an important thing but a very tricky thing to fool with. I
> feel that chose of school subjects should be something that is
> done carefully. A young child given a chose would pick the
> easiest subjects with no foresight into his future. But choose in
> his later years could be very important. To develop his leadership
> qualities. To follow and develop his interests and charictor to his

fillest. So with these facts I come to the conclusion that chose of subjects should not be given until about the age of fifteen. You can not condem or praise what you know little about. Until the age of choise a full and general cericulum should be given. It is not up to the school board to decide your life and until you are old enough to decide it is not your dission either.

This writer is able to express conflicting points of view and weave them into a coherent solution. This type of writing requires holding many different ideas in one's mind at one time and seeing the relationships among them. If a writer's attention is absorbed by the mechanics of writing, it is not possible to hold all of these relations in mind.

One implication of this work is that high-quality writing requires that the writer not have to use much attention for the mechanical aspects of sentence production. Good writing requires that the mechanics of penmanship, spelling, punctuation, and grammar be automatic. Thus, to be a good writer requires much more than having good ideas; it also requires a great deal of well-learned knowledge about the English language.

IMPLICATIONS FOR INSTRUCTION: TRANSLATING

The foregoing review of research on translation makes three points. First, the writer is constrained by many factors, including the mechanics of using proper grammar, spelling, and penmanship. Second, the mechanics of proper sentence writing may overload the writer's attentional capacity, thus interfering with high-level planning and organization. Third, there appears to be a developmental trend in which older writers, who presumably have automated much of the mechanics of writing, are able to write more complex sentences, to integrate the information, and to keep writing until finished.

Writing instruction that emphasizes correct spelling, punctuation, grammar, penmanship, and other mechanics may serve to reduce or eliminate the student's ability to plan. The result can be a mechanically correct composition that lacks coherence. Instead, students may benefit from writing situations in which the mechanical constraints are removed or relaxed (e.g., being free to write rough drafts that may not be mechanically perfect). The promising research on unpolished first drafts suggests that the quality of the final product may be higher if students are not forced to write polished first drafts. Even practice in oral expression—which certainly avoids constraints on spelling and penmanship—may provide needed practice in the translation process. These kinds of relaxations of mechanical constraints seem particularly important for young writers who have not yet automatized many of the mechanical aspects of writing.

Eventually, students need to develop automatic skills in the mechanics of writing such as penmanship (or typing), spelling, grammar, and punctuation. This will free their attentional capacity to concentrate on the relations among ideas in the composition.

WRITING WITH WORD PROCESSORS. A potentially important instructional intervention that may reduce the drudgery of the translation process is learning to use a word processor. The translation process involves putting words on paper. An obvious question concerns whether this process is influenced by whether the words are produced by typing them on a keyboard versus handwriting them. According to a cognitive theory of working memory, the amount of attentional resources are limited. If using one type of the output device—word processor versus pen—places a greater load on working memory than the other, the quality of the written product would suffer. For example, if students lack experience in using a word processor, they have to devote more attentional resource to the mechanics of typing and less to what they are writing. To test this hypothesis, Kellogg and Mueller (1993) compared the writing of students who were asked to compose by longhand, students who were asked to compose on a word processor but who lacked extensive word-processing experience, and students who were asked to compose on a word processor and who possessed extensive word-processing experience. Figure 4–10 shows that the rated quality of the essay (on a 10-point scale) was nearly equivalent for longhand writers and experienced word-processor writers, but that inexperienced word-processor writers produced lower quality essays than did longhand writers.

By the same argument, if younger students have difficulty with the mechanics of handwriting, allowing them to use a word processor might enable them to devote more attention to what they are writing. This inter-

FIGURE 4–10 Quality of essays produced by longhand and by word processors

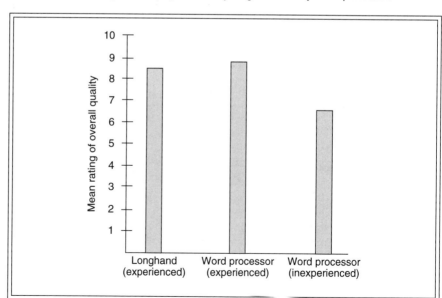

Adapted from Kellogg and Mueller (1993)

vention will work, of course, only if students are well practiced in the use of word processors. In an extensive review of studies comparing writing by longhand and by word processor, Bangert-Drowns (1993) found no significant differences in the quality of writing products in most of the studies. However, overall the word-processing groups had a small advantage. Consistent with the working-memory hypothesis, the advantage of word processing over longhand writing was much greater for elementary school children than for college students, especially when the elementary school students were not highly skilled writers and when they had received extensive practice in using word processors.

These results are consistent with the idea that the translation process is equivalent when writing by pen or by word processor, as long as the writer is skilled in its use. In reviewing research comparing writers who generally possessed these skills, Kellogg (1994) concluded that "word processors and pens are equally effective output devices" (p. 147). However, when a writer lacks skill in using either, the need to focus on correctly using the device detracts from writing a high-quality product. In short, when the translation process requires paying attention to physically writing words, less attention can be paid to what to write.

REVIEWING

WHAT IS REVIEWING?

The third major process in our model of writing is the reviewing process. As Bartlett (1982) points out, this process involves both detecting errors in the text and correcting them.

RESEARCH ON REVIEWING

HOW MANY CHANGES DO STUDENTS MAKE? Gould (1980) presents evidence showing that revision is almost totally absent from adult writing or dictating of simple assignments, such as one-page business letters. Experienced dictators use less than 10% of dictation time on reviewing or revising what they have said. If reviewing is not used often in letter writing, then prohibiting writers from reviewing should not greatly affect their writing performance. To test this idea, Gould (1978b) asked adults to engage in "invisible writing." This invisible writing involved writing with a wooden stylus on a sheet of paper that had carbon paper and another sheet of paper under it so subjects could not see what they had written. Based on the writing of eight business letters, those using invisible writing required about the same amount of time as those using normal writing (10 minutes for invisible writing versus 11 minutes for normal writing), achieved about the same quality ratings from judges (3.0 for invisible writing versus 3.2 for normal writing, with 1 being unacceptable and 5 being excellent), and needed about the same amount of proof-editing changes (almost none for both groups). Similarly, Pianko (1979) reported that college freshmen spent less than 9% of writing time on reading or reviewing what they have written. Apparently, adults often do not review what they have written, especially when the assignment is a fairly short and simple one.

WHAT KINDS OF CHANGES DO STUDENTS MAKE? In a review of the research on revision in writing, Fitzgerald (1987) reported that students mainly make surface and mechanical revisions, suggesting that they generally equate revision with proofreading. In addition, Fitzgerald (1987) found that although teachers rarely ask students to revise what they have written, when they were asked to engage in in-depth revision, their final product was generally improved.

Bartlett (1982) conducted an extensive series of studies of how children in grades three through eight revise text. For example, in one study, fourth- and fifth-graders were asked to revise their own text and text provided by the teacher. Both texts contained syntax errors (such as failure of subject-verb agreement or inconsistent use of verb tense), and referent errors (such as using a pronoun that has an unclear or ambiguous antecedent). Table 4–2 shows that students deteted errors in someone else's text much more easily than errors in their own; in addition, students detected syntax errors more easily than referent errors, especially in their own text.

Children have difficulty not only in detecting referent errors but also in making the appropriate correction. For example, Figure 4–11 shows original versions of text along with revised versions suggested by students. As can be seen, the correction strategies selected were not successful. Bartlett (1982) found that the most commonly used successful strategies for correcting referent errors are the use of pronouns (such as, "One day a man went to the beach. The day was hot and he needed a cool swim.") and use of repetition (such as, "Shortly after Christmas, a young woman moved into the house. The young woman had few possessions and she settled in quickly."). However, in the examples in Figure 4–11 these strategies are not appropriate.

TABLE 4–2	**Percentage of Errors That Were Detected**	
Detecting errors in text	**Referent Errors**	**Syntax Errors**
In writer's own text	17%	53%
In other texts	73%	88%

Adapted from Bartlett (1982)

FIGURE 4–11

Unsuccessful
correction
strategies

Original Text
One day a man left his house. Another man was standing outside. The man took out a letter and gave it to him. They talked for a while and then they got into a car. They were both policemen. They were going to catch a thief.

Attempts to Repeat an Antecedent (60% of Unsuccessful Corrections)
The man took out a letter and gave it to the other man. . . .

Attempts to Differentiate Among Characters (25% of Unsuccessful Corrections)
The man that was outside took a letter and gave it to the other man outside. . . .

Introduction of Nondiscriminating New Information (15% of Unsuccessful Corrections)
Joe left his house. Another Joe was standing outside. Joe took out a letter and gave it to the other Joe. . . .

Adapted from Bartlett (1982)

INDIVIDUAL DIFFERENCES IN REVIEWING. In another experiment reported by Bartlett (1982), children were given eight paragraphs to revise. Each paragraph included an unusual referent error that could not be corrected by the most common strategies of using pronouns or repetition. For example, one of the paragraphs involved what Bartlett called *ambiguous referencing:*

> One day two girls set out for the park.
> She had a bike. . . .

Figure 4–12 summarizes the revision performance of above-average and below-average writers in grades five through seven. As might be expected, above-average writers corrected about twice as many errors as below-average writers, and older writers corrected about twice as many errors as younger writers. However, even the oldest and most able writers successfully corrected only 36% of the referent errors.

Bartlett (1982) also found differences among the correction strategies used by above-average and below-average writers in grades five through seven. Figure 4–13 lists five correction strategies, along with examples of each. Table 4–3 summarizes the proportion of solutions that involved each strategy for above-average and below-average writers. As can be seen, above-average writers tended to rely most heavily on adding descriptive information about both referents or on naming the characters; in contrast, the below-average writers relied on nondefinite referencing or on adding descriptive

FIGURE 4–12 Detection and correction of referent errors

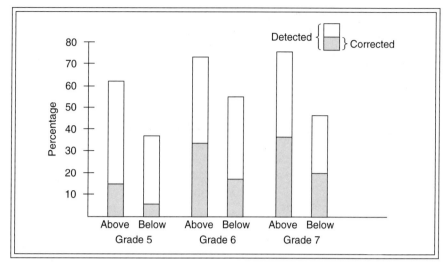

Adapted from Bartlett (1982)

Adapted from Bartlett (1982)

FIGURE 4–13

Successful corrections of a referent error

Original Text
One day two girls set out for the park. She had a bike. . . .

Adding Descriptive Information about Both Referents
One day two girls set out for the park. One was very athletic, and the other hated sports. The athletic one had a bike. . . .

Adding Descriptive Information about One Referent
One day two girls set out for the park. One of the girls was athletic, and she had a bike. . . .

Naming Characters
One day two girls named Sandy and Karen went to the park. Sandy had a bike. . . .

Indefinite Referencing Using Plural Noun
One day two girls went to the park. They had a bike. . . .

Indefinite Referencing Using Singular Noun
One day two girls went to the park. One had a bike. . . .

Adapted from Bartlett (1982)

TABLE 4–3

Differences in correction strategies of good and poor writers

Strategy Used	Percentage of Total Solutions	
	Above-Average Writers	**Below-Average Writers**
Adding descriptive information about both referents	33%	9%
Adding descriptive information about one referent	10%	41%
Naming characters	29%	5%
Indefinite referencing using plural noun	23%	27%
Indefinite referencing using singular noun	6%	18%

Adapted from Bartlett (1982)

information about only one referent. In a follow-up study, Bartlett (1982) found that the performance of adults closely paralleled that of above-average fifth-, sixth-, and seventh-graders. Apparently, good and poor writers differ with respect to both the quantity and quality of their corrections.

Bartlett's research focused on how children revise text containing referent errors, including comparisons of the general revising behavior of skilled and less skilled writers. Using a similar approach, Stallard (1974) compared the writing performance of skilled twelfth-graders versus a randomly selected control group of twelfth-graders. As expected, the skilled writers took more time than the control writers (41 minutes versus 23 minutes) and produced more words (343 words versus 309). However, Stallard also noted that the skilled group conducted three times as many revisions (184 versus 64). In fact, less than half of the control group ever looked back to see what they had written, whereas most of the skilled writers did. Similar differences between the writing processes of skilled and less skilled writers led Hayes and Flower (1986) to conclude that "the more expert the writer, the greater the proportion of writing time the writer will spend in revision" (p. 110).

Additional information concerning the revision process is provided in an analysis of writing by the National Assessment of Educational Progress. As reported by Nold (1981), in the study nine-year-olds and thirteen-year-olds were asked to write a science report about the moon. Students were given 15 minutes to write the report in pencil and an additional 13 minutes to make revisions in pen. One startling finding is that 40% of the nine-year-olds and 22% of the thirteen-year-olds made no revisions during the 13-minute revision period. However, as Nold (1981) points out, many revisions were made during the initial 15-minute writing period.

Table 4–4 lists the types of revisions that were made during the revision period and the percentage of students within each age group who used each type of revision. As can be seen, much attention was paid to

TABLE 4–4	Percentage of Students Making Revision		
Types of revisions made by two age groups	Type of Revision	Nine-Year-Olds	Thirteen-Year-Olds
	Cosmetic	12%	12%
	Mechanical	28%	49%
	Grammatical	22%	37%
	Continuational	20%	22%
	Informational	25%	48%
	Stylistic	26%	53%
	Transitional	6%	24%
	Organizational	7%	18%

Adapted from Nold (1981)

the conventions of written English (e.g., cosmetic, mechanical, and grammatical revisions) by both groups; however, the older writers also tended to show strong interest in making the writing accessible to the reader (e.g., by using stylistic, transitional, and organizational revisions). This result is consistent with Scardamalia et al.'s (1982) finding that young children have difficulty revising their writing for various audiences, whereas fourteen-year-olds do so more successfully.

IMPLICATIONS FOR INSTRUCTION: REVIEWING

In summary, the foregoing review of research makes several points concerning the review process. First, writers often do not review what they have written. Second, when writers are encouraged to review, they fail to detect most of the errors (especially referent errors), and even when they do detect errors they often fail to correct them properly. Third, older or more skilled writers appear to detect and correct far more errors and use more sophisticated review strategies than younger or less skilled writers. Older or more skilled writers also engage in more review than less skilled or younger writers.

These results suggest that students need to be encouraged to review what they have written. Some instruction may be needed in specific strategies for detecting and correcting errors. Checklists or questions can be used to guide a student's review, although the review process should eventually become internalized. The use of word processors may allow for easier review and revision, since students are freed from the need to write each new draft by hand. The difference between a good writer and poor writer is often not in the quality of the first draft but in the number of drafts that are generated. Students need to see how revision can turn a poor paper into an excellent one. Some of these ideas are examined more fully below in our discussion of two instructional programs aimed at improving the revision process—revision training and Writer's Workbench.

REVISION TRAINING. Can students be taught to be more effective reviewers? According to an exemplary study by Fitzgerald and Markman (1987), the answer is yes. In their study, some sixth-grade students received 13 45-minute lessons on the process of revision (revision training group), whereas other sixth-graders spent an equivalent amount of time reading good literature (comparison group). The instruction consisted of four three-lesson units on how to make additions, deletions, substitutions, and rearrangements. In the first day of each unit, the teacher defined the target process (e.g., addition), modeled the process, and led the class in revising an example story. On the second day, students worked in pairs on revising a portion of a text, guided by a step-by-step handout. On the third day, students worked individually on revising a story supplied by the teacher and one they had written themselves. After completing all four units, students received an integrative summary in the 13th lesson.

As a final test, students wrote a first draft of a story (stage 1), marked the original paper for changes (stage 2), made changes on the original paper (stage 3), and wrote a final draft on new piece of paper (stage 4). On average, the revision training group made 23 revisions per 100 words over the course of all four stages, whereas the comparison group made only 16 revisions per 100 words. The revision training group produced 61% more additions, 69% more deletions, 27% more substitutions, and 42% more rearrangements than the comparison group. Importantly, the rated quality of the stories improved from stage one to stage four for the revision training group but not for the comparison group. Fitzgerald and Markman (1987) concluded that "our findings support the utility of direct instruction in revision in writing in the classroom" (p. 18).

THE COMPUTER AS A WRITER'S WORKBENCH. Another way to provide instruction on how to revise prose comes from the use of intelligent computer coaches as editors. For example, one of the first and most studied of these programs was the Writer's Workbench (Macdonald, Frase, Gingrich, & Keenan, 1982). Like many of the commercially available editors that were to follow, the Writer's Workbench is a collection of computer programs that analyze written prose and make suggestions for revisions. The writer's workbench was field-tested at Bell Laboratories with over 1000 users. After a user has typed text into the computer using a standard word-processing system, she can ask the Writer's Workbench program to suggest revisions.

The Writer's Workbench consists of three major parts: a proofreader, a style analyzer, and an on-line English reference guide. The proofreader consists of the following programs:

Spelling: Lists all words that may be misspelled and allows the user to specify any new words (such as jargon or acronyms) to the list of acceptable words.

Punctuation: Lists cases where punctuation may be needed or where existing punctuation may be incorrect.

Double words: Lists all places in which a word is repeated.

Faulty phrasing: Lists phrases that may not be coherent.

Split infinitives: Lists all instances of split infinitives.

An example of the output of the proofreading program is shown in Figure 4–14. As can be seen, the program points out possible errors as well as making suggestions for how to correct the errors.

FIGURE 4–14

Input and output from the proofreader program of the Writer's Workbench.

INPUT: Our report, "The Basic Fundamentals of Computatonal Complexity", is enclosed. Please send any recommended changes at your earliest convenience. thanks.

PROOFER: ———————————— SPELLING ————————————

OUTPUT: Possible spelling errors in examplefile are:

Computatonal   recomended

If any of these words are spelled correctly, later type
            spelladd word1 word2 . . . wordn
to have them added to your spelldict file.

———————————— PUNCTUATION ————————————

The punctuation in examplefile is first described.

2 double quotes and 0 single quotes
0 apostrophes
0 left parentheses and 0 right ones

The program next prints any sentence that it thinks is incorrectly punctuated and follows it by its correction.

line 1
OLD: Our report, "The Basic Fundamentals of Computatonal Complexity",
NEW: Our report, "The Basic Fundamentals of Computational Complexity,"

line 3
OLD: earliest convenience. thanks.
NEW: earliest convenience. Thanks.
For more information about punctuation rules, type:

punctrules

FIGURE 4–14

(continued)

———————— DOUBLE WORDS ————————

For file examplefile:

No double words found

———————— WORD CHOICE ————————

Sentences with possibly wordy or misused phrases are listed next, followed by suggested revisions.

beginning line 1 examplefile
Our report, "The *[Basic Fundamentals]* of Computational Complexity",
is enclosed.

beginning line 2 examplefile
Please send any recommended changes *[at your earliest convenience]*.

file examplefile: number of lines 3, number of phrases found 2

———— Table of Substitutions ————

PHRASE   SUBSTITUTION

at your earliest convenience: use "soon" for "at your earliest convenience"
basic fundamentals: use "fundamentals" for "basic fundamentals"

———————— SPLIT INFINITIVES ————————

For file examplefile:

No split infinitives found

From Macdonald, Frase, Gingrich, and Keenan (1982)

The style analyzer of the Writer's Workbench includes the following programs:

Style: Provides readability indices, measures of average word length and average sentence length, the percentage of verbs in the passive voice, the percentage of nouns that are nominalizations, the number of sentences that begin with expletives, and other such information.

Prose: Compares the style statistics listed above with some standard measures. If the text's measures are outside of the standards, the program prints an explanation of why the text may be hard to read and prints suggested corrections.

Find: Locates sentences with passive verbs, expletives, nominalizations, "to be" verb forms, and other potential problems.

The on-line reference program of the Writer's Workbench contains information on the correct use of 300 commonly misused words and phrases, a computerized dictionary, and other general assistance. Additional programs evaluate the words in the text for abstractness-concreteness, rate the paragraph organization, and detect possible instances of sexist language.

Does the Writer's Workbench help writers detect errors and write better essays? The answers seem to be yes and no, respectively. For example, Hartley (1984) found that although the Writer's Workbench outperformed humans on detecting spelling, punctuation, and style errors, humans outperformed the program on finding ambiguities, factual errors, and controversial points. Importantly, several researchers have found that students who use the Writer's Workbench do not produce higher quality essays than those who do not (Kiefer & Smith, 1983; Pedersen, 1989; Sterkel, Johnson, & Sjorgren, 1986). In reviewing the research on computerized editors, Kellogg (1994) concluded that successful computerized editors need to "duplicate the one-on-one interaction that characterizes a teacher going through a student's document, highlighting problems, explaining why the text may be in error, and offering solutions" (p. 177). More recently, Scardamalia and Bereiter (1994, 1996) have developed a computer-based learning environment called CSILE in which all students may contribute to a communal database on a topic and provide peer commentaries of each others' writing.

BUILDING A WRITING PROGRAM THAT WORKS

THE INSTRUCTIONAL METHOD AND CONTENT OF WRITING PROGRAMS

This chapter has explored three important components in the writing process as well as some possible instructional techniques for improving each component. How could you put this information together into a writing program that works? To answer this question, Hillocks (1984) carefully analyzed experimental studies on writing to determine how and what to teach.

From research on how to teach, Hillocks (1984) identified three general methods of instruction in writing programs:

Natural process mode: The student dominates by initiating most of the writing activity, working at her or his own pace, and seeking feedback, when needed, from other students or the teacher. This approach involves very little guidance from the teacher and is similar to pure discovery methods of instruction.

Presentational mode: The teacher dominates by providing traditional instruction and lectures on how to write, determining the writing topic, and making extensive corrections of student writing. This approach involves very much guidance from the teacher and is similar to rule methods of instruction.

Environmental mode: Student and teacher cooperate in discussing the goals, content, and process of writing a composition. Instead of lecturing, the teacher works with small groups on specific writing projects, helping students to support their assertions with evidence, to predict and counter opposing arguments, to generate appropriate assertions from available data, and so on. Instead of beginning with independent free writing, the student works on specific writing tasks under teacher supervision within small groups. This approach involves intermediate amount of teacher guidance and is similar to guided discovery methods of instruction.

Which method of instruction is most effective? On the average, Hillocks (1984) found that the environmental mode resulted in three times more improvement than the natural process method and four times more improvement than the traditional presentational method. The environmental method provides enough guidance to ensure that students come in contact with specific skills needed for writing and at the same time allows enough freedom to keep students actively involved in the learning process.

From research on what to teach, Hillocks (1984) noted differences in the content of instruction in various writing programs, including the following:

Grammar: The teacher focuses on the mechanics of writing, including defining parts of speech, phrasing sentences, and so on. Usually, the teacher marks every error in a student's writing.

Models: Students are asked to study pieces of good writing as models for their own.

Free writing: Students are asked to write freely about anything they choose.

Sentence combining: Students are asked to build more complex sentences out of simpler ones.

Scales: Students are given a list of questions or a checklist to apply to their own composition or someone else's. Eventually they should internalize this review process.

Inquiry: Students are asked to discuss their own writing process and to improve their strategies for writing. For example, they might be asked to find details to describe a personal experience vividly.

Which kinds of content result in the most improvement in writing? Focusing on sentence combining, scales, and inquiry are the most effective, presumably because they help students acquire skills that are specifically related to composition writing. Focusing on models and free writing is less effective, presumably because the goal of instruction is unclear; focusing on grammar is the least effective of all the approaches, presumably because it draws attention away from the actual writing process. In fact, Hillocks' (1984) analysis of the research shows that in some cases heavy emphasis on grammar may actually decrease the quality of writing. This finding is consistent with the research on translation cited earlier in this chapter, which shows that mechanical constraints can interfere with students' attention to planning a coherent composition. Instead of focusing on grammar as a way of teaching writing, Hillocks (1984) suggests teaching grammar within the context of actual writing.

Hillocks (1984) reports the disturbing fact that the most popular writing programs ignore the available educational research on writing. In spite of findings to the contrary, many writing programs assume that the most effective method of instruction is natural process and that the most effective content is free writing:

> For over a decade, authorities in the field have been caught up in the "writing as process" model, which calls for exploratory talk, followed by free writing, reading by or for an audience of peers, comments from peers, and revision. The teacher's role is simply to facilitate this process—not to make specific assignments, not to help students learn criteria for judging writing, not to structure classroom activities based on specific objectives as in environmental treatments, not to provide exercises in manipulating syntax, not to design activities that engage students in identifiable processes of examining data. In short, this mode . . . studiously avoids the approaches to writing instruction that this report demonstrates to be more effective. (Hillocks, 1984, p. 162)

The approach that Hillocks describes seems to offer too little guidance and may be a sort of reaction against the programs that provided too much guidance in the past. In essence, Hillocks suggests the compromise of using guided discovery methods for teaching writing, in which the teacher provides some scaffolding for students as they learn the basic processes of writing.

COGNITIVE STRATEGY INSTRUCTION IN WRITING

Cognitive Strategy Instruction in Writing (CSIW) is an example of a writing program that seems to follow Hillocks' advice: The method involves some guidance from the teacher and the content involves the basic processes of writing (Englert, Raphael, Anderson, Anthony, & Stevens, 1991). In this chapter, we have seen how each cognitive process in writing—planning, translating, and reviewing—can be taught as a separate component. However, to produce a high-quality essay, writers need to be able to coordinate all three processes. CSIW is a comprehensive program that involves instruction in all of these processes.

The target task in CSIW is to write an essay. For example, suppose you were asked to write an essay explaining how to play a game you know, assuming that the audience does not already know how to play it. Alternatively, suppose you were asked to write a paper comparing how people, places, or things you know are alike and different. These are the kinds of writing assignments that Englert et al. (1991) gave to fourth- and fifth-graders. As you can see, the first one involves an explanation essay, whereas the second one involves writing a compare/contrast essay. Before giving these assignments, however, Englert et al. wanted to use the regular classroom writing time during the academic year to help students improve their writing skills. Based on what you know about cognitive processes in writing, what advice would you give to Englert et al. in preparing students to do well on writing these explanation and compare/contrast essays?

The cognitive model of writing examined in this chapter pinpoints the kinds of cognitive skills that should be part of any writing program. Students need to practice in planning, translating, and revising, as well as in coordinating these processes in actual writing tasks. Because students often fail to engage in appropriate planning (including generating and organizing ideas) and revising processes (including detecting and correcting errors), it is particularly important for students to gain specific experience in how to carry out these processes.

CSIW is a writing program designed to teach students how use and coordinate five writing strategies: plan, organize, write, edit, and revise (Englert et al., 1991). Plan and organize are parts of the cognitive process of planning, write corresponds to the process of translating, and edit and revise are components of the process of revising. The CSIW program does the following:

1. Promotes self-monitoring in which writers learn to "conduct an inner dialogue about the text and its content, the writing process, and the structure of text" (Englert et al., 1991, p. 338).
2. Provides scaffolded instruction that "prompts . . . strategies for planning, organizing, drafting, editing, and revising" (Englert et al., 1991, p. 340).
3. Transforms writing into a collaborative activity through "participation in a writing community" (Englert et al., 1991, p. 340).
4. Situates skills within specific types of text structures such as writing an explanation or a compare/contrast text.

The program is integrated into the regular classroom activities by the teacher, is comprehensive in that it involves all aspects of the writing process, and is individualized in that the teacher provides necessary guidance to students based on their individual needs.

In CSIW, students learn how to use a series of "think-sheets" while writing explanation or compare/contrast texts. The think-sheets are intended to prompt students to engage in cognitive processes that they might otherwise omit, and include the following types:

Plan think-sheet: The purpose of the plan think-sheet is to help students set criteria and generate ideas. For example, students are prompted to write down answers to questions such as "Who am I writing for?," "Why am I writing this?," "What do I know?" (with a list numbered from 1 to 8), "How can I group my ideas?" (with four boxes) and "How can I organize my ideas?" (with four categories: comparison/contrast, explanation, problem/solution, or other). An example is given in Figure 4–15.

Organize think-sheet: The purpose of the organize think-sheet is to help students organize their ideas into an outline. For example, if students have opted for the explanation organization in the plan think-sheet, in the organize think-sheet they will be prompted to specify the subject of the explanation, the material needed, the setting, and the steps in the explanation.

Write think-sheet: The purpose is to assist students as they write their first draft on the write think-sheet, in which they are encouraged to reread their plan and organize think-sheets, flesh out their ideas by using examples, provide engaging introductions and conclusions, and signal the organization of the text to the reader.

Edit/editor think-sheet: The edit think-sheet guides students through self-editing and the editor work-sheet guides students through peer-editing. Both think-sheets ask students to place stars next to parts of the essay they like, place question marks next to parts that are confusing, and to rate the text on several criteria. This phase includes a face-to-face meeting between the writer and the peer editor as they collaborate on improving the paper.

Revision think-sheet: The purpose is to encourage students to reflect on their editing plans. Students list all the suggested revisions and decide on which ones to implement. By carrying out the revisions, they produce a final draft that is published in a class book.

Does CSIW help students to become more effective writers? To answer that question, Englert et al. (1991) compared fourth- and fifth-grade students who participated in the CSIW program throughout the academic year from October to May (treatment group) to equivalent students who participated in the school's regular writing program (comparison group). Students were asked to write essays at the start of the school year as a pretest and toward the end of school year as a posttest. Figure 4–16 shows that the overall quality of the essays (on a three-point scale) improved greatly from pretest to posttest for the treatment group but not for the comparison group. Similarly, ratings of the writer's sensitivity to the

FIGURE 4–15 A plan think-sheet to help students plan their compositions

PLAN

Name _____ Date _____

Topic: _____

Who: Who am I writing for?

_____

_____

Why: Why am I writing this?

_____

_____

What: What do I know? (brainstorm)

1. _____
2. _____
3. _____
4. _____
5. _____
6. _____
7. _____
8. _____

How: How can I group my ideas?

_____	_____

_____   _____

_____   _____

_____	_____

_____   _____

_____   _____

How will I organize my ideas?

_____ Comparison/contrast   _____ Problem/solution

_____ Explanation   _____ Other

Adapted from Englert, Raphael, and Anderson (1989)

FIGURE 4–16 Quality of essays produced by treatment and comparison groups on pretest and posttest

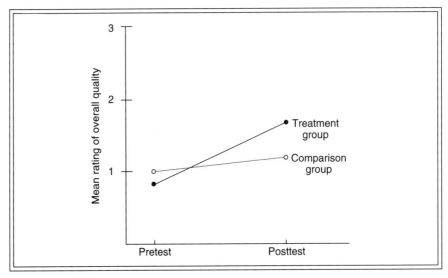

Adapted from Englert et al. (1991)

reader, the writer's organization of the text, and the number of ideas produced by the writer increased greatly for the treatment group but not for the comparison group. Importantly, these same differences in pretest-to-posttest gains between treatment and comparison students were found for learning disabled, low-achieving, and high-achieving students. Overall, these results show that it is possible to design a writing program that works by providing sufficient guidance in using and coordinating the cognitive processes for writing.

CONCLUSION

The research on writing is just beginning to make sense of the writing process. However, even the preliminary research presented in this chapter invites implications for instruction.

First, planning, which includes the development of an organization and the generation of content information, is a major component in writing. Students need explicit and specific training in techniques for organizing compositions, paragraphs, and sentences. Similarly, students need training and practice in how to generate and record information to be used in a composition.

Second, translation is a major writing component that involves converting ideas into words. The translation process relies on mechanical skills, such as handwriting, spelling, punctuation, grammatical sentence construction, and so on. Students need to be freed from the mechanical constraints on translation to concentrate their attentional capacity on planning a coherent composition. For older or more skilled students, the mechanical skills should become automatic; for younger or less skilled students, heavy emphasis on mechanics should not be required in the first draft.

Third, reviewing is a major writing component that involves the detection and correction of errors. The difference between a good composition and a poor composition may depend not on differences in the first draft, but on differences in how subsequent drafts are carried out. Students need explicit and detailed instruction in how to revise, with the ultimate goal of internalizing the revision procedures.

Finally, this chapter has explored the characteristics of effective writing programs. The more successful programs use instructional methods that foster the cognitive processes of writing.

SUGGESTED READINGS

Berieter, C., & Scardamalia, M. (1987). *The psychology of written composition.* Hillsdale, NJ: Erlbaum. (A review of research on writing in school settings.)

Kellogg, R. T. (1994). *The psychology of writing.* New York: Oxford University Press. (A review of research and theory on how people go about the task of writing.)

Levy, C. M., & Ransdell, S. (Eds.). (1996). *The science of writing.* Mahwah, NJ: Erlbaum. (A collection of papers on writing research, including advances in theories of writing.)

CHAPTER 5 Mathematics

CHAPTER OUTLINE

This chapter asks, "What does a student need to know to solve mathematics problems?" The answer to this question includes four components. Linguistic and factual knowledge are needed to help the student translate each sentence of the problem into some internal representation. Schematic knowledge is needed to help the student integrate the information into a coherent representation. Strategic knowledge is needed to help the student devise and monitor a solution plan. Procedural knowledge is needed to help the student carry out the computations required in the plan.

WHAT DO YOU NEED TO KNOW TO SOLVE MATH PROBLEMS?

Suppose I asked you to solve the following problem:

> Floor tiles are sold in squares 30 centimeters on each side. How much would it cost to tile a rectangular room 7.2 meters long and 5.4 meters wide if the tiles cost $.72 each?

What skills must you possess to solve this problem? First, you need to be able to translate each statement of the problem into some internal representation. This translation process requires that you understand English sentences (i.e., you need linguistic knowledge). For example, you need to be able to recognize that the problem contains the following facts: each tile is a 30-by-30-centimeter square, the room is a 7.2-by-5.4-meter rectangle, each tile costs 72 cents, and the unknown is the cost of tiling the room. This translation process also requires that you know certain facts, i.e., you need factual knowledge. For example, you need to know that all sides of a square are equal in length and that there are 100 centimeters in a meter. The top portion of Figure 5–1 presents other examples of mathematical tasks that focus on problem translation. Try these problems to exercise your problem translation skills.

Second, you need to be able to integrate each of the statements in the problem into a coherent problem representation. This problem integration process requires that you must be able to recognize problem types (i.e., you need schematic knowledge). For example, you need to recognize that this problem is a rectangle problem requiring the formula *area = length × width*. Problem integration also involves being able to distinguish between information that is relevant to the solution and information that is not relevant to the solution. The second portion of Figure 5–1 offers examples of mathematical tasks that focus on problem integration. Try these problems to test your problem integration skills.

Third, you need to be able to devise and monitor a solution plan. This solution planning process requires knowledge of heuristics (i.e., strategic knowledge). For example, you need to break the problem into subgoals, such as finding the area of the room, the number of tiles needed, and the cost of those tiles. You also need to be able to monitor what you are doing, such as knowing that when you multiply 7.2×5.4, you are finding the area of the room in meters. The third portion of Figure 5–1 gives examples of mathematical tasks that focus on solution planning and monitoring. Try some of these problems.

Finally, a fourth major component involved in answering the title problem is to be able to apply the rules of arithmetic. For example, you must be able to calculate the answer of $7.2 \times 5.4 = $ _____, or $.72 \times 432 = $ _____. Accurate and automatic execution of arithmetic and algebraic procedures is based on procedural knowledge. The fourth section of

FIGURE 5–1

Skills
involved in
solving math
problems

Problem Translation

Restating the Problem Givens

1. Floor tiles are sold in squares 30 centimeters on each side. How much would it cost to tile a rectangular room 7.2 meters long and 5.4 meters wide if the tiles cost $.72 each?

Which of the following sentences is not true?

a. The room is a rectangle measuring 7.2 meters by 5.4 meters.
b. Each tile costs 30 cents.
c. Each tile is a square measuring 30 centimeters by 30 centimeters.
d. The length of the long side of the room is 7.2 meters.

Restating the Problem Goal

2. Floor tiles are sold in squares 30 centimeters on each side. How much would it cost to tile a rectangular room 7.2 meters long and 5.4 meters wide if the tiles cost $.72 each?

What are you being asked to find?

a. the width and length of the room
b. the cost of each tile
c. the cost of tiling the room
d. the size of each tile

Problem Integration

Recognizing Problem Types

3. Melons were selling three for $1. How many could Larry buy for $4?

Which of the following problems can be solved in the same way as the preceding problem?

a. There were three books for every four students. How many books were there in a class of twenty students?
b. A car travels 25 miles per hour for 4 hours. How far will it travel?
c. John has twenty-five marbles. Sue has twelve marbles. How many more marbles does John have than Sue?
d. If balloons cost 10 cents each and pencils cost 5 cents each, how much do three balloons and two pencils cost?

Recognizing Relevant and Irrelevant Information

4. The manager bought 100 cameras for $3,578. The cameras sold for $6,024. How much was the profit?

(continued)

FIGURE 5–1

(continued)

Which numbers are needed to solve this problem?

a. 100, 6,024, 3,578   c. 100, 3,578
b. 100, 6,024   d. 3,578, 6,024

Determining Information That Is Needed for Solution

5. How much longer is the Mississippi River than the Yangtze River?

   What information is needed to answer this question?

   a. the length of the Mississippi River and the length of the Yangtze River
   b. the location and length of the Mississippi River and the location and length of the Yangtze River
   c. the average rainfall for the Mississippi River and the average rainfall for the Yangtze River
   d. the length of the Yangtze River

Representing a Problem As a Diagram or Picture

6. Mary Jackson earns $215 a week. She pays 30% of this for housing. How much does she pay for housing each week?

Which diagram best represents the problem?

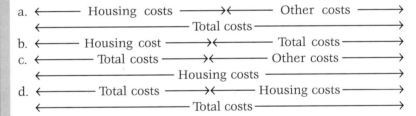

Solution Planning and Monitoring

Representing the Problem As a Number Sentence, Equation, or List of Necessary Operations

7. An insurance agent visited 585 customers. He sold 76 life insurance policies, 97 fire insurance policies, and 208 auto insurance policies. How many policies did he sell in all?

Which number sentence corresponds to this problem?

a. 76 + 97 + 208 =   c. 585 + 76 + 97 + 208 =
b. 585 − 76 − 97 − 208 =   d. 208 − 97 − 76 =

FIGURE 5–1

(continued)

Establishing Subgoals

8. Floor tiles are sold in squares 30 centimeters on each side. How much would it cost to tile a rectangular room 7.2 meters long and 5.4 meters wide if the tiles cost $.72 each?

To answer this question, you need to determine:

a. how many tiles are needed
b. how much longer one side of the room is than the other side
c. how much 100 tiles would cost
d. how much money will be left

Drawing Conclusions

9. The 130 students from Marie Curie School are going on a picnic. Each school bus holds 50 passengers. How many buses will they need?

Rose worked the following problem:

$$\begin{array}{r} 2 \\ 50\overline{)130} \\ \underline{100} \\ 30 \end{array}$$

Look back at the question in the problem. What is the answer?

a. 2   c. 2 3/5
b. 2 R30   d. 3

Solution Execution

Carrying Out Single Calculations

10. $7.2 \times 5.4 = $ _____

The correct answer is:

a. 38.88   c. 311.04
b. 432   d. 28

Carrying Out Chains of Calculations

11. $((7.2 \times 5.4)/(.3 \times .3)) \times .72 = $ _____

The correct answer is:

a. 38.88   c. 311.04
b. 432   d. 28

TABLE 5–1	Component	Type of Knowledge	Examples from the Tile Problem
The four components of mathematical problem-solving	Problem translation	Linguistic knowledge	The room is a rectangle with 7.2-meter width and 5.4-meter length.
		Factual knowledge	One meter equals 100 centimeters.
	Problem integration	Schematic knowledge	Area = length × width
	Solution planning and monitoring	Strategic knowledge	Find the area of the room in meters by multiplying 7.2 × 5.4. Then, find the area of each tile in meters by multiplying 0.3 × 0.3. Then, find the number of tiles needed by dividing the area of the room by the area of each tile. Finally, find total cost by multiplying the number of needed tiles by $.72.
	Solution execution	Procedural knowledge	7.2 × 5.4 = 38.88 0.3 × 0.3 = 0.09 38.88/.09 = 432 432 × .72 = $311.04

Figure 5–1 presents examples of mathematical tasks that focus on solution execution. Go ahead and select your answers.

As the examples show, solving a problem involves more than just getting the final answer. Our componential analysis of the tile problem suggests that there are at least four major components involved in mathematical problem-solving, as summarized in Table 5–1. In this chapter we will take a closer look at each of these four components: (1) translating each statement of the problem; (2) integrating the information into a coherent problem representation; (3) devising and monitoring a solution plan; and (4) accurately and efficiently carrying out the solution plan. (By the way, the answer for the tile problem is $311.04. The answers for the items in Figure 5–1 are: 1, b; 2, c; 3, a; 4, d; 5, a; 6, a; 7, a; 8, a; 9, d; 10, a; 11, c.)

PROBLEM TRANSLATION

WHAT IS PROBLEM TRANSLATION?

The first step in solving the tile problem is to translate each statement into an internal representation. For example, the major statements in the tile problem are: the tiles are squares measuring 30 centimeters by 30 centimeters; the tiles cost 72 cents each; the room is a rectangle measuring 7.2 meters by 5.4 meters, and the cost of tiling the room is unknown. To translate these statements, a problem-solver needs some knowledge of the English language (i.e., linguistic knowledge) and some knowledge about the world (i.e., factual knowledge). For example, linguistic knowledge is required to determine that "floor tiles" and "the tiles" refer to the same thing. Similarly, factual knowledge is required to know that a square has four sides of equal length and that 100 centimeters equals 1 meter.

RESEARCH ON PROBLEM TRANSLATION

COMPREHENDING RELATIONAL SENTENCES. A growing research base suggests that the translation process can be very difficult for students, especially when the problem contains relational statements (i.e., statements that express a quantitative relation between variables). For example, in an analysis of factors that contribute to problem difficulty, Loftus and Suppes (1972) found that the most difficult problems tend to contain relational statements, such as "Mary is twice as old as Betty was 2 years ago. Mary is 40 years old. How old is Betty?"

In another study (Greeno, 1980; Riley, Greeno, & Heller, 1982), children were asked to listen to and then repeat word problems. For example, suppose that the following problem was presented: "Joe has three marbles. Tom has five more marbles than Joe. How many marbles does Tom have?" Children's errors included ignoring the relational statements, such as repeating the problem as follows: "Joe has three marbles. Tom has five marbles. How many marbles does Tom have?"

Adults also seem to have difficulty in translating relational statements. In one study (Soloway, Lochhead, & Clement, 1982), college students were given statements and asked to translate them into equations. For example, suppose the statement was "There are six times as many students as professors at this university." Approximately one-third of the students produced the wrong equation, such as $6S = P$.

Figure 5–2 summarizes the approaches of two students to the students-and-professors problem. One student took a static approach by assuming that P stands for a professor and S stands for the students of that professor. In contrast, another student took a procedural approach by assuming that to determine the number of students, one must perform an operation on the number of professors. According to Soloway et al. (1982), errors in translation occur when students view the relational statement as a static description rather than as a procedural instruction for how to convert one variable into another.

In a related study, Mayer (1982a) asked college students to read and then recall eight algebra story problems. The students made approximately three times as many errors in recalling relational statements (29% errors) than in recalling assignment statements (9% errors). Furthermore, an analysis of the errors revealed that on 20 occasions students converted

FIGURE 5–2

Two approaches to the students-and-professors problem

Problem

"There are six times as many students as professors at this university."

Static Translation

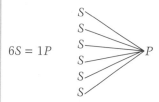

$6S = 1P$

"There are six times as many students, which means it's six students to one professor, and this (points to $6S$) is six times as many students as there are professors (points to $1P$)."

Procedural Translation

$S = 6P$ Take the number of professors | Multiply by 6 | Obtain the number of students "If you want to even out the number of professors, you'd have to have six times as many professors."

a relational into an assignment statement, but that there was only one instance of a student converting an assignment into a relational statement. For example, one student changed the relational statement "the steamer's engine drives in still water at 12 miles per hour more than the rate of the current," into the assignment statement "its engines push the boat at 12 miles per hour in still water." These results suggest that some students may lack the appropriate linguistic knowledge to represent relational statements in memory.

Is difficulty in representing relational statements related to problem-solving performance? In a recent study, Hegarty, Mayer, and Monk (1995), asked students to solve 12 word problems, and later gave a recognition test on four of the problems that contained relational statements. For example, one problem was: "At ARCO, gas costs $1.13 per gallon. This is 5 cents less per gallon than gas at Chevron. If you want to buy 5 gallons of gas, how much will you pay at Chevron?" Table 5–2 lists four alternatives for this problem on the recognition test: the correct answer in which the relational statement is in verbatim form, a literal error in which the meaning of the relational statement is retained but the keyword is changed from "less" to "more," and two kinds of semantic errors in which the meaning of the rela-

TABLE 5–2	Alternatives	Scored As
Which problem did you solve?	At ARCO, gas costs $1.13 per gallon. This is 5 cents less than gas costs at Chevron. If you want to buy 5 gallons of gas, how much will you pay at Chevron?	Correct
	At ARCO, gas costs $1.13 per gallon. Gas at Chevron cost 5 cents more per gallon than gas at ARCO. If you want to buy 5 gallons of gas, how much will you pay at Chevron?	Literal error
	At ARCO, gas costs $1.13 per gallon. Gas at Chevron cost 5 cents less per gallon than gas at ARCO. If you want to buy 5 gallons of gas, how much will you pay at Chevron?	Semantic error
	At ARCO, gas costs $1.13 per gallon. This is 5 cents more than gas costs at Chevron. If you want to buy 5 gallons of gas, how much will you pay at Chevron?	Semantic error

Adapted from Hegarty, Mayer, and Monk (1995)

tional statement is changed. Poor problem solvers produced four times as many literal errors on the recognition test as did good problem solvers (39% versus 9%, respectively). In contrast, good problem solvers produced twice as many literal errors as did poor-problem solvers (44% versus 19%, respectively). These results suggest that successful problem-solvers are much better able than unsuccessful problem solvers to use their linguistic knowledge to determine the meaning of the relational statements.

USING FACTUAL KNOWLEDGE. Factual knowledge is another key component in problem translation. For example, Loftus and Suppes (1972) found that problems involving scale conversion were much more difficult than corresponding problems that did not. Scale conversions require factual knowledge; for example, converting 30 centimeters to .3 meters requires knowing that 100 centimeters equals 1 meter. Bobrow (1968) developed a computer program capable of solving algebra story problems. The program involved two major phases: translation of each statement into an equation and solution of the equations. For the program to translate, a large store of both linguistic and factual knowledge had to be included in the program. For example, the program needed linguistic knowledge, such as "pounds is the plural of pound," and factual knowledge, such as "16 ounces equals 1 pound."

IMPLICATIONS FOR INSTRUCTION: TEACHING PROBLEM TRANSLATION SKILLS

What do successful problem solvers know that unsuccessful problem solvers do not know? The research results suggest that successful problem solvers are more likely than unsuccessful problem solvers to know how to comprehend the sentences in word problems, especially how to comprehend sentences that express a relation between two variables. Apparently, unsuccessful problem solvers may not know how to understand statements such as "the Acme building is 27 feet taller than the Bendex building" or "Elena is 8 cm shorter than Andrea." In short, unsuccessful problem solvers may lack problem translation skills.

Can problem translation skills be taught? Lewis (1989) has developed a two-session instructional program that teaches students how to represent sentences from word problems. In the first session, the instructor demonstrates how each sentence in a series of nine word problems can be classified as an assignment, a relation, or a question, and then students are given a worksheet in which they practice classifying the sentences in eighteen word problems. In the second session, the instructor demonstrates how to diagram each of four sample problems using a simple number-line method, as exemplified in Figure 5–3. For example, the first step is to place the amount Megan has saved on the number line, the second step is to determine whether the amount James saved goes to the left or right of Megan, the third step is to check the placement of James, and the third step is to determine what kind of operation to perform. Then, students receive worksheets in which they diagram eight word problems using the number-line diagram. The problems contain relational statements so students receive practice in recognizing relational statements and representing them on a number line.

Does translation training help students solve word problems? To answer this question, Lewis (1989) asked college students to take a pretest that contained two-step comparison problems (such as the gas problem as shown in Table 5–2) and three-step comparison problems. About one-third of the students made errors on some of the two-step problems, so they could be classified as unsuccessful problem solvers. Lewis' goal was to reduce the errors of these unsuccessful problem solvers, so she invited them to remain in the study. Some of these unsuccessful problem solvers (translation-trained group) received approximately 60 minutes of training across two sessions in which they learned how to recognize and diagram relational sentences from two-step word problems using a number line. Others students (control group) spent an equal amount of time working on the same problems, but their task was merely to judge the difficulty of the problems. Then, the translation-trained and control students took a posttest that contained both two-step and three-step problems.

If translation training helps students to translate the sentences of a word problem and if improper translation is the major impediment to successful problem solving, then unsuccessful problem solvers who receive translation training should show a large pretest-to-posttest decline in errors on

FIGURE 5-3

Worksheet for
learning how
to translate
sentences into
diagrams

Sample Problem

Megan has saved $420 for vacation. She has saved one-fifth as much as James has saved. James has been saving for his vacation for six months. How much has he saved each month?

Diagramming Steps

1. Draw a number line, and place the variable and the value from the assignment statement in the middle of the line.

$420

Megan

2. Tentatively place the unknown variable (James's savings) on one side of the middle.

$420

James   Megan

3. Compare your representation with the information in the relation statement, checking to see if your representation agrees with the meaning of the relation statement. If it does, then you can continue. If not, then try again with the other side.

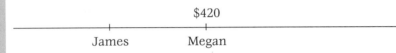

$420

——— x ———

James   Megan   James

4. Translate your representation into an arithmetic operation. If the unknown variable is to the right of the center, then the operation is an increase, such as addition or multiplication. If the unknown variable is to the left of the center, then the operation is a decrease, such as subtraction or division.

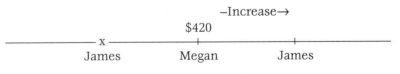

−Increase→

$420

——— x ———

James   Megan   James

Adapted from Lewis (1989)

solving word problems. The left panel of Figure 5–4 shows that the translation-trained group eliminated almost all of its errors on two-step problems on the posttest, whereas the control group did not. Similarly, the right panel of Figure 5–4 also shows that the translation-trained group eliminated most of its errors on three-step problems, whereas the control group did not. These results provide solid evidence that translation training is effective in improving students' problem-solving performance. The improvement occurred both on problems like those presented during training (two-step problems) and on problems that were more complex (three-step problems).

Based on these results, Lewis (1989) concluded that "training aimed at remedying students' erroneous comprehension processes for relational statements can be successful and can result in transfer" (p. 530) to new kinds of word problems. Translation training is consistent with the call for helping mathematics students to build multiple representations of the same problem, such as being able to represent a problem in words, a diagram, and an equation (Grouws, 1992; National Council of Teachers of Mathematics, 1989; Wagner & Kieran, 1989). More recently, Brenner et al. (1997) developed a 20-day program for middle-school prealgebra students that emphasized daily experience in translating among relational sentences, tables, graphs, and equations. Students who participated in the program showed much greater improvements in their ability to understand and solve word problems than did those who received conventional instruction. These results suggest that a major impediment to successful problem solving may be poor problem translation skills. Although translation skills are not typically emphasized in mathematics curricula, there is increasing evidence that translation training can be helpful.

The research summarized in this section suggests that problem translation may be a major source of difficulty in mathematical problem solving. Apparently, many students come to the problem-solving task lacking the

FIGURE 5–4 Percentage of errors on pretest and posttest for translation-trained and control students

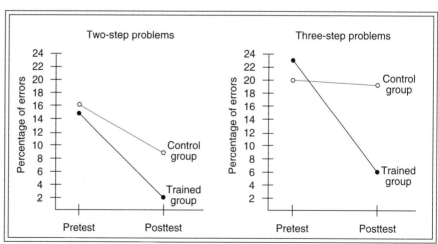

prerequisite linguistic and factual knowledge. One implication of this research is that students may need practice in problem translation, such as paraphrasing statements from the problem.

Let's return to the tile problem described in the introduction to this chapter. The research presented in this section indicates that many students have difficulty in comprehending each major statement in the problem, such as, "Floor tiles are sold in squares 30 centimeters on each side." How can you provide translation training for a problem like the tile problem? Some activities that might encourage the development of translation skills include students restating the problem givens or goals in their own words. In some cases, students could be asked to draw a picture that corresponds to a sentence in the problem, such as the first sentence of the tile problem. Similarly, the first section of Figure 5–1 suggests the use of multiple-choice items to offer practice in recognizing problem givens and goals. These suggestions, of course, are tentative ones that require research verification.

PROBLEM INTEGRATION

WHAT IS PROBLEM INTEGRATION?

The accurate representation of a story problem often requires more than statement-by-statement translation. For example, Paige and Simon (1966) asked students to solve impossible problems such as "The number of quarters a man has is seven times the number of dimes he has. The value of the dimes exceeds the value of the quarters by $2.50. How many of each coin does he have?" (p. 84) Using factual and linguistic knowledge, a person could translate these statements into equations such as

$$Q = 7D$$

$$D(.10) = 2.50 + Q(.25)$$

where Q is the number of quarters and D is the number of dimes. However, if you try to understand how the two statements fit together to form a coherent problem, you might recognize an inconsistency, namely that having more quarters than dimes is inconsistent with the value of the dimes exceeding the value of quarters. In Paige and Simon's study, both types of approaches were observed: some subjects translated each statement separately, while other subjects tried to understand how the statements related to one another.

The foregoing example shows that another important component in the process of understanding a story problem is to put the statements of the problem together into a coherent representation which can be called a *situation model* (Kintsch & Greeno, 1985; Mayer & Hegarty, 1996; Nathan, Kintsch, & Young, 1992). In order to integrate the information in a problem, the problem solver needs to have some knowledge of problem types (i.e., schematic knowledge). For example, you need to recognize that the tile problem is a rectangle problem based on the formula *area = length × width*. This knowledge will help you to understand how the statements in the problem fit together; for example, the situation described in the tile problem consists of a rectangular floor than is covered with square tiles.

RESEARCH ON PROBLEM INTEGRATION

STUDENT SCHEMAS FOR STORY PROBLEMS. According to the cognitive analysis of mathematical problem solving shown in Table 5–1, successful problem solvers need to possess knowledge of problem categories (or schemas). Hinsley, Hayes, and Simon (1977) studied students' schemas for story problems by asking students who were experienced in algebra to sort a series of algebra story problems into groups. Students were quite proficient at this task and reached high levels of agreement. (Table 5–3 shows

TABLE 5–3	Problem Type	Example of Problem
Examples of eighteen problem types	1. Triangle	Jerry walks one block east along a vacant lot and then two blocks north to a friend's house. Phil starts at the same point and walks diagonally through the vacant lot, coming out at the same point as Jerry. If Jerry walked 217 feet east and 400 feet north, how far did Phil walk?
	2. DRT	In a sports car race, a Panther starts the course at 9:00 A.M. and averages 75 miles per hour. A Mallotti starts 4 minutes later and averages 85 miles per hour. If a lap is 15 miles, on which lap will the Panther be overtaken?
	3. Averages	Flying east between two cities, a plane's speed is 380 miles per hour. On the return trip, it flies 420 miles per hour. Find the average speed for the round trip.
	4. Scale conversion	Two temperature scales are established, one, the R scale, where water under fixed conditions freezes at 15 and boils at 405, and the other, the S scale, where water freezes at 5 and boils at 70. If the R and S scales are linearly related, find an expression for any temperature R in terms of a temperature S.
	5. Ratio	If canned tomatoes come in two sizes and the radius of one is two-thirds the radius of the other, find the ratios of the capacities of the two cans.
	6. Interest	A certain savings bank pays 3% interest compounded semiannually. How much will $2,500 be worth if left on deposit for 20 years?
	7. Area	A box containing 180 cubic inches is constructed by cutting from each corner of a cardboard square a small square with sides of 5 inches, and then turning up the sides. Find the area of the original piece of cardboard.
	8. Max-min	A real estate operator estimates that the monthly profit p in dollars from a building s stories high is given by

TABLE 5–3	Problem Type	Example of Problem
(continued)		$p = -2s^2 + 88s$. What height building would he consider most profitable?
	9. Mixture	One vegetable oil contains 6% saturated fats, and a second contains 26% saturated fats. In making a salad dressing, how many ounces of the second must be added to 10 ounces of the first if the percent of saturated fats is not to exceed 16%?
	10. River current	A river steamer travels 36 miles downstream in the same time that it travels 24 miles upstream. The steamer's engines drive in still water at a rate that is 12 miles an hour more than the rate of the current. Find the rate of the current.
	11. Probability	In an extrasensory-perception experiment, a blindfolded subject has two rows of blocks before him. Each row has blocks numbered 1 to 10 arranged in random order. The subject is to place one hand on a block in the first row and then try to place his other hand on the block having the same numeral in the second row. If the subject has no ESP, what is the probability of his making a match on the first try?
	12. Number	The units digit is 1 more than 3 times the tens digit. The number represented when the digits are interchanged is 8 times the sum of the digits.
	13. Work	Mr. Russo takes 3 minutes less than Mr. Lloyd to pack a case when each works alone. One day, after Mr. Russo had spent 6 minutes packing a case, the boss called him away, and Mr. Lloyd finished packing in 4 more minutes. How many minutes would it take Mr. Russo alone to pack a case?
	14. Navigation	A pilot leaves an aircraft carrier and flies south at 360 miles per hour, while the carrier proceeds N30W at 30 miles per hour. If the pilot has enough fuel to fly 4 hours, how far south can he fly before returning to his ship?
	15. Progressions	From two towns 363 miles apart, Jack and Jill set out to meet each other. If Jill travels 1 mile the first day, 3 the second, 5 the third, and so on, and Jack travels 2 miles the first day, 6 the second, 10 the third, and so on, when will they meet?
	16. Progression-2	Find the sum of the first 25 odd positive integers.
	17. Physics	The speed of a body falling freely from rest is directly proportional to the length of time that it falls. If a body was falling at 144 feet per second $4\frac{1}{2}$ seconds after beginning its fall, how fast was it falling $3\frac{3}{4}$ seconds later?
	18. Exponentials	The diameter of each successive layer of a wedding cake is two-thirds the diameter of the previous layer. If the diameter of the first layer of a five-layer cake is 15 inches, find the sum of the circumferences of all the layers.

Adapted from Hinsley, Hayes, and Simon (1977)

the eighteen categories that the subjects used.) Apparently, experienced students come to the problem-solving task with some knowledge of problem types.

Hinsley et al. (1977) also found that students were able to categorize problems almost immediately. For example, as soon as a student has read the first few words of a problem, such as "The area occupied by an unframed rectangular picture," we would expect the student to say, "Oh, it's one of those picture-frame problems." Follow-up studies (Hayes, Waterman, & Robinson, 1977; Robinson & Hayes, 1978) found that students who are experienced in algebra use their schemas to make accurate judgments concerning which information is relevant to a problem and which is not.

Many errors in problem integration occur when a person uses the wrong schema for determining which information is necessary. For example, the following problem used by Hinsley et al. (1977) can be viewed as either a distance-rate-time problem or a triangle problem:

> Because of their quiet ways, the inhabitants of Smalltown were especially upset by the terrible New Year's Eve auto accident which claimed the life of one Smalltown resident. The facts were these: Both Smith and Jones were New Year's babies and each had planned a surprise visit to the other on their mutual birthday. Jones had started out for Smith's house traveling due east on Route 210 just 2 minutes after Smith had left for Jones' house. Smith was traveling directly south on Route 140. Jones was traveling 30 miles per hour faster than Smith even though their houses were only five miles apart as the crow flies. Their cars crashed at the right-angle intersection of the two highways. Officer Franklin, who observed the crash, determined that Jones was traveling half again as fast as Smith at the time of the crash. Smith had been driving for just 4 minutes at the time of the crash. The crash occurred nearer to the house of the dead man than to the house of the survivor. What was the name of the dead man? (p. 102)

Some students interpreted this problem as a triangle problem. For example, they drew triangles and tried to determine the lengths of the two legs and the hypotenuse. One student misread "4 minutes" as "4 miles" and assumed this was the length of one of the legs; another subject assumed "5 miles apart" referred to the length of the hypotenuse. In contrast, other students interpreted this problem as a distance-rate-time problem. For example, one student said: "It looks like a distance problem. So Jones is going east two minutes after Smith is going west. So it might be an overtake problem." Subjects who interpreted the problem as a distance-rate-time problem initially assumed that one driver was going east and the other driver was going west. Apparently, students use either a triangle schema or a distance-rate-time schema as a template for understanding the problem. In all, Hinsley et al. identified 18 basic problem schemas and found that these schemas influence how a subject reads a problem.

In a follow-up study, Mayer (1981b) analyzed the story problems in some typical secondary-school algebra textbooks. Approximately one hundred problem types were found, including many varieties of the eighteen categories that Hinsley et al. (1977) had found. For example, there were at least 12 kinds of distance-rate-time (or motion) problems, including overtake (in which one vehicle starts and is followed later by a second vehicle that travels over the same route at a faster rate), closure (in which two vehicles start at different points and travel toward one another), round trip (in which a vehicle travels to and from point A to B and returns), speed change (in which a vehicle travels at a certain rate for the first leg of a trip and then changes to another rate for the remainder of the trip), and opposite direction (in which two vehicles start at one point and travel in opposite directions). Certain problem types occurred frequently in the textbooks (e.g., more than 25 instances per 1,000 problems), while others were rarely found (e.g., less than 4 instances per 1,000 problems). Table 5–4 lists some common problem types, with similar types grouped into families. The numbers in parentheses indicate the percentage of problems in textbooks that belonged to the category.

In another study (Mayer, 1982b), students were asked to read and then recall a series of eight story problems. The results indicated that students were far more successful at recalling high-frequency problem types than

TABLE 5–4	Family	Category (Percentage of Total)
Some problem types from algebra textbooks	Amount-per-time family	Motion (13%) Current (5%) Work (11%)
	Cost-per-unit family	Unit cost (4%) Coins (7%) Dry mixture (6%)
	Portion-of-total family	Interest/investment (12%) Profit/discount (2%)
	Amount-per-amount family	Direct variation (16%) Inverse variation (3%) Wet mixture (6%)
	Number story family	Part (4%) Age (3%) Consecutive interest (1%)
	Geometry family	Rectangle/frame (3%) Circle (1%) Triangle (1%)

Adapted from Mayer (1981b)

low-frequency types. Figure 5–5 shows the relationship between the frequency of the problem (i.e., how many times per 1,000 problems this type of problem occurred in typical math books) and the probability of correct recall for the problem. As you can see, the probability that a student will correctly recall a problem is strongly correlated with the frequency with which the problem type is represented in typical math textbooks. In addition, an analysis of errors in recall revealed that there was a tendency for subjects to change a low-frequency problem into a similar problem that occurred with higher frequency; in contrast, no high-frequency problems were changed into low-frequency problems by students. Apparently, students possess schemas for some of the more typical problem types. When students are given a problem for which they do not possess an appropriate schema, representation of the problem is in jeopardy.

EXPERT/NOVICE DIFFERENCES IN STUDENT SCHEMAS. Experienced and inexperienced problem solvers differ in the ways they categorize word problems: experienced problem solvers are more likely to focus on the structural features of problems, such as the underlying principle or relation, whereas inexperienced problem solvers are more likely to focus on the surface features, such as the objects described in the problem.

FIGURE 5–5 More common problem types are easier to recall

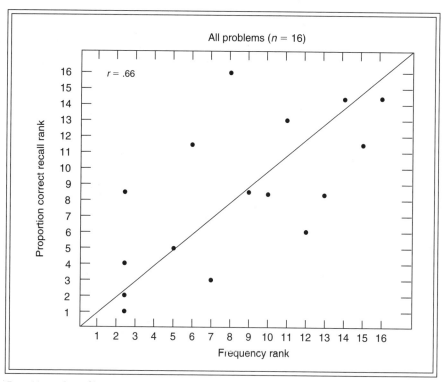

From Mayer (1982b)

For example, Quilici and Mayer (1996) asked students to sort twelve statistics word problems into categories based on similarity, that is, by grouping together problems that could be solved in the same way. Figure 5–6 shows three of the problems used in the study. If a person sorts the problems based mainly on *surface characteristics,* such as the objects described in the problems, then all the problems involving typists will be placed in the same category, all the problems involving rainfall will be placed in the same category, and so on. College students who had no experience in statistics (i.e., novices) tended to group the problems based on surface features; for example, they would put Problems 1 and 2 together because they both involve typists. In contrast, if a person sorts the problems based on *structural features,* such how many groups are involved (i.e., one or two) and the nature of the dependent measure (i.e., categorical or quantitative), the person will sort problems requiring computing a *t*-test into one group, problems requiring the computation of a correlation into another group, and so on. Graduate students who had extensive experience in statistics tended to the group the problems based on structural features; for example, they would put Problems 2 and 3 together because they both deal with correlation. Interestingly, students tended to change from sorting mainly by surface features before taking an introductory course in statistics to sorting at least partially by structural features after taking the course. Apparently, experience in a mathematical domain can help students change the way they organize their schematic knowledge of problem types.

FIGURE 5–6 Three statistics word problems	1. A personnel expert wishes to determine whether experienced typists are able to type faster than inexperienced typists. Twenty experienced typists (i.e., with 5 or more years of experience) and 20 inexperienced typists (i.e., with less than 5 years of experience) are given a typing test. Each typist's average number of words typed per minute is recorded.
	2. A personnel expert wishes to determine whether typing experience goes with faster typing speeds. Forty typists are asked to report how many years they have worked as typists and are given a typing test to determine their average number of words typed per minute.
	3. After examining weather data for the last 50 years, a meteorologist claims that the annual precipitation varies with average temperature. For each of 50 years, she notes the annual rainfall and average temperature.

Adapted from Quilici and Mayer (1996)

Similarly, Silver (1981) asked seventh-graders to sort sixteen story problems into groups. Students who performed poorly in solving story problems tended to group the problems based on their cover stories, such as putting all "money" problems together. Students who performed well in solving story problems tended to group the problems based on their underlying mathematical structure. Apparently, learning to solve story problems successfully is related to the development of useful schemas for problem types.

DEVELOPMENTAL DIFFERENCES IN STUDENT SCHEMAS. The sophistication of students' schematic knowledge may be related to prior experience with story problems. For example, Greeno and his colleagues (Greeno, 1982; Riley et al., 1982) have identified three types of arithmetic word problems:

> **Cause/change problems,** such as "Joe has two marbles. Tom gives him four more marbles. How many marbles does Joe have now?"
> **Combination problems,** such as "Joe has two marbles. Tom has four marbles. How many marbles do they have altogether?"
> **Comparison problems,** such as "Joe has two marbles. Tom has four more marbles than Joe. How many marbles does Tom have?"

As you can see, all three of these problems involve the same underlying computations (2 + 4 = _____). However, Greeno and his colleagues found that the problems differed greatly in difficulty. Children in grades K–3 all performed well on cause/change problems. However, children in grades K and 1 performed poorly on combination and comparison problems, while children in grades 2 and 3 performed well on them. One way to interpret these data is to say that the younger children have only one schema for word problems (i.e., the cause/change schema) and that they try to apply this schema to all word problems. In contrast, the older children seem to have developed different schema for different problem types (i.e., they have added schemas for combination and comparison problems). Thus many errors on comparison problems seem to occur because students lack appropriate schemas rather than because students lack appropriate computational skill.

A CLOSER LOOK AT THE PROBLEM INTEGRATION PROCESSES OF SUCCESSFUL AND UNSUCCESSFUL PROBLEM-SOLVERS. Lewis and Mayer (1987) proposed that many errors in problem-solving occur mainly because of a superficial integration process in which students use key words in problems to signal which arithmetic operations to perform. For example, consider the two versions of the butter problem shown in Figure 5–7. On the top is a consistent version of the butter problem because the key word ("less") primes the appropriate arithmetic operation (subtraction); the other is an inconsistent version of the butter problem because the key word ("less") primes an inappropriate arithmetic operation (subtraction instead of addition of 65 and 2). In-depth analyses of students' problem solving revealed that students made many errors on inconsistent

FIGURE 5–7

Consistent
and
inconsistent
versions of
the butter
problem

Consistent Version

At Lucky, butter costs 65 cents per stick.
Butter at Vons costs 2 cents less per stick than butter at Lucky.
If you need to buy 4 sticks of butter,
how much will you pay at Vons?

Inconsistent Version

At Lucky, butter costs 65 cents per stick.
This is 2 cents less per stick than butter at Vons.
If you need to buy 4 sticks of butter,
how much will you pay at Vons?

Adapted from Hegarty, Mayer, and Monk (1995)

problems in which focusing on key words led to the wrong answer, but almost no errors on consistent problems in which focusing on key words led to the correct answer (Lewis & Mayer, 1987; Verschaffel, De Corte, & Pauwels, 1992). When students made errors, they tended to perform the arithmetic operation primed by a key word, such as subtracting 2 from 65 and multiplying the result by 4 in the butter problem. These results implicate a faulty problem integration process as a major culprit in producing problem-solving errors.

Successful and unsuccessful problem solvers may engage in quite different processes for representing word problems such as the two versions of the butter problem shown in Figure 5–7 (Hegarty et al., 1995; Mayer & Hegarty, 1996; Mayer & Lewis, 1987). When confronted with a word problem, unsuccessful students may be more likely to use a direct translation approach in which they select numbers from the problem and use key words in the problem to determine which arithmetic operations to perform. Students using a direct translation approach are likely to extract the numbers "65 cents," "2 cents," and "4 sticks." The key word "less" primes the arithmetic operation of subtraction, so the first step is to subtract 2 from 65. The key words "how much" primes the arithmetic operation of multiplication, so the next step is to multiple the result by 4. In contrast, successful students may be more likely to use a problem model approach in which they construct a mental model of the situation that is described in the problem statement. Students using a problem model approach integrate the sentences by determining that "this" refers to butter at Lucky.

To examine more closely differences in how successful and unsuccessful problem-solvers represent word problems, Hegarty et al. (1995) monitored the eye movements of eight successful and eight unsuccessful problem solvers as they read word problems from a computer screen and formulated a solution plan. All students carefully read the four lines of the problem and then went back to reread certain parts of the problem. Unsuccessful problem solvers tended to look back at numbers and key words far more often than did successful problem solvers; in contrast, successful problem solvers tended to frequently reread the variable names (e.g., "Vons" and "Lucky") and other words before rereading the numbers in the problem. These findings indicate that unsuccessful problem solvers are more likely to use a direct translation approach to problem integration, whereas successful problem solvers are more likely to use a problem model approach.

IMPLICATIONS FOR INSTRUCTION: TEACHING PROBLEM INTEGRATION SKILLS

When confronted with a problem, students must determine what information is needed to solve it and then locate that information in the problem. If the problem contains irrelevant information, students must ignore it. If the problem lacks essential information, students must recognize that it cannot be solved.

For example, consider the three problems in Figure 5–8. Determine whether each problem has (1) sufficient information (i.e., enough information to solve the problem); (2) irrelevant information (i.e., information that is irrelevant to the solution); or (3) missing information (i.e., not enough information to solve the problem). The correct answers are that problem 1 has sufficient information, Problem 2 has irrelevant informa-

---

FIGURE 5–8

Does the problem have sufficient, irrelevant, or missing information?

For each problem indicate whether:
a. It contains enough information to be able to solve the problem,
b. It contains information that is irrelevant for the solution of the problem (if so, please underline the unnecessary information), or
c. It does not contain enough information to be able to solve the problem (if so, please specify the additional information needed to solve the problem).

Problems
1. A rectangular lawn is 12 meters long and 5 meters wide. Calculate the area of a path 1.75 meters wide around the lawn.
2. The length of a rectangular park is 6 meters more than its width. A walkway 3 meters wide surrounds the park. Find the dimensions of the park if it has an area of 432 square meters.
3. The lengths of the sides of a blackboard are in a 2:3 ratio. What is the perimeter (in meters) of the blackboard?

Adapted from Low and Over (1993)

tion, and Problem 3 has missing information. If you are like most of the high school students tested by Low and Over (1989, 1990, 1993; Low, 1989), you made errors on more than half of the problems, such as failing to recognize a piece of irrelevant information or that an additional piece of information was needed.

The type of task exemplified in Figure 5–8—asking a student to judge whether the information presented in a problem corresponds to the information needed to solve the problem—represents a crucial test of a student's schematic knowledge. To make judgments about the relevance of information, a student needs to construct an integrated representation of the problem. Low and Over (1989, 1990, 1993; Low, 1989) found that high school students often are unable to use schematic knowledge about common problem types such as rectangle, interest, and distance problems.

Is problem-solving performance related to the ability to detect whether a problem contains sufficient, irrelevant, or missing information? On some of the problems that Low and Over (1989) presented to students, they were asked to identify information that was missing or what information was not needed; on other problems (which contained sufficient or irrelevant information), the students were asked to compute a solution. As expected, performance on judging whether problems contained missing or irrelevant information correlated highly ($r = .9$) with ability to solve problems, such that students who performed well on solving problems also tended to perform well judging whether problems contained missing or irrelevant information and those who performed poorly on problems also tended to perform poorly on making judgments. These results support the contention that problem integration skills are an important component in mathematical problem solving.

If the ability to make relevance judgments is highly related to success in solving word problems, and if many high school students perform poorly on making relevance judgments, then teaching students how to judge the relevance of problem information should lead to improved problem-solving performance. This was the premise behind an instructional study involving high school students reported by Low (1989). Some students (relevance-trained group) were given 80 minutes of training in recognizing whether word problems contained sufficient, irrelevant, or missing information, and in specifying which information was irrelevant or missing. In all, students classified each of 27 problems and subsequently received feedback from the teacher concerning how to classify the problems. For example, in modeling her rationale for classifying a problem as having missing information, the teacher would say: "This is an area-of-rectangle problem. Since area equals length multiplied by width and only length is given, the information provided is insufficient for solution." In contrast, other students (conventional group) received 80 minutes of conventional instruction during which they solved problems similar to the sufficient problems given to the relevance-trained group and received feedback from the teacher concerning how to calculate a solution to the problems. Other students (control group) received no instruction.

Does relevance training affect students' ability to solve word problems? To help answer this question, students were given a pretest and posttest in which they were asked to solve word problems that contained either sufficient or irrelevant information. On the pretest, lower-ability students in each group solved about one-fourth of the problems. However, on the posttest, students in the conventional and control groups showed modest gains of about 10 percentage points whereas the relevance-trained group showed a much larger increase of about 25 percentage points. As you can see, training in how to judge the relevance of problem information was more effective than instruction in generating solutions in improving problem-solving performance. These results encourage the idea that students can learn problem integration skills that significantly improve their problem-solving performance.

This section has provided some research evidence that errors occur when students lack a schema or use the wrong schema for organizing a problem. How could you provide schema training? Some textbooks organize practice problems so that all problems on a page are solvable by the same procedure. This homogeneous organization fails to give students practice in recognizing different problem types. A greater mixture of problems in each exercise would encourage students to learn how to discriminate among different types of problems.

Let's return to the tile problem. Some techniques for helping students learn problem types include asking students to draw an integrated diagram of the problem, to sort the problems into categories, or to determine which information is irrelevant. The second part of Figure 5–1 offers multiple-choice items aimed at fostering these skills. As with the suggestions given in the previous section, these also require research verification.

Schema training is not the same as training students to recognize key words. For example, some students learn to categorize problems on the basis of superficial key words, such as, "If the problem says 'more,' then add the numbers in the problem," and "If the problem says 'less,' then subtract the second number from the first." This system is a poor one because it does not encourage the student to understand and represent the problem. It also can lead to errors such as the one in the inconsistent version of the butter problem in Figure 5–7. Students need to see that key word methods do not always lead to the correct answer. Instead of relying on key words, students should be encouraged to represent the problem in their own words.

In summary, when students represent a problem, they must engage in problem translation and problem integration. The foregoing two sections have provided examples of how failures in problem-solving often occur because of students' lack of schematic, linguistic, or factual knowledge. Instructional techniques that help students acquire such knowledge must be recognized as a crucial aspect of mathematics instruction. One promising sign is that items testing problem representation are beginning to appear on standardized mathematics tests.

SOLUTION PLANNING AND MONITORING

WHAT IS SOLUTION PLANNING AND MONITORING?

The next component in solving a mathematics story problem is to devise and monitor a plan for solving the problem. For example, in the tile problem at the beginning of this chapter, the plan might involve breaking the problem into subproblems: First, find the area of the room by multiplying room length by room width; second, find the area of a single tile by multiplying tile length by tile width; third, find the number of tiles needed by dividing area of the room by the area of one tile; fourth, find the cost of the tiles by multiplying the number of tiles by the cost per tile. As you can see, this solution plan involves four parts; in solving the problem, you must monitor where you are in the plan. In addition, you must be able to make scale conversions where needed, such as converting meters to centimeters or dollars to cents.

DEVISING A SOLUTION PLAN

When you are confronted with a problem you have never seen before, where does the idea for a solution plan come from? In his classic book *How to Solve It,* Polya (1945) offered the following advice for devising a solution plan: "If you cannot solve the proposed problem try to first solve some related problem. Could you imagine a more accessible related problem?" (p. xvii) Once the student finds a related problem that he or she has solved before, Polya (1945) asks: "Could you use it? Could you use its results? Could you use its method? Should you introduce some auxiliary element in order to make its use possible?" (p. xvii). In short, Polya (1945) concluded that "it is often appropriate to start work with the question: Do you know a related problem?" (p. 9). According to Polya (1945), "the main achievement in the solution of a problem is to conceive of the idea of a plan" (p. 8), and the planning process should begin with the question "Do you know a related problem?" (p. 9).

For example, consider the frustrum problem in Figure 5–9. You are given the values of the lower base *(b)*, upper base *(a)*, and height *(h)* of a frustrum of a right pyramid, and are asked to find the volume of the frustrum. If you are like most students who encountered this problem in Polya's geometry classes, you have never seen this problem before. Do you know how to solve a related problem? Most geometry students know how to find the volume of a right pyramid using the following formula: volume equals one-third of the product of the area of the base and the height of the pyramid. Can you use this related problem to solve the frustrum problem? Imagine completing the pyramid as shown in the bottom of Figure 5–9. Since you

FIGURE 5–9

The frustrum
problem

Here's a problem to solve:
Find the volume F of the frustrum of a right pyramid with a square base. Given the altitude h of the frustrum, the length a of the a side of its upper base, and the length b of a side of its lower base.

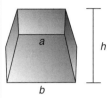

Here's a hint to help you devise a plan:
If you cannot solve the proposed problem, look around for an appropriate related problem. For example, do you know how to find the volume of a pyramid? If so then you know that the procedure for computing the volume of a pyramid is to multiply the area of the base times the height and divide the result by 3.

Here's a flash of insight provoked by the related problem:
To find the volume of the frustrum, subtract the volume of big pyramid from the volume of the small pyramid.

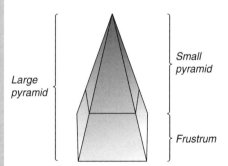

Here's how to develop the plan based on the procedure for a related problem:
The volume of the big pyramid is $b^2(h + x)/3$ and the volume of the small pyramid is $a^2(x)/3$ where b is the base of the big pyramid, a is the base of the small pyramid, x is the height of the small pyramid, and (h + x) is the height of the big pyramid.

Adapted from Polya (1945, 1965)

know how to use the formula to find the volume of the big pyramid (with *a* as its base) and the small pyramid (with *b* as its base), you can find the volume of the frustrum by subtracting the volume of the small pyramid from the volume of the large pyramid. Now your plan is taking shape: find the volume of the large pyramid, find the volume of the small pyramid, and subtract the smaller from the larger to get the volume of the frustrum.

As you can see, this process of devising a plan depends on several heuristics: (1) finding a related problem; (2) restating the problem; and (3) breaking the problem into subgoals. In the frustrum problem, a related problem you know how to solve is finding the volume of a right pyramid. Before you can use the formula, however, you must restate the problem as: "Find the difference between the volume of the big pyramid and the small pyramid." Finally, you need to break your solution to subgoals—such as finding the volume of large pyramid, finding the volume of the small pyramid, and subtracting the volume of the small pyramid from the volume of the large pyramid. To accomplish these goals, you need to break each down further into finding the values for base and height, and plugging them into the formula for volume.

Although Polya's ideas have been influential, especially among some mathematics educators, you might wonder whether there is any evidence that problem-solving heuristics for planning can be taught. To help answer this question, Schoenfeld (1979, 1985) taught students how to use problem-solving heuristics including finding a related problem, restating the problem, and breaking the problem into subgoals. Students who received practice in using these kinds of heuristics improved from 20% correct on a pretest to 65% on a posttest, whereas control students who received practice in solving problems without heuristics training averaged 25% correct on both tests. Although the sample size was small in this study, the results suggest that it is possible to help people improve the way they devise plans for solving mathematics problems.

USING WORKED-OUT EXAMPLES. Polya's suggestion, based on his practical experience in teaching mathematics, corresponds to current cognitive theories of analogical transfer. When a student is confronted with a mathematics problem that she has never seen before, how does she figure out how to solve it? Where does a creative solution plan come from? According to analogical transfer theory, a student solves a new problem (called a *target*) by remembering another problem (called a *base*) that she can solve, by abstracting a solution method from the base, and then by mapping that solution method to the target. There are three steps in the process of analogical transfer:

recognition—in which a student identifies a related problem (called a *base*) that can be solved;

abstraction—in which a student abstracts a solution method or principle from the base; and

mapping—in which a student applies that method or principle to the target.

The most commonly used technique in mathematics textbooks for helping students acquire a useful collection of base problems is to provide worked-out examples (Mayer, Sims, & Tajika, 1995). For example, consider the worked-out distance-rate-time problem in the top of Figure 5–10. Do you think that studying this example will help students solve an equivalent test problem, such as the one shown at the bottom of Figure 5–10?

To examine this question, Reed, Dempster, and Ettinger (1985) asked students to solve some word problems after they had studied both equivalent and unrelated worked-out examples. Students who studied equivalent examples performed poorly (25% correct) on the test problems, even though the test problems could be solved using the same solution method as in example problems they had just studied; unsurprisingly, students who studied unrelated examples also performed poorly (18% correct).

Why did students in the equivalent-example group often fail to transfer their learning of example problems to the solution of a new equivalent problem? There are two major obstacles to problem-solving transfer. The first obstacle is that students may not be able to abstract the solution method from the worked-out example. To overcome this obstacle, Reed et

FIGURE 5–10

A short worked-out example and an equivalent test problem

Here's a (short) worked-out example:

PROBLEM:

A car traveling at a speed of 30 miles per hour (mph) left a certain place at 10:00 A.M. At 11:30 A.M., another car departed from the same place at 40 mph and traveled the same route. In how many hours will the second car overtake the first car?

ANSWER:

The problem is a distance-rate-time problem in which distance $(D) =$ rate $(R) \times$ time (T).

Because both cars travel the same distance, the distance of the first car (D_1) equals the distance of the second car (D_2). Therefore $D_1 = D_2$, or $R_1 \times T_1 = R_2 \times T_2$, where $R_1 = 30$ mph, $R_2 = 40$ mph, and $T_1 = T_2 + 3/2$ hr. Substituting gives the following:

$$30 \times (T_2 + 3/2) = 40 \times T_2$$
$$30\,T_2 + 45 = 40\,T_2$$
$$T_2 = 4.5 \text{ hr}$$

Can you solve this problem?
A car travels south at the rate of 30 mph. Two hours later, a second car leaves to overtake the first car, using the same route and going 45 mph. In how many hours will the second car overtake the first car?

Adapted from Reed, Dempster, and Ettinger (1985)

al. (1985) provided an expanded version of the worked-out example that included a verbal explanation for each step in the solution processes. The second obstacle is that students might not realize that the worked-out example is relevant to solving the test problem. To overcome this obstacle, Reed et al. (1985) presented the corresponding worked-out example along with each test problem so students could refer to the example as they solved the test problem. In this situation, students given equivalent worked-out examples performed well (69% correct), but students given unrelated examples did not (17%).

Students also have difficulty knowing how a particular worked-out example (i.e., base problem) is related to a new test problem (i.e., target problem). For example, how would you go about solving the following grocer problem:

> A grocer mixes peanuts worth $1.65 a pound and almonds worth $2.10 a pound. How many pounds of each are needed to make a mixture worth $1.83 a pound?

If you are like most students in a study conducted by Reed (1987), you were not able to solve this problem. However, now study the worked-out solution of the nurse problem in Figure 5–11. Do you see the connections between the nurse problem and the grocer problem? To help you map the correspondences between the two problems, fill in the blanks in Table 5–5. If you are like most students in Reed's (1987) study, you were able to solve the grocer problem after studying the worked-out nurse problem.

To examine more closely how successful and unsuccessful problem-solvers study and use worked-out examples in textbooks, Chi and her colleagues (Chi, Bassok, Lewis, Reimann, & Glaser, 1989) asked students to read a physics lesson that included three worked-out word problems and then take a test on solving similar problems. Students were asked to talk aloud as they studied the examples, which included one computing the mass of a block suspended by two springs. The top table in Table 5–6 shows that students who performed well on the problem-solving test (i.e., successful problem-solvers) tended to make more statements as they read the worked-out examples than did students who performed poorly on the problem-solving test (i.e., unsuccessful problem-solvers). Their statements included self-explanations, such as "Umm, this would make sense because since they're connected by a string that doesn't stretch"; monitoring statements, such as "I can see how they did it"; and paraphrases, such as "Okay, so three forces are on the two strings." The bottom table in Table 5–6 shows that successful problem solvers use worked-out examples differently than unsuccessful problem solvers when they are allowed to refer to them during the problem-solving test: Unsuccessful problem solvers tended to reread worked-out examples as if they were looking for general guidance, whereas successful problem solvers tended to check the worked-out examples for specific pieces of information, such as "I'm looking at the

FIGURE 5–11

A worked-out example of the nurse problem

A nurse mixes a 6% boric acid solution with a 12% boric acid solution. How many pints of each are needed to make 4.5 pints of an 8% boric acid solution?

The problem is a mixture problem in which two quantities are added together to make a third quantity. The two component quantities are the 6% and 12% solutions.

The total amount of acid in the combined solution must equal the total amount of acid in the two component solutions. The amount of acid is found by multiplying the percentage of acid in a solution by the quantity of the solution. If we mix p pints of 6% solution with $4.5 - p$ pints (since we want a total of 4.5 pints) of 12% solution, the 6% solution will contribute $.06 \times p$ pints of acid. The 12% solution will contribute $.12 \times (4.5 - p)$ pints of acid. The first two lines of the table show this information.

Kind of Solution	Quantity of Solution (Pints)	Percentage of Acid	Quantity of Acid (Pints)
6% acid	p	6%	$.06 \times p$
12% acid	$4.5 - p$	12%	$.12 \times (4.5 - p)$
8% acid	4.5	8%	$.08 \times 4.5$

The bottom line shows that the combined solution consists of 4.5 pints of 8% acid, or $.08 \times 4.5$ pints of acid. Since the total amount of acid in the combined solution must equal the total amount in the two component solutions:

$$.06 \times p + .12 \times (4.5 - p) = .08 \times 4.5$$
$$\text{Solving for } p \text{ yields:}$$
$$.06p + .54 - .12p = .36$$
$$.18 = .06p$$
$$p = 3 \text{ pints of 6\% solution}$$
$$1.5 \text{ pints of 12\% solution}$$

Adapted from Reed (1987)

TABLE 5-5

Can you map the nurse problem onto the grocer problem?

Mapping Test: Fill in the Corresponding Values and Expressions

Nurse Problem	Grocer Problem
1. 6% acid	1. _____
2. 12% acid	2. _____
3. 8% acid	3. _____
4. $4.5 - p$ pints	4. _____
5. 4.5 pints	5. _____
6. 4.5 pints $\times$ 8% acid	6. _____

Correct Answers for Mapping Test

Nurse Problem	Grocer Problem
1. 6% acid	1. $1.65
2. 12% acid	2. $2.10
3. 8% acid	3. $1.83
4. $4.5 - p$ pints	4. $30 - A$
5. 4.5 pints	5. 30
6. 4.5 pints $\times$ 8% acid	6. $30 \times \$1.83$

Note: Solution equation for the grocer problem is: $\$1.65 \times A + \$2.10 \times (30 - A) = \$1.83 \times 30$. ($A$ = pounds of peanuts.)

Adapted from Reed (1987)

TABLE 5-6

Differences between how successful and unsuccessful problem solvers study and use worked-out examples

Average Number of Statements Made While Studying Examples

Type of Statement	Type of Problem Solver	
	Successful	Unsuccessful
Explaining	15	3
Monitoring	20	7
Paraphrasing	16	7

Average Number of Uses of Example While Solving a Problem

Type of Use	Type of Problem Solver	
	Successful	Unsuccessful
Rereading	.6	4.2
Checking	1.0	.3

Adapted from Chi, Bassok, Lewis, Reimann, and Glaser (1989)

formula here trying to see how you solve for [force 1] given the angle." These results suggest that worked-out examples are most helpful when students actively try to abstract the underlying rules or principles.

Overall, the research on worked-out examples continues to demonstrates the persistent finding that the road to problem-solving transfer is a rocky one (Salomon & Perkins, 1989). In particular, students need help in learning how to abstract a solution from a worked-out example, and how to make connections between an example and a new problem.

ATTITUDES FOR MATHEMATICAL PROBLEM-SOLVING. Student attitudes about problem-solving may also influence the way they plan a method for reaching a solution. Perhaps the most destructive belief concerning the planning process is the idea that math problems must be solved by applying meaningless procedures. Schoenfeld (1992) summarizes this belief as follows: "Ordinary students cannot expect to understand mathematics; they expect simply to memorize it and apply what they have learned mechanically and without understanding" (p. 359). For example, Lester, Garofalo, and Kroll (1989) reported that many third-graders believed that "all story problems could be solved by applying the operations suggested by the key words present in the story (e.g., *in all* suggests addition, *left* suggests subtraction, *share* suggests division)" (p. 84). As a consequence of this belief, these students "did not bother to monitor their actions or assess the reasonableness of their answers because they saw no need to do so" (Lester et al., p. 84). Where did such a bizarre belief come from? According to Lester et al. (1989), such a belief was well-founded because "most of the story problems to which these children had been exposed could be answered correctly by applying their key-word method" and in many cases "teachers had taught them to look for key-words" (p. 84).

Another common belief that prevents students from using productive planning processes is the idea that "students who have understood the mathematics they have studied will be able to solve any assigned problem in five minutes or less" (Schoenfeld, 1992, p. 359). The effect of this attitude is that students will give up on a problem if they are unable to solve it within a few minutes. For example, when Schoenfeld (1988) asked high school students how long it should take them to solve a typical homework problem, the average estimated time was two minutes. When he asked them how long they would work on a problem before giving up, the average estimated time was twelve minutes. The belief that all math problems can be solved quickly is based on students' experience in mathematics classes: "Students who have finished a full twelve years of mathematics have worked thousands upon thousands of 'problems'—virtually none of which were expected to take the students more than a few minutes to complete" (Schoenfeld, 1988, pp. 159–160). In monitoring their problem solving, students are likely to quit when they reach a major obstacle even though they might have solved the problem if they had persevered.

IMPLICATIONS FOR INSTRUCTION: TEACHING FOR PLANNING

When confronted with a new word problem, some students do not know what to do, even though they may know how to carry out the required arithmetic. For example, consider the following problem:

> Christine borrowed $850 for one year from the Friendly Finance Company. If she paid 12% simple interest on the loan, what was the total amount she repaid?

This is a multi-step problem because it involves two steps—finding the amount of interest owed by multiplying $850 by .12, and finding the total amount repaid by adding the result to $850. In spite of years of training on word problems, most U.S. high school seniors fail to solve such multistep word problems such as this one (Dossey, Mullis, Lindquist, & Chambers, 1988). Interestingly, almost all of these students can solve basic arithmetic problems, such as $604 - 207 = \underline{\hspace{1cm}}$.

Not knowing what to do reflects a lack of strategic knowledge, and in particular, a failure in planning. National assessments of mathematics achievement show that conventional instruction in word-problem-solving is not equipping students with the planning skills they need (Dossey et al., 1988).

How can we help students to develop appropriate planning skills? A team of researchers called the Cognition and Technology Group at Vanderbilt has developed a video-based program for helping students learn how to plan solutions to mathematics problems (Bransford et al., 1996; Cognition and Technology Group at Vanderbilt, 1992; Van Haneghan et al., 1992). The materials consist of a series of video episodes of *The Adventures of Jasper Woodbury,* each lasting 15 to 20 minutes. In each episode, the character is faced with a challenge that requires mathematical problem solving, such as planning a trip, generating a business plan based on statistics, and using geometry meaningfully. Working in small groups, the students in the class solve the problem and then see another video showing how the character solved the problem.

For example, in the episode "Rescue at Boone's Meadow," Jasper's friend Larry teaches Emily how to fly an ultralight airplane in a scene that provides information about the plane's payload, fuel capacity, fuel consumption, speed, and landing capabilities. Later, in a restaurant, Jasper tells Emily and Larry about his planned fishing trip to Boone's Meadow, noting that there is a landing strip next to where he plans to park his car and that the hiking distance to Boone's Meadow is 18 miles. On the way from the restaurant, Emily and Larry stop to weigh themselves. Jasper is next seen happily fishing at Boone's Meadow when he discovers a wounded bald eagle and through a radio is able to get this information to Emily. In the final scene, Emily is in a veterinarian's office, where she learns about eagles and consults a map on the wall showing that there are no roads leading to Boone's Meadow. The problem is how to save the eagle.

Working in groups to solve the problem, students must consider a range of possibilities and variables. For example, the ultralight aircraft needs to fly a greater distance than normal to get to the rescue site; to fly a greater distance, more fuel must be added, but this would increase the overall weight, which in turn would require a change in pilots. Although students can usually generate an answer within about 30 minutes, they are encouraged to work longer to develop a better solution. In the process of problem-solving, they often review parts of the video to check or gather information. They also work on alternative versions of the problem. In all, they spend about a week on each episode.

Does participating in the Jasper series affect students' planning skills? To examine this question, 10 classrooms of fifth- and sixth-graders (Jasper-trained group) received instruction in three or four Jasper adventures for three to four weeks, whereas 10 matched classrooms (control group) received their regular instruction, which focused on word problems. To measure their planning skills, all students took a planning test before and after instruction, consisting of problems, such as shown in Figure 5–12. As you see, the test included questions about how to plan a solution to a word problem (Question 1) and how to break a problem into parts (Question 2).

FIGURE 5–12

Can you devise a solution plan for this problem?

JILL'S TRIP PROBLEM

Jill lives in Carson City. She wants to drive her car from her house to a friend's house in Meridien. As shown on the map, Jill can take the road from Carson City to Johnstown and Johnstown to Meridien. Her car is filled with gasoline and ready to go. There is a gas station in Carson City, Ceymore, and Meridien, but there is not one in Johnstown. Jill plans to leave on her trip at 8:00 in the morning.

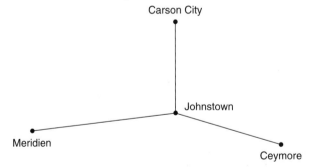

Question 1: What does Jill need to think about to figure out how long it will take her to make the trip?

Question 2: Jill divides the distance from Carson City to Meridien (120 miles) by the speed she will drive (60 miles per hour). Why does she do this?

Adapted from Cognition and Technology Group at Vanderbilt (1992)

Although both the Jasper-trained group and the control group scored about the same on the pretest (i.e., achieving scores of approximately 20% correct), the Jasper-trained group performed much better than the control group on the posttest (i.e., achieving approximately 40% correct compared to 25% for the control group). These results show that training with the Jasper adventures resulted in a large improvement in students' planning performance, whereas conventional training in word problems did not.

Why does the Jasper series improve students' planning skills? *The Adventures of Jasper Woodbury* is based on three principles that distinguish it from conventional mathematics programs:

Generative learning: Students learn better when they actively construct their own knowledge rather than when they passively receive information from the teacher.

Anchored instruction: Students learn better when material is presented within an interesting situation rather than as an isolated problem.

Cooperative learning: Students learn better when they communicate about problem-solving in groups rather than when they work individually.

Although it is not possible to isolate the features of the Jasper series that are responsible for its effectiveness, the program is based on a combination of generative, anchored, and cooperative methods of teaching and learning. In summary, as one reviewer has noted, the Jasper series "uses videodisc computer technology as a vehicle for changing the fabric of instruction, away from transmission and toward active problem solving in realistic contexts" (Lehrer, 1992, p. 287). Additional research is needed, but this promising project encourages the development of other programs based on the same instructional principles.

This section has examined both heuristics that help students devise solution plans and obstacles that may impede successful planning. Heuristics for planning include using a related problem, restating the problem, and breaking the problem into subgoals. Obstacles to planning include difficulties in finding a related problem, reliance on meaningless solution procedures, and a failure to persevere. How can you provide strategy training? It is important for students to recognize that there may be more than one right way to solve a problem and that finding a solution method can be a creative activity. Students need to be able to describe their solution methods and to compare their methods with those used by other students. Some researchers have been successful in explicitly teaching strategies for problem-solving, such as asking students to write a list of operations (or a number sentence) necessary for solving a problem, to list the subgoals needed in a multistep problem, or to draw a conclusion based on the partial completion of a solution plan. Sample multiple-choice items are given in the third section of Figure 5–1.

In summary, devising and monitoring a solution plan are crucial components in mathematical problem-solving. Students and teachers need to recognize that they should pay as much attention to process (i.e., their solution strategy) as to product (i.e., the final numerical answer). Research is needed to verify the preceding suggestions for improving students' strategic planning skills in mathematics.

SOLUTION EXECUTION

WHAT IS SOLUTION EXECUTION?

Once you have understood the tile problem presented at the beginning of this chapter and devised a plan for solving it, the next major component is to carry out your plan. For a problem like the tile problem, you need to be able to carry out arithmetic operations such as $7.2 \times 5.4 = \underline{\hspace{1cm}}$ or $.72 \times 432 = \underline{\hspace{1cm}}$. As you can see, problem execution requires procedural knowledge (i.e., knowledge about how to carry out a procedure such as addition, subtraction, division, or multiplication).

The acquisition of computational procedures involves a progression from naive procedures to more sophisticated procedures, and from tedious application of procedures to automatic application. In summary, as children gain experience, their procedures become more sophisticated and automatic. With experience students develop a collection of procedures that can be selected for various computational problems.

RESEARCH ON SOLUTION EXECUTION

DEVELOPMENT OF EXPERTISE FOR SIMPLE ADDITION. As an example of the development of expertise in computation, let's consider a child's procedure for solving single-column addition problems of the form,

$$m + n = \underline{\hspace{1cm}}$$

where m and n are single-digit positive integers whose sum is less than 10.

Fuson (1982, 1992) has identified four major stages in the development of computational expertise: counting-all, counting-on, derived facts, and known facts. The counting-all procedure involves setting a counter to 0, incrementing it m times, and then incrementing it n times. For the problem $2 + 4 = \underline{\hspace{1cm}}$, the child might put out one finger and say "1," put out another finger and say "2," pause, put out a third finger and say "3," put out a fourth finger and say "4," put out a fifth finger and say "5," and put out a sixth finger and say "6."

The counting-on procedure involves setting a counter to m (or n) and incrementing it n (or m) times. For the problem $2 + 4 = \underline{\hspace{1cm}}$, the child might put out two fingers and then say "3, 4, 5, 6," as each of four additional fingers was put out. One version of this approach is what Groen and Parkman (1972) call the "min model," which involves setting a counter to the larger of m or n and then incrementing the counter by the smaller number. For the problem $2 + 4 =$ _____, the child might put out four fingers and then say "5, 6," as each of two additional fingers is put out.

The derived facts procedure involves using one's knowledge of number facts to figure out answers for related problems. For example, the first number facts that a child learns are usually the doubles, such as $1 + 1 =$ _____, $2 + 2 =$ _____, $3 + 3 =$ _____, and so on. For the problem, $2 + 4 =$ _____, a student might say: "I can take 1 from the 4 and give it to the 2. That makes $3 + 3$, so the answer is 6." In this example, the child knew that the sum of 3 plus 3 is 6, but did not directly know the answer for 2 plus 4.

The known facts procedure, also called retrieval, involves having a ready answer for each number fact. For example, drill and practice with flash cards is generally aimed at helping students acquire rapid responses for a set of basic facts. For the problem, $2 + 4 =$ _____, the child would say "6."

As you can see in this progression, the child's early procedures for single-digit addition are based on counting. The child can treat addition as if it were an extension of what the child already knows about counting. With more experience, the counting procedures can become more efficient, such as the use of a counting-on procedure instead of a counting-all procedure. With even more experience, some of the facts become automatic, and eventually all may become automatic.

What evidence is there for stages in the development of computational expertise? One method for studying students' solution procedures is to observe carefully what children do as they solve addition problems; in particular, we should listen to what they say and watch their fingers. Another method is to measure the time it takes to solve addition problems. Figure 5–13 summarizes the counting-all and counting-on (min version) procedures, with boxes representing actions and diamonds representing decisions. For example, we could make the following predictions concerning response times for each procedure. For the counting-all procedure, response time should be a function of the sum of $m + n$. For the problem $2 + 4 =$ _____ or $4 + 2 =$ _____, the child must increment a counter six times. For the min version of the counting-on procedure, response time should be a function of the smaller number (m or n). For the problem $2 + 4 =$ _____ or $4 + 2 =$ _____, the child must increment two times. For the derived facts procedure, response time should be fastest for the problems that are already known. Thus doubles (like $2 + 2 =$ _____ or $3 + 3 =$ _____) should yield the fastest response times when they become memorized. For the known facts procedure, response time should be the same for all problems since the child is simply "looking up" the answer in memory.

To determine which procedures children use as they begin formal instruction in computation, Groen and Parkman (1972) asked first-graders to answer a series of single-column addition problems. Their response time performance could best be described by the min model of the counting-on procedure. Figure 5–14 shows the response time for problems that the min model says require 0 increments (such as $1 + 0 =$ _____ or $5 + 0 =$ _____), 1 increment (such as $5 + 1 =$ _____ or $6 + 1 =$ _____),

FIGURE 5–13 Counting-all and counting-on procedures for simple addition

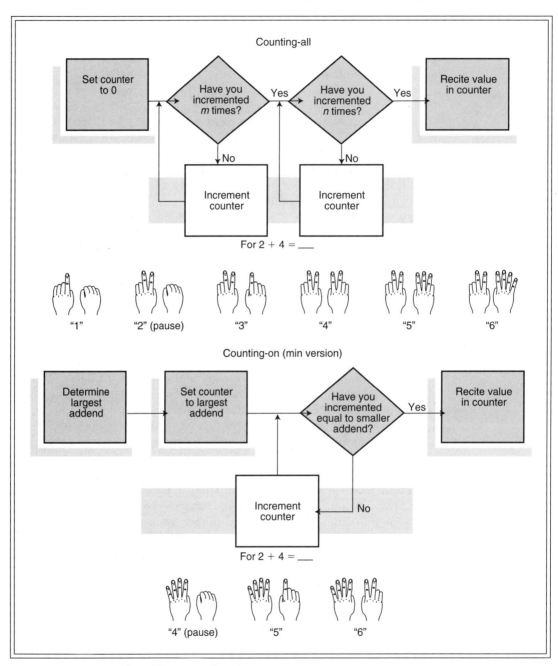

Adapted from Mayer (1992)

FIGURE 5–14 Response time depends on the number of increments required by the min model

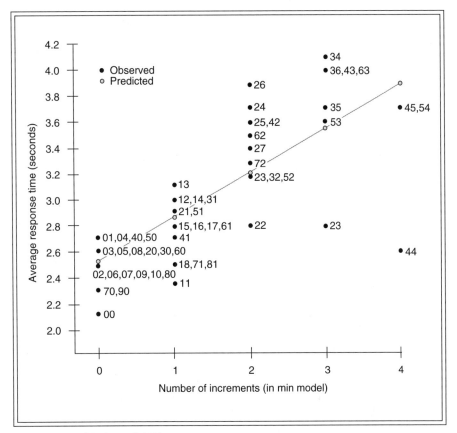

From Groen and Parkman (1972)

2 increments (such as 5 + 2 = _____ or 6 + 2 = _____), 3 increments (such as 5 + 3 = _____ or 6 + 3 = _____), and 4 increments (such as 5 + 4 = _____ or 4 + 5 = _____). As shown, response time generally increases by about one-third second for each additional increment in the value of the smaller number. Thus most problems seem to be solved by setting a counter to the larger number and incrementing it by the smaller number. However, you might note that there is some evidence that doubles (0 + 0 = _____, 1 + 1 = _____, 2 + 2 = _____, and so on) were answered rapidly regardless of the number of increments; this suggests that doubles might already be well-memorized number facts (requiring a known facts procedure), while other problems require a counting procedure.

Parkman and Groen (1971) also found that a min model best fit the performance of adults. However, the time needed for an adult to make an increment was one-fiftieth second, compared to one-third second for first-graders. Since it is unlikely that a person can count silently at a rate of fifty increments per second, Parkman and Groen (1971) offered an alternative explanation: for almost all problems, adults have direct access to the answer in their memories (i.e., on most problems, adults use a known facts approach), but on a few problems they fall back to a counting procedure. Ashcraft and Stazyk (1981) have accounted for the performance of adults by assuming that they must "look up" answers in a complicated network. Thus adults apparently use some version of a known facts approach, while first-graders seem to be using some version of a counting approach.

SELECTION OF ADDITION PROCEDURES. Students seem to progress through a series of mathematical discoveries, inventing progressively more efficient procedures for solving simple arithmetic problems. Does a child's procedural knowledge consist mainly of the more efficient methods that have replaced the earlier ones or of an ever-increasing collection of procedures ranging from the least to the most mature? To answer this question, Siegler (1987) asked kindergartners, first-graders, and second-graders to solve forty-five addition problems, such as "If you had 8 oranges and I gave you 7 more, how many would you have?" and "What is 8 plus 7?" After giving each answer, the students were asked to describe verbally how they solved the problem.

Children reported using five kinds of procedures: guessing (or not responding), counting-all, counting-on (min version), derived facts, and known facts. Table 5–7 shows the percentage of time students at each grade level used each of the procedures. Most children reported using at least three procedures, and at no age was one procedure used most of the time. Did the children accurately describe their solution procedures? Siegler (1987) found that on problems for which children reported using a counting-on procedure, the min model was a good predictor of their solution times, but on problems for which they reported using other strategies, the min model was not a good predictor. In reviewing these results, Siegler and Jenkins (1989) concluded that "these and a variety of other data converged on indicating that children used the strategies they reported using and that they employed them on those trials where they said they had" (p. 25).

Overall, these results suggest that students build an arsenal of addition procedures, choose procedures independently for different addition prob-

TABLE 5–7	Addition Procedure				
Percentage of time that kindergartners, first-graders, and second-graders use each of five procedures for simple addition	Grade	Guessing	Counting-all	Counting-on	Derived Facts	Known Facts
	K	30%	22%	30%	2%	16%
	1	8%	1%	38%	9%	44%
	2	5%	0%	40%	11%	45%

Adapted from Siegler (1987)

lems. Interestingly, children use a known-facts approach (which can also be called *retrieval*) for easy problems, but for hard problems they rely on what Siegler and Jenkins (1989) call "back-up strategies" (such as derived facts or counting). In deciding whether to use counting-all or counting-on (min version), students are more likely to use counting-on (min version) when one of the addends is smaller, such as 9 + 2, than when the two addends are close in value, such as 5 + 6. As you can see, this choice makes sense, because it is easier to use a counting-on (min version) when one addend is smaller. Siegler and Jenkins (1989) argue that rather than using a single procedure for all addition problems, children "behave adaptively . . . in choosing among alternative . . . strategies" (p. 29).

COMPLEX COMPUTATIONAL PROCEDURES. Once a child has achieved some level of automaticity in carrying out simple procedures (e.g., single-column addition or subtraction), these procedures can become components in more complex computational procedures. For example, solving a three-column subtraction problem such as

$$456 - 321 = \underline{\hspace{2cm}}$$

requires the ability to solve single-digit subtraction problems such as 6 − 1 = _____, 5 − 2 = _____, and 4 − 3 = _____. The procedure for three-column subtraction is summarized in Figure 5–15, where the boxes represent processes, the diamonds represent decisions, and the arrows show where to go next. As shown, one of the skills required to use this procedure is the ability to carry out single-column subtraction (e.g., see step 2c).

Figure 5–15 diagrams the procedure that children are supposed to acquire; however, some students acquire a flawed version. For example, a student may have a procedure for three-column subtraction that contains one small "bug" (i.e., one of the steps in the student's procedure might be different from the corresponding step of the procedure in Figure 5–15). A student who uses such a "buggy" procedure (i.e., a procedure with one or more bugs in it) may be able to answer some problems correctly but not others.

Consider the following problems:

564	722	821	954	349
−472	−519	−431	−233	−123
112	217	410	721	226

As you can see, the student who solved these problems obtained correct answers for two out of the five. A more precise way of characterizing the student's performance is to say that the student is using a procedure that has a very common "bug" in it: at steps 2a, 2b, and 2c, the student subtracts the smaller number from the larger number, regardless of which one is on top in the problem statement. Brown and Burton (1978) have argued that a student's knowledge of subtraction procedures can be described by listing which bugs (if any) are found in the student's possesses. This example involves a very common bug, which Brown and Burton call "subtract smaller from larger."

FIGURE 5–15 A procedure for three-column subtraction

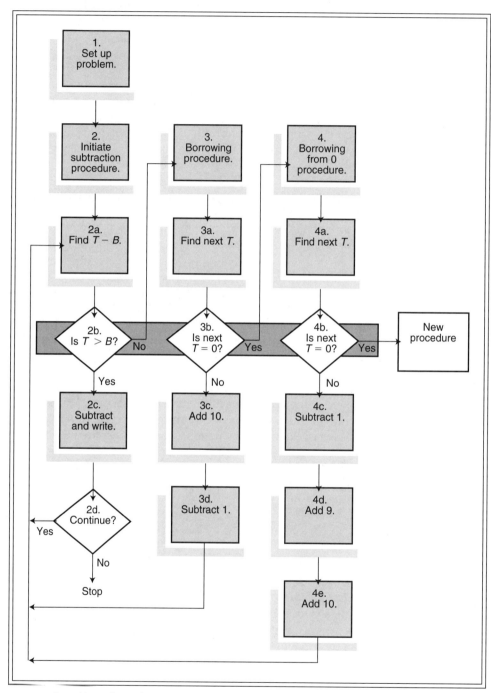

From Mayer (1981a)

According to Brown and Burton (1978), errors in subtraction may occur because a student consistently uses a flawed procedure, not because a student cannot apply a procedure. To test this idea, Brown and Burton gave a set of 15 subtraction problems to 1,325 primary-school children, and developed a computer program called "BUGGY" to analyze each student's subtraction procedure. If all the student's answers were correct, BUGGY would conclude that the student was using the correct procedure (shown in Figure 5–15). If there were errors, BUGGY would attempt to find one bug that could account for them. If no single bug could be identified, BUGGY would evaluate all possible combinations of bugs that could account for the errors. Table 5–8 shows some of the most common bugs; for example, 54 of the 1,325 students behaved as if they had the "smaller-from-larger" bug.

Although the BUGGY program searched for hundreds of possible bugs and bug combinations, it was able to find the subtraction procedure (including bugs) for only about half of the students. The other students

TABLE 5–8 Some subtraction bugs	Number of Occurrences in 1,325 Students	Name of Bug	Example	Description
	57	Borrow from 0	103 − 45 ⎯⎯ 158	When borrowing from a column whose top digit is 0, the student writes 9, but does not continue borrowing from the column to the left of 0.
	54	Smaller from larger	253 − 118 ⎯⎯ 145	The student subtracts the smaller digit in each column from the larger, regardless of which one is on top.
	10	$0 - N = N$	140 − 21 ⎯⎯ 121	Whenever the top digit in a column is 0, the student writes the bottom digit as the answer.
	34	$0 - N = N$ *and* move over zero	304 − 75 ⎯⎯ 279	Whenever the top digit in a column is 0, the student writes the bottom digit as the answer. When the student needs to borrow from a column whose top digit is 0, he or she skips that column and borrows from the next one.

Adapted from Brown and Burton (1978)

seemed to be making random errors, were inconsistent in their use of bugs, or may have been learning as they took the test. Thus Brown and Burton's (1978) work allows for a precise description of a student's procedural knowledge—even when that knowledge is flawed.

IMPLICATIONS FOR INSTRUCTION: TEACHING FOR EXECUTING

How can we help students to build a useful base of procedural knowledge? For nearly 100 years, drill-and-practice has been the dominant instructional method for teaching arithmetic procedures. In drill-and-practice, a student is given a simple problem and asked to give a response, such as, "What is 2 plus 4?" If the student gives the correct response, the student receives a reward, such as the teacher saying, "Right!" If the student gives the wrong response, the student receives a punishment, such as the teacher saying, "Wrong!" When you use flash cards, with the question on one side and the answer on the other, you are learning by drill-and-practice. When you sit in front of a computer screen that presents problems and gives feedback, you are learning by drill-and-practice. When you answer a series of exercise problems in a textbook and then check your answers, you are learning by drill-and-practice.

Although drill-and-practice can be an effective method for teaching procedural knowledge, it may not be the only worthwhile method. A major problem is that learning procedural knowledge—such as how to add and subtract—can become isolated from conceptual knowledge—such as what a number is—so that mathematics becomes a set of meaningless procedures for students.

Case and his colleagues (Case & Okamoto, 1996; Griffin, Case, & Capodilupo, 1995; Griffin, Case, & Siegler, 1994) have argued that the learning of basic arithmetic procedures must be tied to the development of central conceptual structures in the child. According to this view, the most important conceptual structure for learning arithmetic procedures is a mental number line. Case and his colleagues developed a test of students' knowledge of a mental number line that included their ability to compare two numbers, to visualize the number line, to count, and to determine the magnitude specified by number words. When they gave the test to six-year-olds of low socioeconomic status (SES), only 32% demonstrated an acceptable knowledge of the number line; however, 67% of high-SES six-year olds demonstrated such knowledge. More importantly, 25% of the low-SES children and 71% of the high-SES children could solve simple addition problems, such as 2 + 4 = _____.

Why do some students have difficulty with simple addition? According to Case and his colleagues, the source of the difficulty is that students lack a representation of a mental number line. If this is true, the instructional implication is clear: Teach students to construct and use mental number lines as a prerequisite for learning arithmetic procedures. This is the approach taken in a math readiness program called "Rightstart" (Griffin &

Case, 1996; Griffin et al., 1994, 1995). The program consists of 40 half-hour sessions in which students learn to use a number line by playing a series of number games. For example, in one game two students each roll a die and must determine who rolled the higher number. The student who rolled the higher number then moves his or her token along a number-line path on a playing board. The first student to reach the end of the path wins. These games promote skills such as comparing the magnitude of two numbers, counting forward and backward along a number line, and making one-to-one mapping of numbers onto objects when counting.

Does number-line training help students learn arithmetic procedures? To answer this question, researchers (Griffin & Case, 1996; Griffin et al., 1994, 1995) gave one group of low-SES first-graders the Rightstart training (treatment group), whereas another group of similar children received their regular mathematics instruction (control group). First, there was overwhelming evidence that number-line training helped students build conceptual knowledge of number lines. On a posttest of number-line knowledge, 87% of the treatment group and 25% of the control group demonstrated skill on number-line tasks such as determining which of two numbers was smaller. Second, there was evidence that number-line training helped students learn arithmetic procedures. On a posttest with simple addition, 82% of the treatment group and 33% of the control group gave correct answers. Third, treatment students were more successful than control students in learning mathematics in school: 80% of the treatment group and 41% of the control group mastered first-grade mathematics units on simple addition and subtraction. Griffin and Case (1996) noted that "a surprising proportion of children from low-income North American families—at least 50% in our samples—do not arrive in school with the central cognitive structure in place that is necessary for success in first grade mathematics," so "their first learning of addition and subtraction may be a meaningless experience" (p. 102). However, they argued that this problem can be overcome with a relatively modest instructional program aimed at promoting the conceptual knowledge that underpins arithmetic procedures.

In reviewing the Rightstart program, Bruer (1993) argued for the importance of connecting procedural and conceptual knowledge:

> Without this understanding [of the mental number line], [students'] basic number skills remain recipes, rather than rules for reasoning. If they don't understand how number concepts and structures justify and support these skills, their only alternative is to try to understand school math as a set of arbitrary procedures. Why arithmetic works is a mystery to them. . . . For mathematics to be meaningful, conceptual knowledge and procedural skills have to be interrelated in instruction. (p. 90)

Number-line training is an important demonstration of the value of helping students to make connections between arithmetic procedures and number concepts.

What can you do to improve training in computational procedures? This question was addressed early in the history of educational psychology by Thorndike (1925), who argued for the importance of practice with feedback, as exemplified in the last portion of Figure 5–1. Thus, to acquire skill in solving computation problems, students need practice in solving computation problems. In addition, students need feedback on whether their answers are correct. This advice has become very well accepted in educational psychology and is amply supported by research. However, more recent research has shown that students tend to develop new arithmetic procedures by using their previously learned procedures and conceptual knowledge of numbers. For example, Resnick (1982) has argued that procedural knowledge should be tied to a learner's conceptual knowledge by making computation more concrete.

CONCLUSION

Let's return one final time to the tile problem described at the opening to this chapter. To solve that problem, a person needs several kinds of knowledge: linguistic and factual knowledge for problem translation, schematic knowledge for problem integration, strategic knowledge for solution planning and monitoring, and procedural knowledge for solution execution.

A review of mathematics textbooks and achievement tests reveals that procedural knowledge is heavily emphasized in school curricula (Mayer, Sims, & Tajika, 1995). For example, students are given drill-and-practice in carrying out computational procedures. In this chapter, we refer to this type of instruction as solution execution. However, systematic instruction in how to translate problems, how to make meaningful representations of problems, and how to devise solution plans is not always given.

Problem translation involves converting each statement into an internal representation, such as paraphrase or diagram. Students appear to have difficulty in comprehending simple sentences, especially when a relationship between variables is involved, and students often lack specific knowledge that is assumed in the problem (e.g., the knowledge that a square has four equal sides). Training in how to represent each sentence in a problem is an important and often neglected component of mathematics instruction.

Problem integration involves putting the pieces of information from the problem together into a coherent representation. Students appear to have trouble with unfamiliar problems for which they lack an appropriate schema. Training for schematic knowledge involves helping students to recognize differences among problem types.

Solution planning and monitoring involve devising and assessing a strategy for how to solve the problem. Students appear to have trouble describing the solution procedure they are using, such as spelling out the subgoals in a multistep problem. In addition, students often harbor unproductive attitudes, such as the idea that a problem has only one correct solution procedure. Strategy training is needed to help students focus on the process of problem solving in addition to the product of problem solving.

These three types of training complement the fourth component in mathematics instruction, solution training. All four components are needed for students to become productive mathematical problem-solvers.

Although this chapter has focused on just one type of mathematics problem, many of the concepts apply to other kinds of mathematics problems as well. The tile problem was selected as an example because it is representative of the type of story problems that are found in secondary-school mathematics courses. A major theme of this chapter has been that there is more to mathematics than learning to get the right answer (i.e., more than learning number facts and computational procedures). This chapter has provided examples of the important role played by linguistic and factual knowledge, schematic knowledge, and strategic knowledge, as well as procedural knowledge.

SUGGESTED READINGS

Bruer, J. T. (1993). *Schools for thought.* Cambridge, MA: MIT Press. (Chapter 4 presents an excellent summary of cognitive research on making mathematics meaningful.)

Campbell, J. I. D. (Ed.). (1992). *The nature and origins of mathematical skills.* Amsterdam: North-Holland. (A description of various research programs on mathematical thinking and its development.)

Grouws, D. A. (Ed.). (1992). *Handbook of research on mathematics teaching and learning.* New York: Macmillan. (A collection of twenty-nine papers reviewing a broad range of research in mathematics education.)

CHAPTER 6 Science

According to the conceptual-change approach to science education, science learning involves helping learners change their existing conceptions rather than solely add new information to their memories. What cognitive processes are involved in learning a new scientific principle? In this chapter we explore four cognitive processes in science learning: recognizing that one's current conception is inadequate to explain one's observations, inventing a new conception that better fits the observed data, applying one's conception to solve a new scientific problem, and developing expertise in scientific reasoning. In addition, this chapter examines techniques for fostering each of these four processes.

THE INTUITIVE PHYSICS PROBLEM

Figure 6–1 shows a bird's-eye view of a curved metal tube. A metal ball is put into the end indicated by the arrow. The ball is then shot through the tube at a high speed, so that it comes out the other end of the tube. Your job is to use a pencil to draw the path that the ball will follow after it comes out of the tube. (You can ignore the effects of air resistance.)

Instructions and diagrams like these were used in a study by McCloskey, Caramazza, and Green (1980). They found that college students tended to give two kinds of answers to the problems. Some students drew a curved line, as shown at the left side of Figure 6–2. Others drew a straight line, as shown at the right of Figure 6–2. Does your answer correspond to either of these drawings?

Now consider the two explanations shown in Figure 6–3. The first explanation states that the ball acquires a "force" or "momentum" as it moves through the curved tube, and that this force causes the ball to continue its curved path for some time after it emerges from the tube. In contrast, the second explanation states that the ball will continue at a constant speed in a straight line until some force acts on the ball. Choose the explanation that corresponds most closely with your conception of motion.

If you drew a curved line, as shown in the left side of Figure 6–2, your answer is consistent with that given by the majority of college students in the McCloskey et al. (1980) study. Similarly, if you selected the first explanation in Figure 6–3, you are in agreement with a student who had completed one year of high school physics and one year of college physics.

FIGURE 6–1 Where will the ball go?

You are looking down on the curved metal tube shown below. Assume that a metal ball is put in the end with the arrow, and that the ball is shot through the tube at a high rate of speed. Your task is to draw a line corresponding to the path that the ball will follow once it leaves the tube.

Adapted from McCloskey et al. (1980)

FIGURE 6–2 Two possible answers to the tube problem

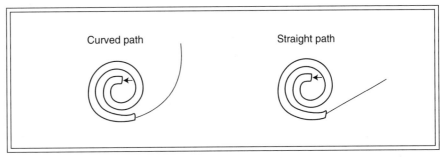

Adapted from McCloskey et al. (1980)

However, this answer is incorrect and seems to be based on a medieval conception of motion called the "theory of impetus"—the idea that when an object is set into motion it acquires a force or impetus that keeps it moving, at least until the impetus gradually dissipates. For example, this idea was popular in the fourteenth century writings of Buridan (cited in McCloskey, Caramazza & Green, 1980). In contrast, the correct answer, based on modern Newtonian conceptions of motion, is the straight path shown on the right-hand side of Figure 6–2 and the second explanation in Figure 6–3. The Newtonian concept is that an object in motion will continue until some external force acts upon it.

The point of this demonstration is not to show that people don't understand physics but rather that students approach learning and thinking in physics, or any science, with certain preexisting conceptions. An impor-

FIGURE 6–3

Two possible explanations for the tube problem

Student A
"The momentum that is acquired as it went around here (through the tube), well, the force holding it has given it angular momentum, so as it comes around here (out of the tube), it still has some momentum left, but it loses the momentum as the force disappears."

Student B
"The ball will continue to move in a line away from here (end of tube). It will keep going until some force acts on the ball. If no force acts on the ball, it will just continue."

Adapted from McCloskey et al. (1980)

tant educational implication of this demonstration is that instruction should take into account the fact that students already possess intuitions or conceptions about science. Thus, instruction cannot be viewed as providing knowledge about an entirely new topic; rather, instruction involves beginning with the learner's existing "intuitive physics" (or "intuitive science") and trying to change or build upon those conceptions.

CONCEPTUAL-CHANGE THEORY

Research on science education has encouraged a shift from a traditional to a conceptual-change view of learning (Carey, 1986; Posner, Strike, Hewson, & Gertzog, 1982; Strike & Posner, 1985, 1992). According to a traditional view, learning involves adding more and more facts to one's memory. In contrast, the conceptual-change view is that learning occurs when one's mental model (or naive conception) is replaced by a new one. According to *conceptual-change theory,* learning involves three steps:

Recognizing an anomaly: Seeing that your current mental model is inadequate to explain observable facts; that is, realizing that you possess misconceptions that must be discarded.

Constructing a new model: Finding a more adequate mental model that is able to explain the observable facts; that is, replacing one model with another.

Using a new model: When confronted with a problem, using your new model to discover a solution; that is, being able to operate your new model mentally.

As you can see, mental models are at the heart of conceptual-change theory. A mental model is a cognitive representation of the essential parts of a system as well as the cause-and-effect relations between a change in the state of one part and a change in the state of another part (Gentner & Stevens, 1983; Halsford, 1993; Mayer, 1992). For example, you are using a mental model—albeit a discredited one—when you think of force as a sort of constant pushing that keeps an object moving. If you find that this model fails to generate correct predictions on problems such as the ones you just tried, then you need to find a new mental model, such as the idea that force is like a single kick that changes the speed of an object by a certain amount.

This chapter explores four aspects of how students learn science. First, students must overcome their misconceptions that conflict with school science, that is, they need to discard their existing mental models. Second, students must replace their misconceptions with new conceptions; that is, they must find new mental models. Third, students must develop skills in thinking scientifically; that is, they need to use their new mental models. Fourth, students must acquire content knowledge that will allow them to begin to change from being novices to being experts.

RECOGNIZING ANOMALIES: DISCARDING A MISCONCEPTION

THEORY: KNOWLEDGE AS DESCRIPTION VERSUS EXPLANATION

Historians of science have distinguished between two goals of science— *description* versus *explanation* (Bronowski, 1978; Kearney, 1971; Westfall, 1977). According to the traditional view, the goal of science is to describe the natural world, including descriptions of the relations among variables that can be stated as laws, such as *force = mass × acceleration.* It follows that the goal of science education is to help students learn facts about the natural universe. To accomplish this goal, science books and encyclopedias keep growing in length.

In contrast, according to the conceptual-change view, the goal of science is not only to describe but also to explain the natural universe, including the mechanisms underlying the descriptive laws. For example, to understand Newton's laws of motion, one's conception of motion must change from seeing rest as the natural state of objects to seeing movement at a constant velocity as the natural state. The study by McCloskey et al. (1980) shows that students may enter the learning situation with certain preexisting conceptions (or misconceptions) of science, so the first step in science education should be to help students recognize the inadequacies of their conceptions.

In their theory of conceptual change, Posner et al. (1982) point to detection of anomalies as the first step in science learning.

> There must be dissatisfaction with existing conceptions. [S]tudents
> are unlikely to make major changes in their concepts until they
> believe that less radical changes will not work. . . . [A]n individual
> must have collected a store of . . . anomalies and lost faith in the
> capacity of his current concepts to solve these problems. (p. 214)

The first step toward meaningful learning is to recognize that one's current conceptions are unable to explain the available data.

In this section, let's pursue the second view of science education by focusing on learning explanations rather than solely on learning descriptions. In particular, additional examples of misconceptions of physics will be presented, and educational implications will be drawn.

RESEARCH ON LEARNERS' MISCONCEPTIONS OF PHYSICS

THE CLIFF PROBLEM. Consider a cartoon character who runs over a cliff and falls into the valley below, as shown in Figure 6–4. With a pencil, draw the path that the falling body will follow. Figure 6–5 shows four possible answers:

FIGURE 6–4 How does a moving object fall over a cliff?

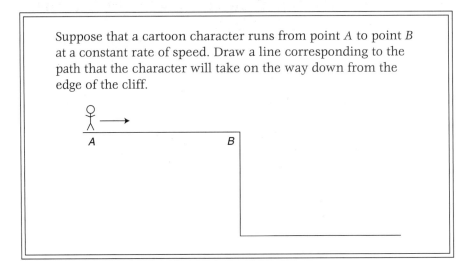

Suppose that a cartoon character runs from point *A* to point *B* at a constant rate of speed. Draw a line corresponding to the path that the character will take on the way down from the edge of the cliff.

FIGURE 6–5 Four paths for a falling body

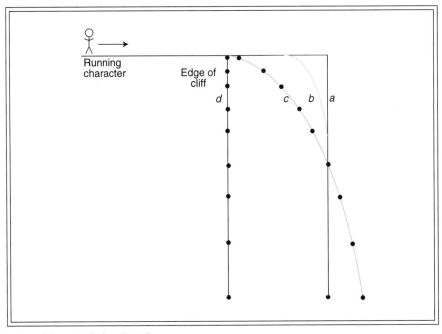

Adapted from McCloskey (1983)

1. It will go on for some horizontal distance and then fall straight down.
2. It will go on for some horizontal distance and then gradually arc downward.
3. It will immediately arc downward, maintaining a constant forward speed and an accelerating downward speed.
4. It will fall straight down as soon as it leaves the edge of the cliff.

Does your answer correspond to any of these four alternatives?

When high school and college students were asked to make predictions in a similar task, 5% opted for the first answer (these may have been fans of the "Road Runner"), 35% opted for the second, 28% selected the third, and 32% chose the fourth (McCloskey, 1983).

The correct answer is the third—the object will continue to move at the same rate horizontally, since no force has changed its horizontal movement, and will move downward at an accelerating rate, since gravity is acting on it. This answer is based on the modern Newtonian conception of motion—an object will stay in motion unless some force acts upon it.

An alternative conception, similar to the medieval concept that a moving object acquires some internal momentum or "impetus" that keeps it in motion until the momentum is dissipated, is consistent with the first and second answers. This view was expressed by the student who said, "It's something that carries an object along after a force on it has stopped. Let's call it the force of motion. It's something that keeps the body moving" (McCloskey, 1983, p. 125). Thus this student seems to believe that a moving object requires a force to keep it moving. Students also seem to believe that the ball will drop when the momentum is dissipated: "I understand that friction and air resistance adversely affect the speed of the ball, but not how. Whether they absorb some of the force that's in the ball . . ." (McCloskey, 1983, p. 126). As can be seen, students are expressing the medieval impetus theory that a moving object is kept moving by its own internal force and that movement is affected as the internal force dissipates. This view, while intuitively appealing, is inconsistent with the modern Newtonian view that objects do not require any force to continue moving at a constant speed (or to remain at rest). Instead, an external force is required to alter the velocity of a moving (or resting) body.

THE BALL PROBLEM. As another example of students' misconceptions of motion, consider the problem shown in Figure 6–6. In this problem, suppose that you are running forward at a constant speed with a heavy ball in your hand. As you are running, you drop the ball. Where will the ball land? Choose a line in Figure 6–7 corresponding to the path that the ball will take once you drop it.

As in the study involving the cliff, the most popular answer was consistent with the impetus theory—49% of the students predicted that the ball would fall straight down. Six percent thought the ball would move backward as it fell, and only 45% gave the Newtonian answer that the ball would move forward as it fell. In fact, the ball will continue to move

FIGURE 6–6 Where will the ball fall?

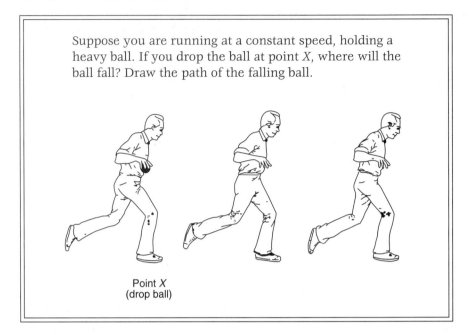

Suppose you are running at a constant speed, holding a heavy ball. If you drop the ball at point X, where will the ball fall? Draw the path of the falling ball.

Point X
(drop ball)

forward at the same rate as the runner and will move downward at an accelerating rate. Using a similar task, Kaiser, Proffitt, and McCloskey (1985) found that elementary school children were far more likely to give incorrect answers than adults.

You may be wondering whether training in physics helps to reduce learners' misconceptions of motion. To examine this question, McCloskey (1983) gave a modified version of the ball problem to college students who

FIGURE 6–7 Three possible paths for a falling ball

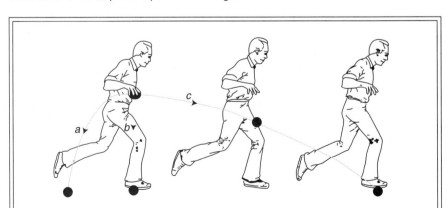

Adapted from McCloskey (1983)

FIGURE 6–8 The coin problem

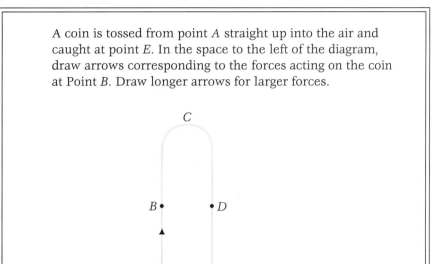

A coin is tossed from point *A* straight up into the air and caught at point *E*. In the space to the left of the diagram, draw arrows corresponding to the forces acting on the coin at Point *B*. Draw longer arrows for larger forces.

had taken no physics courses and to college students who had taken at least one physics course. In this study, 80% of the nontrained students thought the ball would drop straight down, whereas only 27% of the physics-trained group opted for this "impetus" view; alternatively, 13% of the nontrained students thought the ball would continue forward after being dropped, compared to 73% of the trained group. Thus, while training in physics shows some positive effect, more than one-quarter of the trained students still held non-Newtonian conceptions of motion. In addition, McCloskey (1983) noted that some ideas are particularly resistant to instruction, such as the belief that impetus acquired when an object is set into motion serves to keep the object in motion. For example, 93% of the students held this belief prior to instruction in physics, and 80% retained it even after instruction.

THE COIN PROBLEM. Clement (1982) provides additional evidence concerning students' preconception that "motion implies a force." For example, a group of college engineering students, most with previous course work in high school physics, was given the coin problem shown in Figure 6–8.

Figure 6–9 shows both the correct answer on the left and the most typical incorrect answer on the right. The overwhelming majority of students (88%) gave incorrect answers based on the idea that if an object is moving upward, there must be some force acting on it. A typical student explanation is as follows:

FIGURE 6–9 Two answers to the coin problem

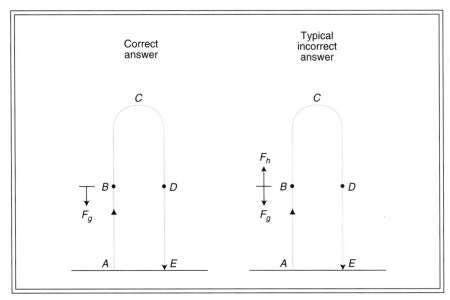

Adapted from Clement (1982)

So there's the force going up and there is the force of gravity pushing it down. And the gravity is less because the coin is still going up until it gets to C. [Draws upward arrow labeled "force of the throw" and shorter downward arrow labeled "gravity" at point B in the figure.] If the dot goes up, the force of the arrow gets less and less because gravity is pulling down on it, pulling down. (Clement, 1982, p. 68)

THE ROCKET PROBLEM. Another problem from Clement's (1982) study is shown in Figure 6–10. Figure 6–11 shows the correct answer, based on Newtonian physics, on the left, and the most common incorrect answer on the right. As in the coin problem, the overwhelming majority of students opted for incorrect answers. Apparently, students come to college with the preconception that motion implies a force, which can be summarized as follows: if an object is moving, there is a force acting upon it; changes in speed or direction occur because the force increases or decreases.

Does a college course in mechanics affect students' conceptions of motion? Table 6–1 shows the percentage of correct answers on the coin and the rocket problems for students before and after a mechanics course. As can be seen, the course tends to double the number of correct responses; however, the error rates are still over 75%. Thus preconceptions built up over a lifetime seem resistant to schooling.

FIGURE 6–10 What is the path of the rocket?

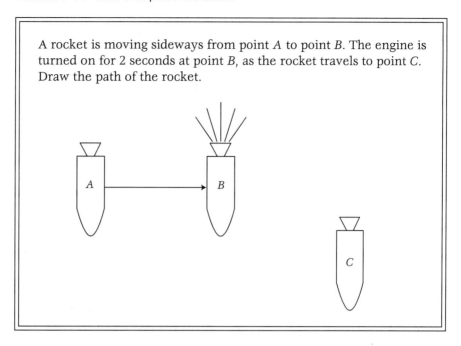

A rocket is moving sideways from point *A* to point *B*. The engine is turned on for 2 seconds at point *B*, as the rocket travels to point *C*. Draw the path of the rocket.

FIGURE 6–11 Two answers to the rocket problem

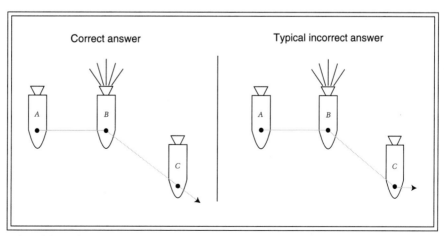

Correct answer   Typical incorrect answer

Adapted from Clement (1982)

TABLE 6–1		Percentage Correct on Coin Problem	Percentage Correct on Rocket Problem
Correct conceptions of motion before and after instruction	Before instruction	12%	11%
	After instruction	28%	23%

Adapted from Clement (1982)

OTHER MISCONCEPTIONS. Similarly, misconceptions have been observed in students' understanding of other scientific concepts, including gravity (Gunstone & White, 1981), acceleration (Trowbridge & McDermott, 1981), density (Novick & Nussbaum, 1978, 1981), living versus nonliving (Carey, 1985; Tamir, Gal-Choppin, & Nussinovitz, 1981), chemical equilibrium (Wheeler & Kass, 1978), heat (Erickson, 1979), and the earth as a cosmic body (Nussbaum, 1979; Vosniadou & Brewer, 1992). For example, Nussbaum (1979) found evidence of a developmental progression in children's conception of the earth as a cosmic body. Fourth-graders viewed the earth as flat, with "down" being toward the "bottom" of the cosmos. Sixth-graders envisioned the earth as round, but "down" still referred to a direction with respect to some cosmic "bottom." Eighth-graders viewed the world as round and tended to see "down" as a direction with respect to the center of the earth. These were the dominant views at each age level, but there was also much variation within each age group.

In reviewing the research on misconceptions of elementary school children (ages eight to eleven), Osborne and Wittrock (1983) found the following examples: "light from a candle goes further at night," "friction only occurs between moving surfaces," "electric current is used up in a light bulb," "a worm is not an animal," "gravity requires the presence of air," "force is a quantity in a moving object in the direction of motion," and "the bubbles in boiling water are bubbles of air." In addition, they reported that as children get older—and presumably learn more school science—some of their misconceptions actually increase before ultimately improving by ages sixteen to eighteen. However, in another review of misconceptions studies, Eylon and Linn (1988) found that adults possess many misconceptions, including the ideas that heat and temperature are the same, that heavier objects displace more liquid than lighter objects, and that objects move in the direction they are pushed.

IMPLICATIONS FOR INSTRUCTION: CONFRONTING STUDENTS' MISCONCEPTIONS

The research on students' misconceptions of scientific principles is both frustrating and challenging for science teachers. The results are frustrating because they suggest that students come to the science classroom with many preconceptions that are somewhat resistant to traditional instruction. However, the results are also challenging because they suggest a technique for teaching that is aimed specifically at helping students to revise their scientific intuitions and conceptions.

Consider the following two scenarios. In classroom A, the teacher lectures on the nature of heat flow and gives a demonstration. The teacher pours some water into one beaker and some oil into another, places a thermometer into each beaker, puts the beakers on a hot plate, and turns the hot plate on. Within a few minutes the water is boiling, and the teacher asks a student to read the thermometers on the two beakers. Then, he explains why the oil is hotter than the water. Pleased that the class has learned an important lesson, the teacher dismisses the class.

In classroom B, the teacher has reason to suspect that students harbor misconceptions concerning the mechanisms underlying heat flow. She takes two beakers, fills one with water and one with cooking oil, places a thermometer in each, and puts both beakers on a hot plate. She tells the class that she is going to turn on the hot plate until the water boils and asks them to predict how the temperatures will compare when the water reaches a boil. Some students predict that the oil temperature will be lower because "it has not boiled yet." Other students predict that the temperatures will be the same because both beakers have been heated on the hot plate for the same amount of time. Then, students observe what happens by reading the two thermometers when the water is boiling and discover that the oil is hotter than the water. Finally, they must explain why their predictions conflicted with their observations. Both predictions are based on concepts that the teacher would not expect and that would not be exposed through the demonstration method. Although many students recognize that their current theory of heat and temperature is inadequate, few are able to generate an explanation that the teacher would accept. In spite of the students' failures to generate correct predictions, the teacher is pleased. She has exposed a major misconception. That is enough for today, and tomorrow she will help students build an explanation.

The scenario in classroom A is based on the view of science learning as the addition of facts to one's repertoire, whereas the scenario in classroom B follows from the conceptual-change view of science learning. White and Gunstone (1992) refer to the second scenario as predict-observe-explain (POE) and point out its advantages over the demonstration method used in the first scenario. In the predict-observe-explain method, students predict what will happen, observe what happens, and explain why their observations conflict with their predictions. As Clement (1982) and Posner et al. (1982) point out, it is not appropriate to assume that the student's mind is a blank slate. Instead, instructional techniques should take a student's beliefs into account. Much of science instruction involves helping students to change their preconceptions of science. For example, Minstrell (cited in McCloskey, 1983) has developed a technique for directly challenging students' misconceptions of motion. Students are presented with problems, such as the ones in the Figures 6–1, 6–4, 6–6, 6–8, and 6–10, and are asked to verbalize their conceptions. The students' conceptions can then be compared to Newtonian conceptions, and the differences can be explicitly pointed out. Minstrell has been successful in changing students' intuitive physics from the medieval impetus view to the modern Newtonian view.

When students' conceptions of real-world physical events conflict with the conceptions underlying school science, students have several options. A common strategy used by students is to learn one set of rules for school science and another for the real world (West & Pines, 1985). In contrast, some students may discard their preexisting conceptions and replace them with concepts that are consistent with current scientific theories.

To induce this second kind of learning, Champagne, Gunstone, and Klopfer (1985) have developed an instructional program called *ideational confrontation*. Students are first asked to make predictions about a common physical situation, such as the motion of an empty versus a loaded sled going downhill. Next they develop theoretical explanations to support their predictions. Then the instructor demonstrates the physical situation and provides a scientific explanation. In the ensuing discussions, students must reconcile their predictions with the actual results and must replace their ineffective conceptions with new ones. It is clear from the work of Champagne et al. (1985) that instructional procedures like ideational confrontation require a great deal of time and planning, but there is some evidence that the procedure can be effective. Science instruction needs to make use of techniques that will help students discard misconceptions and replace them with correct conceptions of science.

This approach to teaching science is consistent with the general prescription proposed by Ausubel (1968) in his classic book *Educational Psychology:*

> If I had to reduce all of educational psychology to just one
> principle, I would say this: The most important single factor
> influencing learning is what the learner already knows.
> Ascertain this and teach him accordingly. (p. vi)

In science education, this means that the teacher must begin by helping students to recognize the anomalies between what their theories predict and what really happens.

INITIATING CONCEPTUAL CHANGE: CONSTRUCTING A NEW CONCEPTION

THEORY: LEARNING AS ASSIMILATION VERSUS ACCOMMODATION

The traditional and cognitive change approaches to science education offer two fundamentally different views of how students learn—by assimilation versus by accommodation. According to the traditional view, students learn by assimilation; that is, they fit new information into their existing knowledge. For example, if a student learns that water boils at 212 degrees, she can connect this to her existing conception that heat causes temperature change. This results in a modest form of conceptual change—the existing concepts remain the same, but new information is connected to them. The assimilation view is incomplete because it cannot account for radical forms of conceptual change, such as replacing the impetus theory with the Newtonian theory of motion.

In contrast, conceptual-change theory posits that learning can sometimes involve accommodation rather than assimilation. In accommodative learning, the student "must replace or reorganize his central concepts" because the student's "current concepts are inadequate to allow him to grasp some new phenomenon successfully" (Posner et al., 1982, p. 212). In short, the learner must build a new conception that can accommodate the newly presented information. For example, if a student believes that "equal heat produces equal temperature," she will have to replace that concept when she learns that the same amount of heat results in lower temperature when it is applied to a beaker of water than when it is applied to a beaker of oil.

Unfortunately, simply recognizing an anomaly does not guarantee that a student will find an adequate new conception. Posner et al. (1982, p. 214) posit three characteristics of a new conception in accommodative learning. The new conception must be:

Intelligible: The learner must grasp how the new conception works.
Plausible: The learner must see how the new conception is consistent with other knowledge and explains the available data.
Fruitful: The learner must be able to extend the conception to new areas of inquiry.

In short, the new model must make sense to the learner and be useful in solving old and new problems.

Analogies are a major vehicle for lending meaning to a new conception, so they are instrumental in initiating the process of conceptual change. An analogy occurs when a learner can construct a mapping between the parts and relations of a model (which can be called a *base*) and the corresponding parts and relations in a natural system (which can be called a *target*). Gentner (1983, 1989) has proposed a structure-mapping theory in which the objects, attributes, and relations of a base system are matched to the corresponding objects, attributes, and relations of a target system.

For example, consider the electrical circuit shown at the left of Figure 6–12, which consists of a battery, wires, and a resistor. To understand how this system works, a learner could view an electrical circuit as an hydraulic system (or a water-flow system), as shown at the right of Figure 6–12. As you can see, the battery is analogous to a pump, the wire is analogous to a pipe, the resistor is analogous to a constriction in the pipe, and electron flow is analogous to water flow. A relational principle such as "current increases with voltage" is analogous to saying "water flow

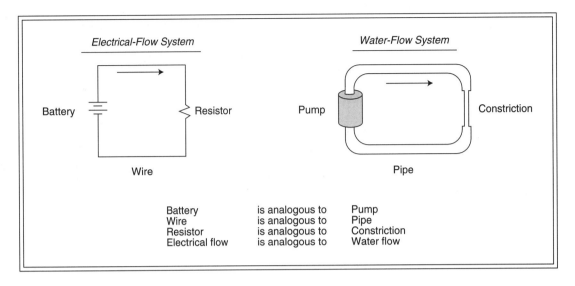

increases with water pressure"; similarly, the relational principle "current decreases with resistance" is analogous to saying "water flow decreases with pipe narrowness." Some of the mappings between the water-flow system and the electrical-flow system are summarized in Figure 6–12. To use an analogical model effectively, a learner must focus on aspects of the model that are relevant and ignore those that are irrelevant. For example, the learner must ignore the characteristics of water, which would, of course, prove to be disastrous if literally applied to an electrical circuit. Gentner and Gentner (1983) and White (1993) found that students often report using a water-flow analogy to solve problems involving electrical circuits or to understand the formal description in Ohm's law: *current = voltage/resistance.* If a student determines that current is like water flow, voltage is like water pressure, and resistance is like a constriction in a pipe, then the learner can use the water-flow analogy to understand the mechanism explaining Ohm's law.

In this section, we explore research and practice in how analogical models can be used to promote conceptual change.

RESEARCH ON EFFECTIVE ANALOGICAL MODELS

What makes a good analogical model? To help answer this question, please read the pump passage in Figure 6–13 and then try to answer the following question: Suppose you push down and pull up on the pump handle several times but no air comes out. What could be wrong? If you experience difficulty in solving this problem, refer to the pump model shown in Figure 6–14. In the pump model, the pump has been simplified so the learner can see that the valves work like one-way doors and the piston in

FIGURE 6-13

A verbal explanation of how a bicycle tire pump works

Bicycle tire pumps vary in the number and location of the valves they have and in the way air enters the cylinder. Some simple bicycle tire pumps have the inlet valve on the piston and the outlet valve at the closed end of the cylinder. A bicycle tire pump has a piston that moves up and down. Air enters the pump near the point where the connecting rod passes through the cylinder. *As the rod is pulled out, air passes through the piston and fills the areas between the piston and the outlet valve. As the rod is pushed in, the inlet valve closes and the piston forces air through the outlet valve.**

*Key information is in italics.
From World Book Encyclopedia (1990)

FIGURE 6-14 Coordinating verbal and visual explanations of how a bicycle tire pump works

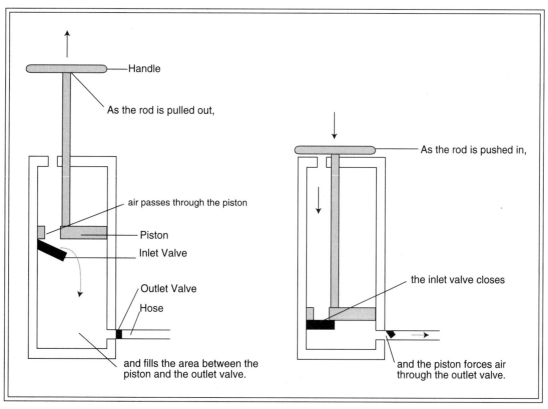

Adapted from Mayer and Gallini (1990)

the cylinder works like a syringe. This may help the learner to build connections between actions stated in the passage, such as "the inlet valve closes," and a mental model of the system, such as a mental image of a one-way door in the pump being forced closed.

If you are like the students in the studies by Mayer and Gallini (1990), you found that the pump model helped you understand how pumps work. Mayer and Gallini (1990) found that students who looked at a model like the one in Figure 6–14 while reading a passage about how pumps work generated nearly twice as many creative solutions to problems as students who read the passage without seeing the model. In a review of nineteen studies, Mayer (1989, 1993) found that when a pictorial model was added to textbook passages on how various systems worked, subsequent problem-solving performance was improved by an average of over 60%.

Although visual models can be effective aids in promoting conceptual change, they are rarely used. In an analysis of science textbooks, Mayer (1993) found that although almost 50% of the space was devoted to illustrations, less than 10% presented analogical models. Similarly, in his survey of 43 science textbooks, Glynn (1991) reported that "elaborate analogies . . . were relatively rare" (p. 228). Glynn, Yeany, and Britton (1991) point out that

> the present science textbooks and methods of instruction do not yet take into account recent discoveries in the psychology of how students learn science. Discoveries about the constructive nature of students' learning, about students' mental models, and about students' misconceptions have important implications for teachers. (p. 5)

In summary, science educators are being asked to accept a new conception of "learning science as a process of construction and reconstruction of personal theories and models" (Glynn et al., 1991, p. 16).

IMPLICATIONS FOR INSTRUCTION: PROMOTING CONCEPTUAL CHANGE

The implications of research on analogical models in science are straightforward: "Science teachers should view instruction as a process of helping students acquire progressively more sophisticated theories of science phenomena" (Glynn et al., 1991, p. 16). How can teachers put this advise into practice? For example, given that students enter the science classroom with serious misconceptions about motion, how can teachers foster conceptual change? What kinds of experiences can foster conceptual change in sixth-graders? How can we reduce or eliminate students' misconceptions? Is it possible to design instruction that will help students to perform better than untrained students on a test of physics concepts?

In an effort to answer these questions, White (1993) designed a computer-based microworld called "ThinkerTools," which is intended to help students acquire the concepts of motion and force. Consistent with the conceptual-change theory proposed by Posner and his colleagues (1982), White gives students experience in making predictions about motion that fail and in developing progressively more sophisticated mental models of how the physical world works. Rather than beginning with a formal statement of the laws of motion, such as $F = ma$, instruction is based on qualitative reasoning about how a microworld works.

Students learn to solve problems in a progression of increasingly sophisticated microworlds. The instructional cycle for each microworld in ThinkerTools consists of four phases—motivation, model evolution, formalization, and transfer. In the motivation phase, the teacher asks students to make predictions about real-world physics problems such as the following:

> Imagine that we have a ball resting on a frictionless surface and we blow on the ball. Then, as the ball is moving along, we give it a blow, the same size as the first, in the opposite direction. What will be the effect of this second blow on the motion of the ball? (White, 1993, p. 10)

The teacher tabulates the students' answers and their reasons. For example, some of the most common answers are that the second blow will (1) make the ball turn around and move in the direction of second blow; (2) make the ball slow down; and (3) make the ball stop. This exercise is designed to motivate students to find out who is right and why.

In the model evolution phase of ThinkerTools, groups of two or more students solve problems presented on a computer screen, as shown in Figure 6–15. In the problem in Figure 6–15, the students' job is to make the dot (specified as a large gray circle) hit the target (specified as a large X) at a speed of four units. If the students succeed, the dot returns to its starting position in preparation for a new problem; if the students fail, the dot crashes into a wall and explodes. There is no gravity or friction to consider, and the students can affect the movement of the dot by using a joystick. Whenever the students pull the joystick in one of the four directions—right, left, up, or down—and pushes the firing button, the dot receives one unit of push in the direction indicated by the joystick. On the screen, a flaming arrow next to the dot indicates the direction of the push, and a swooshing sound indicates that the dot has received a push. Motion is represented by (1) the dot's movement; (2) small dots, called wakes, that are produced on screen at regular time intervals to indicate the history of the dot's movement; and (3) a sort of speedometer, called a datacross, that shows the speed of the dot in each of the four directions. In another exercise, the students' job is to move the dot along an L-shaped path using the joystick.

FIGURE 6–15 A computer-based game for learning physics

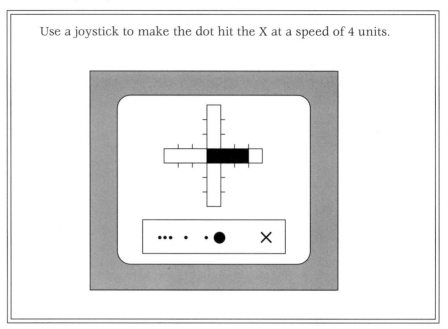

Use a joystick to make the dot hit the X at a speed of 4 units.

Adapted from White (1993)

In the formalization phase of ThinkerTools, small groups of students work at a computer to determine the validity of each of a set of laws, such as the following:

1. If a dot is moving to the right and you apply an impulse to the right, the dot will speed up. [Correct but not general.]
2. Whenever you apply an impulse to the dot, it changes speed. [Correct but not precise.]
3. If you keep giving the dot impulses in the direction that it is moving, it keeps speeding up. If you keep giving it impulses in the direction opposite to that in which it is moving, it slows down, stops, and goes the other way. [Correct, but neither precise nor general.]
4. You can think of the effect of an impulse as adding to or subtracting from the speed of the dot. If applied in the same direction that the dot is moving, it adds a unit of speed; in the opposite direction, it subtracts. [Correct for the one-dimensional micro-world shown in Figure 6–15; this is a useful law because it allows precise predictions for any sequence of impulses.]
5. Whenever you give the dot an impulse to the left, it slows down. [Not correct when the dot is moving left or stopped.]

6. Whenever you give the dot an impulse, it speeds up. [Not correct when the impulse is applied in the direction opposite the dot's motion.]
7. Unless you keep applying impulses to the dot, it will slow down. [Not correct because there is no friction in the microworld.] (White, 1993, p. 13)

Then, the teacher leads a class discussion of whether each law is correct or incorrect, and which of the correct laws is the most useful in generating precise solutions to a variety of problems. Rule 4 is typically selected as the most useful rule because it is correct, precise, and general.

In the transfer phase of ThinkerTools, students are asked to explain how the rule they selected as the most useful relates to a real-world problem such as the one given during the motivation phase. For example, if rule 4 is selected as the most useful rule, students can show how it predicts that the second blow will cause the ball to stop. In addition, they can experiment with real objects or with the microworld. For example, by adding friction to the microworld, they can find that the second blow makes the ball turn around and change direction—a prediction that many students made initially. Thus, they can see that the rules they have developed apply to a frictionless world but not to a world with friction.

After working in a one-dimensional microworld, students move to a two-dimensional world in which the dot can move up and down as well as right and left. Then, the student moves to a microworld in which continuous forces can be created by holding down the button on the joystick to release an impulse every 3/4 of a second. Finally, the students learn about a microworld that involves gravity and that focuses on problems concerning the trajectories of dots.

Does experience with ThinkerTools foster conceptual change in science students? To examine this question, White (1993) gave a test of physics concepts to a group of sixth-graders who had received the ThinkerTools curriculum every school day for 45 minutes over a two-month period (trained group) and to an equivalent group of sixth-graders who had no physics experience (control group). Figure 6–16 shows some of the items on the test, in which students are asked to make predictions about the paths and velocities of moving objects. If the students entered the physics classroom with misconceptions about motion, then we would expect the control group to perform poorly on the test. If experience in the ThinkerTools microworld helps students to change incorrect conceptions into correct ones, then we would expect the trained group to perform well on the test. Consistent with these predictions, the control students gave correct answers to 44% of the problems, whereas trained students gave correct answers to 66%. In summary, these results demonstrate that a carefully planned set of experiences can foster conceptual change in students.

FIGURE 6–16 Sample questions from a test of physics concepts

Suppose that we are trying to get an ice hockey puck to travel along the track shown below. At the beginning of the track, somebody hits the puck in the direction shown. (*Note*: Each hit of the puck has the same intensity.) In which direction—*A*, *B*, or *C*— will somebody need to hit the puck so that it makes the first turn?

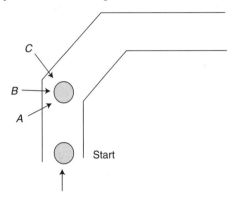

Imagine that you kick a ball sideways off a cliff. Which path will the ball take as it falls to the ground?

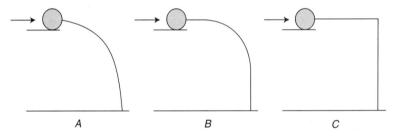

Suppose that two identical boats are trying to cross two identical rivers. The only difference is that one river has a current flowing and the other does not. Both boats have the same motors and leave at the same time. Which boat gets to the other side first?

1. The one crossing the river without a current flowing.
2. The one crossing the river with a current flowing.
3. Both boats get to the other side at the same time.

Adapted from White (1993)

DEVELOPING SCIENTIFIC REASONING: USING A NEW CONCEPTION

THEORY: SCIENTIFIC REASONING AS HYPOTHESIS-TESTING VERSUS HYPOTHESIS CREATION

The previous two sections have shown how conceptual change depends on anomalies and analogies, respectively. The next step in the process of conceptual change is application—being able to use one's knowledge to reason scientifically through experiments. This section compares two views of scientific reasoning.

According to the traditional approach, scientific reasoning is a process of hypothesis-testing in which a learner systematically tests each possible hypothesis. Systematic hypothesis-testing is at the heart of Piaget's (1972; Inhelder & Piaget, 1958) formal operational thought and represents a well-recognized form of scientific reasoning. Formal operational thought, expected to occur during adolescence, is the highest level of cognitive development. It involves the ability to think in terms of abstractions, symbols, probabilities, and proportions, and to consider many variables or dimensions at the same time. Each of these skills is a crucial component in scientific tasks such as understanding the principles of motion in physics.

Conceptual-change theory suggests a second kind of scientific reasoning—hypothesis creation. What happens in situations where systematic hypothesis-testing fails? When your pool of hypotheses is exhausted, you need a new way of looking at the problem that will allow you to generate new hypotheses. Hypothesis creation occurs when a learner has rejected all hypothesis derived from one conception of the problem, and now must generate new hypothesis based on a new conception of the problem. According to conceptual-change theory, an account of scientific reasoning that ignores hypothesis creation is incomplete.

RESEARCH ON STUDENTS' SCIENTIFIC THINKING

HYPOTHESIS-TESTING. Most science textbooks and instructional programs assume that high school and college students are capable of scientific thinking. However, there is some startling evidence that some students may enter the science classroom without the prerequisite skills required for scientific thought. For example, many researchers have measured the proportion of college students consistently using formal thought for scientific tasks to be as low as 25% to 50% (Cohen, Hillman, & Agne, 1978; Griffiths, 1976; Kolodiy, 1975; Lawson & Snitgen, 1982; McKinnon & Renner, 1971).

In a major study, Karplus and his colleagues (Karplus, Karplus, Formisano, & Paulsen, 1979) developed two tasks to measure secondary school students' ability to engage in formal thinking—the proportional reasoning task and the control-of-variables task. These tasks were administered to 3,300 secondary school students (generally thirteen to fifteen years old) in seven industrialized countries: Denmark, Sweden, Italy, United States, Austria, Germany, and Great Britain. Figure 6–17 shows an example of a proportional reasoning task, called the paper clip problem. Students are shown sheets of paper containing two stick figures, Mr. Tall and Mr. Short. When the heights of these two characters are measured using rows of large round buttons, it is found that Mr. Tall is six buttons tall and Mr. Short is four buttons tall. Then the students are asked to measure the height of Mr. Short using standard paper clips (the answer is 6), and to figure out the height of Mr. Tall in paper clips as well. In addition, students are asked to explain how they figured out the height of Mr. Tall.

Student answers can be classified as follows:

Intuitive: This approach either does not fully use the available data or uses the data in an illogical way. Examples of students' intuitive explanations include, "The way I got that Mr. Tall is 12 paper clips is I just doubled 6 buttons," and "I added 6 and 4 together."

Additive: This approach uses a single difference between Mr. Tall and Mr. Short (such as their height difference in buttons) uncoordinated with other differences, and solves the problem by adding this difference to some number. For example, one student said, "If Mr. Tall is 6 buttons and Mr. Short is 4 buttons, that is a difference of 2. Now Mr. Short is 6 paper clips tall, so I took the 2 and added it to 6 and got 8."

FIGURE 6–17 A proportional reasoning task: The paper clip problem

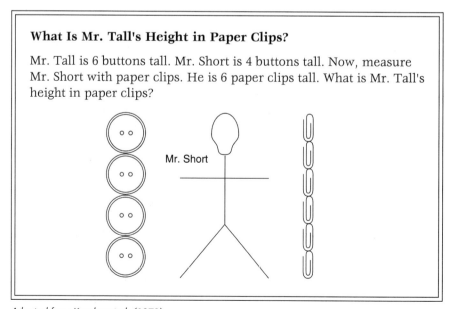

What Is Mr. Tall's Height in Paper Clips?

Mr. Tall is 6 buttons tall. Mr. Short is 4 buttons tall. Now, measure Mr. Short with paper clips. He is 6 paper clips tall. What is Mr. Tall's height in paper clips?

Mr. Short

Adapted from Karplus et al. (1979)

Transitional: This approach partially uses proportional reasoning, but fails to generate a completely correct procedure. For example, one student said, "I divided 4 into 6; 4 is how many buttons Mr. Short is and 6 is the amount of paper clips, and I got 1 1/2. Then I added 6, the amount of buttons of Mr. Tall, to 1 1/2 and got 7 1/2."

Ratio: This is the correct procedure for answering the paper clip problem, and involves deriving a proportion or ratio, and using the proportion to generate the answer. For example, one student said, "I got this by putting their height in buttons into a fraction (4/6) and by putting their height in paper clips into a fraction (6/x) and solved it. The result is 9." Another example is, "1 button = 1 1/2 paper clips; 1 1/2 × 6 = 9."

The results of the study are not encouraging. Figure 6–18 shows the percentage of U.S. students using each of the four strategies (based on two proportional reasoning tasks). As can be seen, very few students use the ratio procedure, with the most commonly used method being the intuitive strategy.

FIGURE 6–18 Performance of U.S. students on a proportional reasoning task

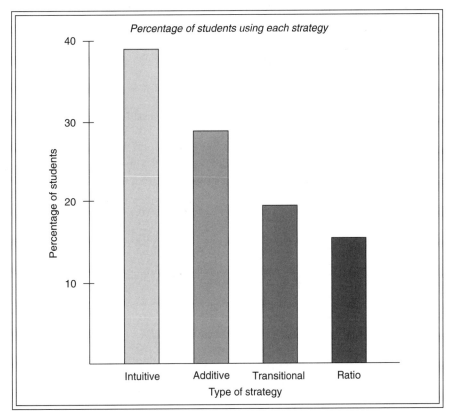

Adapted from Karplus et al. (1979)

The same general pattern of results was obtained in each of the seven countries that Karplus et al. (1979) studied. However, students in selective European schools scored much higher than Americans in ratio thinking (e.g., 75% consistently used ratio in a selective British school and 64% in a selective German school). In a pilot study, Karplus et al. (1979) found that 92% of the students from a highly selective Chinese elementary school used proportional reasoning in tasks like the paper clip problem.

Another problem used by Karplus et al. (1979), is the control-of-variables task. In this problem, the student is shown a track with a target ball in it, as shown in Figure 6–19. The student is told that if she rolls another ball down the track, it will collide with the target and make it move some distance. The student has the option of using a heavy metal ball or a light glass ball (both of equal size), and of placing it either high, medium, or low in the track. They are then asked a series of questions to determine whether they understand how to control variables during experimentation, such as:

> Suppose you want to know how much difference the weight of the ball makes in how far the target goes. You are going to use two balls on the target. Where would you start the heavy ball? Where would you start the light ball? Please explain your answers carefully. (p. 101)

Karplus et al. (1979) discovered that students gave three types of answers to this question:

FIGURE 6–19 A control-of-variables task: The track problem

A heavy- or lightweight ball may be placed in either a high, medium, or low position on the track. How does the weight of the ball affect how far the target ball will move?

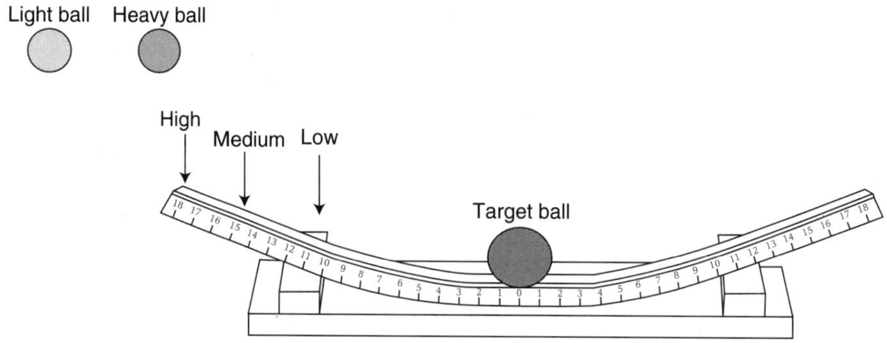

Adapted from Karplus et al. (1979)

Intuitive: This approach allows for any starting position. For example, one student said, "I would start the heavy sphere at medium to see if, even though the sphere is heavy, it will make a difference. I started the light one at high so it would pick up speed and knock the ball far."

Transitional: This approach calls for starting the balls at the same position, but does not provide a complete rationale. For example, a student explained, "Start them at the same place and give them the same speed, then measure how far the target goes up the other side."

Control: This approach calls for starting the balls at the same place and stating that equality of conditions is crucial. For example, one student reasoned, "The main reason of this experiment is the weight difference, so you would have to keep all other factors the same."

Figure 6–20 shows the percentage of U.S. students who used each approach to a control-of-variables problem. The results of this study, like those of the proportional reasoning study, are not encouraging. Again, similar patterns were obtained in each of the industrialized countries studied.

These results, based on a large sample of students, clearly corroborate the findings of other researchers that the development of formal thought cannot be assumed to be complete in adolescents. Overall, Karplus et al. (1979) found 251 students (or about 7% of their sample) who consistently

FIGURE 6–20 Performance of U.S. students on a control-of-variables task

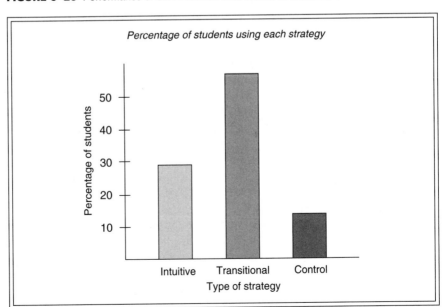

Adapted from Karplus et al. (1979)

used a ratio strategy on the paper clip task and a control strategy on the track task; in contrast, they identified 422 students (or about 14%) who consistently used intuitive reasoning on all clip-task questions and all track-task questions. Based on their total sample of 3,300 students, Karplus et al. (1979) found that about 37% of eighth-graders do not use formal operational thinking in either the proportional reasoning or control-of-variable task, and that another 36% fail to use formal operational thinking on both types of tasks. Thus the majority of eighth-graders do not consistently show evidence of formal operational reasoning.

HYPOTHESIS CREATION. How do people make scientific discoveries? For example, suppose that you wanted to discover how the genes in the simple bacterium *E. coli* control the production of glucose, which is needed for the bacterium to live. When lactose is present, the *E. coli* secretes enzymes, called beta-gal, that convert the lactose into glucose. The top panel of Figure 6–21 shows some of the genes that may be involved in glucose production: the beta-genes produce beta-gal, which converts lactose into glucose, whereas the I-gene, P-gene, and/or O-gene may be involved in controlling the beta genes.

Let's try an experiment that is simulated on a computer screen. Suppose you allow 100 micrograms of lactose, represented as a large white square, to enter the *E. coli*. As soon as the lactose is under the beta genes, they produce 50 micrograms of beta-gal, represented as small black rectangles. The beta-gal (small black rectangles) breaks the lactose (large white rectangle) into glucose, which is represented as white triangles. This reaction takes about 12 seconds and is summarized in the bottom three panels of Figure 6–21.

Suppose that you can conduct experiments by manipulating three variables and seeing the results simulated on the screen. First, you select one of six amounts of lactose to be input—0, 100, 200, 300, 400, or 500 micrograms. Second, you select one of four types of mutations—normal *E. coli*, I-gene mutation, P-gene mutation, or O-gene mutation. In this experiment, only one gene can be mutated on a chromosome. If a gene is mutated, it does not work. Third, you select one of two chromosome structures—haploid, which contains one set of genes, and diploid, which contains two sets of genes so a gene can be mutated on one chromosome but not the other and vice versa. If the I-gene, P-gene, or O-gene controls the beta genes by chemical signal, then the beta-genes will produce beta-gal as long as one of the two chromosomes contains the needed genes. If the I-gene, P-gene, or O-gene controls the beta-genes by physical contact, then beta-gal will be produced only when the activator gene is on the same chromosome as the enzyme-producing genes. For each experiment, you learn how much beta-gal was produced. The goal is to determine what controls how much beta-gal is produced.

What is your initial hypothesis? If you are like the subjects in a study conducted by Dunbar (1993), you might begin by hypothesizing that one of the genes (such as the P-gene) activates the production of beta-gal. Based on the first study, in which 100 units of lactose were input and 50 units of

FIGURE 6–21 How do genes in *E. coli* control production of glucose?

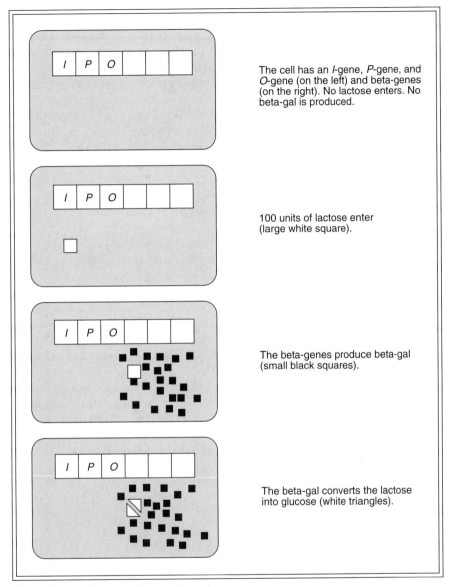

The cell has an *I*-gene, *P*-gene, and *O*-gene (on the left) and beta-genes (on the right). No lactose enters. No beta-gal is produced.

100 units of lactose enter (large white square).

The beta-genes produce beta-gal (small black squares).

The beta-gal converts the lactose into glucose (white triangles).

Adapted from Dunbar (1993)

beta-gal were output, you may have the idea that when a certain amount of lactose is input, the beta-genes in normal *E. coli* will produce half that amount of beta-gal. To test your hypothesis, you introduce 200 micrograms of lactose into a haploid with a P-gene mutation. If the P-gene activates the production of beta-gal, then no beta-gal should be produced. However, when you conduct the experiment you find that 100 micrograms of beta-gal were produced, the same amount as you would expect for normal *E. coli.*

Undaunted, you may now try a new hypothesis—namely, that the I-gene activates beta-gal production. However, when 200 micrograms of lactose are put into a haploid with a mutated I-gene, 876 micrograms of beta-gal are produced. Clearly, the hypothesis is not supported. Similarly, to test the hypothesis that the O-gene activates the beta-genes, you put 200 micrograms of lactose into a haploid with a mutated O-gene. In contrast to your prediction, 527 micrograms of beta-gal are produced. These results are summarized in Table 6–2. Overall, normal E. coli and E. coli with P-gene mutations produce an amount of beta-gal that is half the amount of lactose added; E-coli with a mutated I-gene produces 527 units of beta-gal, regardless of how much lactose is added; and E-coli with a mutated O-gene produces 876 micrograms of beta-gal, regardless of how much lactose is added.

Dunbar (1993) found that all 20 of the subjects in his experiment began with the hypothesis that one of the genes—either I, O, or P—detected the presence of lactose and activated the beta-genes to produce of beta-gal. However, these hypothesis generated predictions that conflicted with the results—in no case did a mutated gene result in zero production of beta-gal. After an hour of experimentation, most of the subjects concluded that all three genes worked in combination as activators, a conclusion that is inconsistent with the data but consistent with their initial view that the genes are activators.

In contrast, seven subjects constructed a radically different hypothesis that involved inhibition, and of these, four subjects actually discovered the correct hypothesis—that the I- and O-genes worked together as inhibitors as follows: when no lactose is present, the I-gene sends an inhibitor that binds to the O-gene, blocking the production of beta-gal by the beta-genes. When lactose is introduced, the inhibitor (which is produced by the I-gene) binds with the lactose and not the O-gene. Thus, the beta-genes are no longer inhibited, so they produce beta-gal. After the beta-gal converts all of the lactose to glucose, the E. coli returns to the inhibited state until more lactose is added. A Nobel Prize was awarded to Jacques Monod and Francois Jacob in 1965 for the discovery of this mechanism.

TABLE 6–2

Results of experiments with E. coli

Cell Type	Mutated Genes	Amount of Lactose Input	Amount of Beta-Gal Output
Haploid	None	100	50
Haploid	P	200	100
Haploid	I	200	876
Haploid	O	200	527

Adapted from Dunbar (1993)

FIGURE 6–22

Two approaches to scientific discovery

AN ACTIVATION-THEORY STUDENT SEEKS TO CONFIRM A HYPOTHESIS

"Right now, my objective is to find a way such that nothing is produced. That's my objective. Um. Ok. So, so far I've tried the combinations of *O* absent. I've tried the combination of *I* absent. *O* absent, *I* absent. Uh . . . *I* present, *O* present, *P* present, it gives me 200. If I take away the *P*, it gives me 876. No, if I take away *I*, it gives me a much much greater amount. . . . Question: How to . . . how to make nothing appear? Have I tried all the combinations?"

AN INHIBITION-THEORY STUDENT SEEKS TO EXPLAIN A DISCREPANCY

"As long as there's lactose present there's beta; you can break it down into glucose. In this case [points to the result for the *I*-gene mutant] they seem to be unregulated. They produce this much [points to an output of 876]. Why do they produce 876?"

From Dunbar (1993)

Why did some students retain their initial activation theory of how genes control enzyme production, whereas other people are able to invent a new theory based on inhibition? Both groups conducted about the same number of experiments, but they differed in their goals. The activation-theory people focused on trying to find a situation in which no beta-gal was produced, that is, on finding a situation that confirmed their hypothesis. The inhibition-theory people focused on trying to discover why *E. coli* with mutated I-genes or O-genes produced such large outputs of beta-gal, that is, on finding an explanation for an anomaly. Sample comments that subjects made as they solved the problem are given in Figure 6–22. These results are consistent with the findings from other research on scientific reasoning in which unsuccessful problem-solvers displayed *confirmation bias*—a strategy of trying to find evidence to support one's theory (Klahr & Dunbar, 1988; Klayman & Ha, 1987). Chinn and Bewer (1993) identified six strategies that science students use to discount anomalous data and therefore avoid conceptual change.

IMPLICATIONS FOR INSTRUCTION: TEACHING SCIENTIFIC REASONING

In essence the science educator is confronted with two different conceptions of scientific inquiry: scientific reasoning as the systematic testing of hypotheses and scientific reasoning as the creation of hypotheses.

Although Piagetian research on formal operations emphasized the generality of hypothesis-testing strategies (Inhelder & Piaget, 1958), more recent research on conceptual change has pointed to the domain specificity of scientific discovery (Carey, 1986; West & Pines, 1985). For example, Kuhn, Amsel, and O'Loughlin (1988) note:

> The lack of generality of formal operational strategies across a range of content . . . has left science educators wondering whether it is reasonable to suppose that they reflect developmental stages in scientific thinking, appropriate as the focus of attention of educators wishing to design curricula to develop scientific thinking skills. (p. 232)

According to the systematic testing view, students need training in how to systematically test their hypotheses, including training in how to control for extraneous variables. In short, they must overcome unsystematic or illogical hypothesis-testing. According to the conceptual-change view, students need to learn to seize on discrepancies or anomalies as interesting facts to be explained, and to seek alternative theories that can better account for the data. In other words, they need to overcome the tendency to seek data that confirm their theory and to ignore discrepant data.

TEACHING HYPOTHESIS-TESTING. An important educational question that emerges from this research is whether scientific thinking can be taught. To address this question, Lawson and Snitgen (1982) used an inquiry-based approach to a college course entitled "Biological Science for the Elementary Teacher." Students were given problems, asked to generate experiments, carry them out, and to compare their results with other students. For example, students were asked to determine the energy source(s) for growing plants. This required systematically varying variables such as watering, lighting, and soil composition, and noting their effects on various seed parts. Concepts relevant to the control of variables were introduced during the discussion and applied in subsequent experiments. A similar procedure was used to introduce examples of proportional reasoning.

Students were given pretests and posttests. Figure 6–23 shows that there were substantial pretest-to-posttest gains in performance on tests of proportional reasoning and control-of-variables—both of which were explicitly taught as part of the inquiry-based course; however, scores on tests of conservation of weight and volume were not affected by instruction and were not explicitly part of the instruction. These results are promising because they suggest that scientific reasoning can be taught through a carefully planned inquiry-based approach to science, and are consistent with previous experiments that successfully increased scientific thinking (i.e., formal thinking) in science students (Lawson & Wollman, 1976;

FIGURE 6–23 Changes in scientific thinking following training

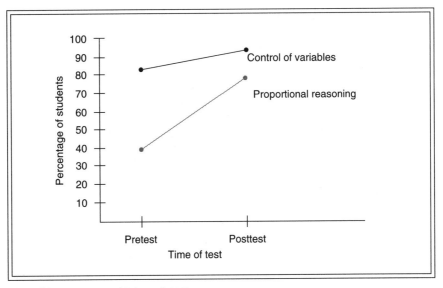

Adapted from Lawton and Snitgen (1982)

McKinnon & Renner, 1971; Wollman & Lawson, 1978). However, the findings must be viewed critically in light of the fact that no control group received noninquiry training.

Hands-on experience is sometimes viewed as a guaranteed means of fostering creativity in students; similarly, the quality of a school's science program is often measured by the amount of laboratory experience given to students. Yet the research presented in this section implies that hands-on laboratory work can be unproductive, especially when students do not approach problems scientifically. It is not lab activity per se that induces science learning; instead, students must be encouraged to think scientifically about situations, to control variables, to test hypotheses, and so on. Thus, while lab experience is an important component in school science programs, it must be administered in a way that fosters scientific thinking rather than blind activity.

TEACHING HYPOTHESIS CREATION. Scientific thinking requires a sensitivity to evidence that refute one's theory. However, Kuhn et al. (1988) found that students often misunderstood the distinction between theory and data. For example, students ranging in age from eight years old to adult were asked to determine which features of tennis balls—such as size, texture, or color—affected the quality of a player's serve. When asked to state whether a certain piece of evidence supported or refuted their theory, students of all ages had difficulty. When asked to suggest evidence that would refute their theory, many were unable to do so. These results are consistent with the idea that many students view data only as evidence that could support rather than refute a theory.

Can students learn to change their view of scientific experimentation? Carey, Evans, Honda, Jay, and Unger (1989) developed a three-week science unit for seventh-graders that focused on students' beliefs about formulating and testing hypotheses. As part of the unit, students made and tested hypotheses about why bread dough rises. They began with the question, "What makes bread rise?" The teacher mixed yeast, flour, sugar, salt, and warm water in a flask with a corked top. Soon the mixture began to bubble and the cork flew off. The next question was "Why do yeast, flour, sugar, salt, and warm water produce a gas?" The students conducted experiments using various combinations of ingredients, but their goal seemed to be to reproduce the bubbling phenomenon. They worked unsystematically and failed to determine which ingredients are needed to produce bubbles. When the teacher asked the students to draw conclusions from their experiments, they were unable to do so. Next the teacher helped the class design well-controlled experiments that revealed that the bubbling is caused by only yeast, sugar, and water. The teacher continued the lesson by emphasizing that the goal of experimentation is to determine why these ingredients produce bubbling. The act of constructing an explanation required the students to consider theories such as the bubbles are caused by a chemical reaction involving the three ingredients or the bubbles are caused by the process of the yeast eating the sugar and producing gas as a result of the metabolism. Here the class learned to seek evidence that could refute or support each theory. Experiments were designed and conducted, and the students had to determine how the results related to the possible explanations. Throughout the lesson, the students were learning that the goal of experimentation is to explain why something happened rather than to produce a certain result.

Carey et al. (1989) assessed the effectiveness of their lesson by interviewing students before and after instruction. Students were asked about the purpose of science, experiments, hypotheses, research ideas, and results. Figure 6–24 lists several levels of answers for the various questions in the interview. For example, a low-level answer concerning experimentation is that "an experiment is when you try something new"—that is, an activity that is not guided by a question or idea. A high-level answer is that "an experiment is when scientists test to see if they need to change their idea." Figure 6–25 summarizes the pretest to posttest gains for each topic. Overall, scores improved substantially, showing that the instructional program was successful in changing students' scientific thinking. Success in teaching of scientific thinking skills has been reported by a growing number of researchers (Eylon & Linn, 1988; Halpern, 1992). These results encourage a revision of science education curricula to emphasize the nature of scientific reasoning as a creative process.

FIGURE 6–24

A survey about
scientific
thinking

The goals of science are:

_____ (1) to discover new things, e.g., "to find a cure for cancer"

_____ (2) to find out how things work, e.g., "to find out how animals get oxygen"

_____ (3) to explain why things are the way they are, e.g., "to explain why the dinosaurs became extinct"

An experiment is:

_____ (0) when you try something new

_____ (1) when scientists try to find out about the thing they're experimenting on

_____ (2) when scientists test to see if their idea is right

_____ (3) when scientists test to see if they need to change their idea

Scientists do their work by:

_____ (0) doing experiments on whatever they feel like

_____ (1) gathering new information, e.g., "putting things under microscopes to see how they behave"

_____ (2) gathering information for a purpose, e.g., "walking through a forest, finding something new, and trying to learn more about it"

_____ (3) creating ideas and testing them, e.g., "probably thinking up an idea, and then building an experiment out of the idea"

An unexpected result shows:

_____ (1) that something needs to be changed to make the experiment come out right

_____ (2) that either the experiment or the scientist's idea must be changed

_____ (3) that the scientist's idea must be changed to fit with the new result

Note: To determine overall score, add the number of points on each item

Adapted from Carey et al. (1989)

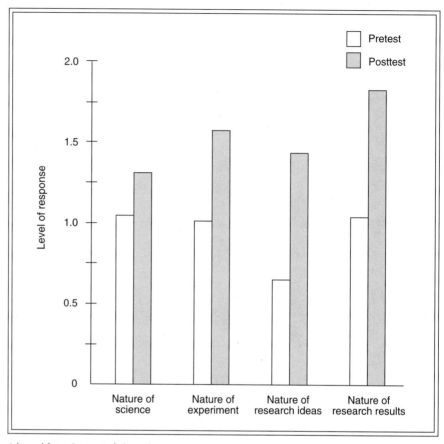

FIGURE 6–25 Pretest and posttest scores of students given a lesson on scientific thinking

Adapted from Carey et al. (1989)

BUILDING SCIENTIFIC EXPERTISE: LEARNING TO BUILD AND USE SCIENTIFIC KNOWLEDGE

THEORY: QUANTITATIVE VERSUS QUALITATIVE DIFFERENCES

The foregoing sections show that science learning involves recognizing one's misconceptions, building new conceptions, and using the new conceptions in scientific reasoning. Another approach to the study of science learning involves comparing novices, such as students in a beginning science course, to experts, such as established scientists. The main question addressed in this approach is, What do experts know that novices do not?

Experts and novices may differ *quantitatively*—in terms of how much they know—as well as *qualitatively*—in terms of what they know. According to a traditional view of cognitive growth, experts simply know more about a domain than novices. For example, an experienced physicist knows more facts and formulas about the physical world than a first-year physics student. In contrast, according to the cognitive-change view, in addition to possessing more facts, an expert's knowledge is qualitatively different from a novice's knowledge. For example, an experienced physicist is not only faster in solving problems but goes about solving problems in a different way than a first-year physics student.

These two contrasting views have important implications for instruction. If becoming an expert is mainly a process of acquiring more and more information, then instruction should emphasize the acquisition of facts and formulas. Instead, if the development of expertise involves a progressive restructuring of knowledge, then instruction must help students not only to acquire facts but also to reorganize their knowledge in useful ways. In short, if experts look at problems differently than novices do, then instruction should encourage novices to think like experts. Research comparing expert and novice physicists provides convincing evidence that the expert-novice shift involves a qualitative change rather than solely a quantitative one (Carey, 1986).

RESEARCH COMPARING NOVICE AND EXPERT PHYSICISTS

Let's begin with a typical problem similar to those found in first-year physics courses (Larkin, McDermott, Simon, & Simon, 1980a, 1980b)—the car problem in Figure 6–26. This problem comes from a domain in physics called *kinematics*. Kinematics involves the study of motion, and the kinematics chapter in a physics textbook generally contains about a dozen formulas expressing relations among variables such as time, distance, average velocity, initial velocity, terminal velocity, and acceleration. Some potentially useful formulas for the car problem are listed in Figure 6–26.

If you have had an introductory physics course and are willing to engage in some serious thinking, you may be able to solve this problem. However, if you are an experienced physicist who has spent many years studying and using physics, you can probably solve this problem almost immediately without much effort. For example, Larkin et al. (1980a, 1980b) found that first-year physics students took four times longer than physics professors to solve problems like this one. This difference in performance prompts the question of what an expert knows about physics that a novice does not.

Mayer (1992) has identified four types of knowledge involved in physics expertise:

Factual knowledge: Basic knowledge of physics, including physical laws such as *force = mass × acceleration*.

Semantic knowledge: Knowledge of the concepts that underlie the variables in physical laws, such as knowing what force, mass, and acceleration mean.

Schematic knowledge: Knowledge of problem types, such as knowing whether a given problem involves conservation of momentum.

FIGURE 6–26 The car problem

A car traveling 25 meters per second is brought to rest at a constant rate in 20 seconds by applying the brake. How far did it move after the brake was applied?

Here are some useful equations:

1. distance = average speed × time
2. final speed = initial speed + (acceleration × time)
3. average speed = (initial speed + final speed)/2
4. distance = (initial speed × time) + 1/2(acceleration) × time^2
5. final speed^2 – initial speed^2 = 2(acceleration × distance)

Adapted from Larkin, McDermott, Simon, and Simon (1980b)

Strategic knowledge: Knowledge of how to generate and monitor plans for solving a problem, such as working backward from the goal to the givens.

In this section, we examine how expert physicists differ from novice physicists in terms of factual knowledge, semantic knowledge, schematic knowledge, and strategic knowledge. These differences are summarized in Table 6–3.

TABLE 6–3	Type of Knowledge	Novices	Experts
Expert versus novice differences in physics	Factual knowledge	Possess small functional units of knowledge	Possess large functional units of knowledge
	Semantic knowledge	Build naive representations	Build physics-based representations
	Schematic knowledge	Categorize based on surface similarities	Categorize based on structural similarities
	Strategic knowledge	Work backward from unknown to givens	Work forward from givens to unknown

Adapted from Mayer (1992)

EXPERT/NOVICE DIFFERENCES IN FACTUAL KNOWLEDGE. Why do experts solve the car problem so much more quickly than novices? One possibility is that experts' factual knowledge is stored more accessibly than novices'. Suppose, for example, that novices store factual knowledge in small or separate units, such as individual formulas:

Formula 1: distance = average speed × time

Formula 3: average speed = (initial speed + final speed)/2

whereas experts store such factual knowledge in large or interconnected units such as combined formulas:

Formulas 1–3: distance = [(initial speed + final speed)/2] × time

Experts can thus work more quickly than novices on problems requiring the use of many equations because they do not have to retrieve as many pieces of information. If experts look for a formula involving distance, they can find what they need by retrieving one large formula, whereas novices would first retrieve formula 1 and then need to search for a formula involving average speed (i.e., formula 3).

In order to examine this hypothesis about expert/novice differences, Larkin (1979) presented kinematics problems like the car problem to first-year physics students (novices) and physics professors (experts). The subjects were asked to "think aloud" as they described what was going on inside their heads as they solved the problem. An analysis of their *thinking-aloud protocols*—the transcripts of what they said as they worked—revealed that experts and novices both generated several formulas but at different rates. Novices produced formulas individually, at a random rate, suggesting that the formulas are stored separately in memory. In contrast, experts produced formulas in clusters, generating some in a rapid burst, followed by a delay and then another burst of multiple formulas. This pattern suggests that experts store their factual knowledge in large units consisting of two or more formulas.

These results are summarized in the top row of Table 6–3: Novices store their factual knowledge of physics as individual equations that are separate from one another (i.e., small units) whereas experts possess interconnected solution equations that can be accessed as a whole (i.e., large units). Thus, while novices have to proceed step-by-step and do a lot of checking, experts are able to solve the problem all at once using a more integrated procedure.

EXPERT/NOVICE DIFFERENCES IN SEMANTIC KNOWLEDGE. A second kind of knowledge needed to solve the car problem is semantic knowledge, that is, knowledge of concepts underlying the problem situation. Physicists need to know not only the formulas but also what the terms in the formulas mean and how they relate to descriptions in physics problems. For example, consider the three-cart problem in Figure 6–27. What do you see when you look over this problem?

FIGURE 6–27 The three-cart problem

What constant horizontal force F must be applied to the large cart (of mass M) in the figure below so that the smaller carts (mass m_1 and m_2) do not move relative to the large cart? Neglect friction.

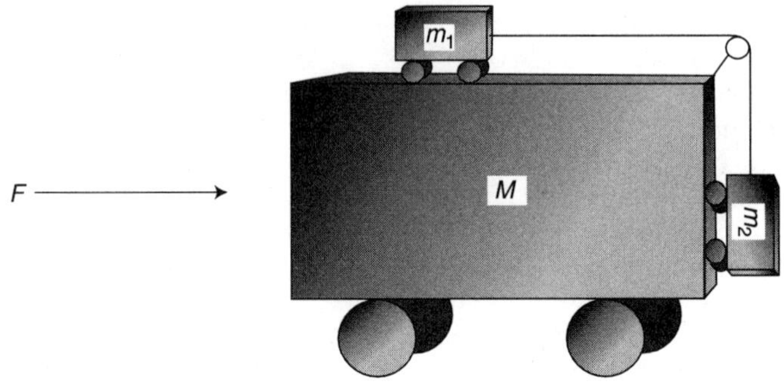

Adapted from Larkin (1983)

If you are like the novices in a study by Larkin (1983), you see the most obvious surface entities: a large cart, two small carts, some ropes, and a pulley. This view is not much help in determining which formulas to use to solve the problem because it does not allow you to make a connection between the surface features of the problem and the underlying physics principles. For example, here's how a typical first-year physics student got stuck in trying to solve the three-cart problem (Larkin, 1983, p. 81):

> Well, I'm right now trying to reason why it isn't going to move. . . .
> Once I visualize it, I can probably get started. But I don't see how it is going to work.

Based on students' thinking-aloud protocols, Larkin (1983) concluded that novices build naive representations of the problem that are not semantically related to physics concepts.

In contrast, if you are like the experts in Larkin's (1983) study, you may be able to see the physics concepts, such as forces, underlying the problem. For example, a typical expert saw beyond the surface features of the problem (Larkin, 1983):

> Well, with a uniformly accelerating frame of reference, all right?
> So that there is a psuedo-force on m_1 to the left that is just
> equivalent, just necessary to balance out the weight of m_2. (p. 81)

According to Larkin's analysis of thinking-aloud protocols, experts tend to build physics-based representations. Instead of seeing ropes and carts, they see an object at rest on an accelerating frame of reference, and they see two forces acting on the small cart—on the left is a psuedoforce caused by the motion of the large cart acting to the left and on the right is a tension force caused by the connection to the pulley.

The second row of Table 6–3 summarizes the conclusion that the novice's representation of the problem is based on surface features, whereas the expert's representation is based on underlying physics conceptions. The expert is better able than the novice to access the appropriate formulas by virtue of being able to view the problem in terms of its underlying physics variables.

EXPERT/NOVICE DIFFERENCES IN SCHEMATIC KNOWLEDGE. A third kind of knowledge needed to solve physics problems is schematic knowledge, that is knowledge of problem types. For example, suppose that you are given several physics problems, such as those in Figure 6–28, and asked to sort them into groups.

Did you put problems 1 and 2 into the same category, and problem 3 into a different category. That's what happened when Chi, Feltovich, and Glaser (1981) asked eight undergraduates (novices) to categorize 24 similar problems like those found in Figure 6–28. According to Chi et al. (1981), the novices sorted the problems based on surface similarities, that is, on the physical characteristics of the objects. For example, novices placed problems involving blocks on an inclined plane (such as problems 1 and 2) in one category, problems involving springs (such as problem 3) in another category, problems involving pulleys in another, and so on. When the novices were asked to justify putting problems 1 and 2 in the same category, they emphasized the similarities in their physical features, saying, "These deal blocks on an inclined plane," or "blocks on inclined planes with angles," or "inclined plane problems."

In contrast, when Chi et al. (1981) asked eight advanced physics graduate students (experts) to sort the problems, they placed problems 2 and 3 into one category and problem 1 into a different one. If you did the same, you are thinking like an expert. According to Chi et al. (1981), experts cat-

FIGURE 6–28 Which two problems belong in the same category?

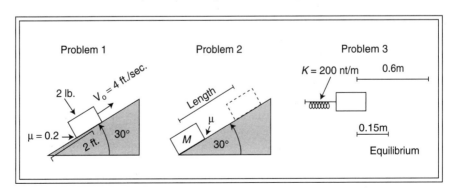

Adapted from Chi, Feltovich, and Glaser (1981)

egorize the problems based on structural similarities, that is, on the physics principle required to solve them. For example, problems 2 and 3, although involving different objects, both are based on the law of conservation of energy, so experts put them together. When asked to explain why they placed problems 2 and 3 in the same category, experts gave answers such as, "conservation of energy," or "work-energy theorem," or "These can be done from energy considerations; either you should know the principle of conservation of energy or work is lost somewhere."

In summary, experts and novices seem to possess different categories for problems. As shown in the third row of Table 6–3, novices base their categories on surface similarities, whereas experts base theirs on structural similarities.

EXPERT/NOVICE DIFFERENCES IN STRATEGIC KNOWLEDGE. A fourth difference between experts and novices concerns their solution strategies. For example, suppose I were to ask you to describe what you are thinking as you solve the car problem shown in Figure 6–26. When Larkin et al. (1980a, 1980b) asked first-year physics students (novices) to do this, they tended to work backward from the goal to the given. When dealing with the car problem, a novice begins by asking, "What am I trying to find?" and determines that the main unknown is the distance the car travels. Then, the novice decides to use Formula 1 because it is the best-known formula involving distance. The next step is to look for the values of average speed and time in the problem. The novice finds average time—20 seconds—but not average speed. Again, the novice asks, "What am I trying to find?" and decides that it is average speed. She remembers a formula involving average speed—namely, formula 3—and then searches for the values of initial speed and final speed. She finds initial speed (25 meters per second) but becomes confused, not realizing that the final speed must be 0 meters per second. Having failed to solve formula 3, the novice looks for another formula involving distance and finds formula 4. Trying to solve for distance in formula 4, she sees that the problem contains values for initial speed (25 meters per second) and time (20 seconds) but not for acceleration. Her next goal is to find an equation involving acceleration, so she selects formula 2. This time she also finds values for initial speed, final speed, and time, and therefore is able to compute a value for acceleration using formula 2. She now can plug this value into formula 4 and derive a value for distance. Thus, the novice works backward, beginning with what she is trying to find and moving toward the givens. In the process she uses formulas 1, 3, 4, 2, and 4, in that order.

In contrast, when Larkin et al. (1980a, 1980b) asked experienced physicists to solve this problem, they tended to work forward from the givens to the unknown. For example, an expert begins by using formula 3, which calls for adding initial speed (25 meters per second) to final speed (0 meters per second), and dividing the sum by 2 to determine average speed (12.5 meters per second). Then, the expert plugs the newly calculated value of average speed (12.5 meters per second) and the value of time (20 seconds) from the problem into formula 1, yielding a value for distance: $12.5 \times 20 = 250$ meters. Thus, the expert solves the problem by working forward, that is, by systematically combining the given values to produce a calculated value of the unknown.

As a way of further testing these observations, Larkin et al. (1980a, 1980b) produced a computer program that simulates the problem-solving performance of experts and novices. The expert program works forward and uses large functional units, while the novice program works backward and uses small functional units. The main output of the program is a listing of the order in which formulas were used. The output of the expert program is fairly consistent with that of human experts, and the output of the novice program is fairly consistent with that of the human novices. Thus there is some reason to believe that the simulations correctly describe expert/novice differences.

Why do experts work forward whereas novices work backward? The choice of strategy may be influenced by the way that the subjects store their factual knowledge. If experts store knowledge in large units, as previously described, then they can simply plug values into a large solution formula. However, if novices store knowledge in small units, as previously described, they must figure out how to put the equations together, a process that lends itself to working from the unknown back to the goal. This difference in expert versus novice strategies is summarized in the fourth row of Table 6–3. However, subsequent research in other domains, such as medical expertise, reveals that even experts may work backward when they are given an unfamiliar problem (Groen & Patel, 1988). For first-year physics problems, experts work forward more often than novices because problems that are unfamiliar for novices, and therefore require a backward-moving strategy, are often familiar for experts, and therefore require a forward-moving strategy.

IMPLICATIONS FOR INSTRUCTION: FOSTERING SCIENTIFIC EXPERTISE

Research on expertise raises the practical question of how a teacher could help a student move from novice to expert status. Shavelson (1972, 1974) has provided an interesting analysis of changes in the way that students structure their knowledge of physics following instruction. In one study, high school students in the trained group read lessons about Newtonian physics over the course of five days, while control students did not receive physics instruction. Students were given pretests and posttests measuring achievement and knowledge structure.

The achievement test measured retention of material from the lesson, using a standard multiple-choice format. As expected, the control group did not show a significant pretest to posttest gain (30% to 32%), but the trained group did show a significant pretest to posttest gain (33% to 54%).

The knowledge structure test listed fourteen key concepts. For each key concept, the subject was given one minute to write down all the words he could think of. The fourteen key concepts are momentum, inertia, power, mass, time, work, weight, acceleration, force, distance, velocity, impulse, speed, and energy. Based on the word association responses given for the knowledge structure test, Shavelson was able to determine how strongly each of fourteen key words was related to each of the other words. For example, if a subject listed many of the same words for force and mass, then a relatedness index would indicate that these two concepts were highly related. As expected, the pretest results indicated that subjects entered the study with preexisting conceptions of Newtonian mechanics terms; clusters of terms were related by the students, although not in the way that Newtonian physics prescribes. The knowledge structure test was given after each of the five lessons. As Figure 6–29 shows, the relatedness index increased each day for the trained group but remained low throughout the study for the control group. In addition, Shavelson derived the expert word-association responses based on the actual relations expressed in physics equations. Figure 6–29 demonstrates that the difference between the expert knowledge structure and that of the trained group decreased with each day of instruction; in contrast, the control group showed no change. These results are consistent with the idea that training in physics not only enhances general achievement but also influences the way in which knowledge is organized in memory. With training, the students are less likely to organize key concepts based on their underlying meanings and more likely to relate them based on the rules of physics.

What are the instructional implications of this line of research? Simon (1980) suggests that science training should have two basic goals: to provide a rich knowledge base (e.g., lots of experience with the major formulas in kinematics), and to develop general problem-solving strategies relevant to the science (e.g., how to recognize problem types and work forward). Simon (1980) argues that there is no substitute for experience, and Hayes (1985) estimates that to become an expert in a field requires approximately ten years of study. In addition, to achieve expertise one must have extensive experience with worked-out examples done by experts (Simon, 1980).

A major controversy in science education concerns the relative merits of teaching the fruits of scientific research (science facts) versus teaching how to do science (scientific thinking). The research on expertise suggests that facts and hands-on experience alone are not sufficient. Students need both a certain amount of basic factual knowledge as well as training in problem-solving skills that can applied to this knowledge. Unfortunately, many science textbooks contain large numbers of relatively isolated facts about the physical world. Student memorization of a large number of such facts should not be the main goal of science instruction. Instead, the goal must be to help students understand the physical and natural events in the world. This goal requires well-organized knowledge as well as practice in scientific problem-solving.

FIGURE 6–29 Changes in knowledge structure following physics instruction

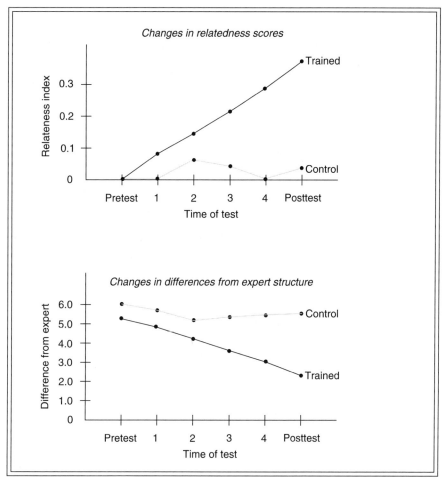

Adapted from Shavelson (1972)

CONCLUSION

The traditional view of science learning involves adding more and more information to one's memory. According to the cognitive-change view, however, learning occurs when one's knowledge is radically restructured; that is, when one's current conception (or mental model) is replaced with a new one. Conceptual change involves three steps—recognizing an anomaly, constructing a new model, and using a new model.

This chapter examines four aspects of conceptual change in science learning. First, learners enter the science classroom with many preexisting misconceptions or incomplete conceptions that conflict with the teacher's conceptions. Conceptual-change theory emphasizes that the goal of science is explanation rather than solely description of the natural universe. Students often develop naive conceptions of physics, based on the idea that "motion implies force." For example, this explanation leads them to predict that when a rolling object falls off a cliff it will go straight down. Instruction is needed to help learners recognize when their conceptions are inadequate to explain the available data and need to be discarded. A technique for helping students recognize anomalies is the predict-observe-explain method, in which students predict the outcome of a simple experiment, observe that the outcome conflicts with their prediction, and then try to explain the discrepancy.

Second, learners must replace their misconceptions with new conceptions; that is, they must find a new mental model that explains the data better than their previous one. According to conceptual-change theory, science learning depends on accommodation rather than solely assimilation. Accommodative learning occurs when a learner builds a new analogy between the scientific system (called the target) and a more familiar model (called the base), such as viewing an electrical circuit as a hydraulic system. Providing an analogy can be an effective instructional aid. For example, student understanding of radar is enhanced by comparing how radar works to how a thrown ball bounces off a remote object. Science instruction should help students build a progression of increasingly more powerful explanations of various natural phenomenon. For example, the microworld ThinkerTools helps students to explore the laws of motion and, thereby, to replace their naive conceptions with Newtonian conceptions of motion.

Third, students need to develop scientific thinking skills, such as how to use their conceptions to solve problems. Conceptual-change theory emphasizes scientific discovery in addition to more routine thinking involving the systematic testing of hypotheses. In particular, students must learn to search for new models that will explain phenomenon rather than for evidence that will support their current theory. Piagetian-inspired research on formal operations shows that students often enter the science classroom without the skills needed for systematic scientific reasoning, including how to control variables and how to think in terms of proportions and probabilities. In addition, research on scientific discovery reveals that students often see their goal as trying to create a certain phenomenon rather than to explain the mechanism that produces the phenomenon; in short, students seek to provide evidence that supports their current theory rather than evidence that refute it and support a competing theory. There is encouraging evidence that both kinds of scientific reasoning can be taught, and that students can learn techniques that improve their performance on control-of-variables tasks and that help them view scientific reasoning as a search for a new explanation of data.

Finally, students need to acquire the knowledge needed to change from novices to experts. Consistent with conceptual-change theory, the learner who enters as a novice is qualitatively different from the expert. If we take a snapshot of the novice's knowledge structure before instruction and the expert's knowledge structure after extensive experience, we find four major differences: (1) novices organize factual knowledge in small units, whereas experts build large units; (2) novices possess semantic knowledge that encourages them to build naive representations of problems, whereas experts build physics-based representations; (3) novices have schematic knowledge in which problems are categorized based on surface similarities, whereas experts focus on structural similarities; and (4) novices' strategic knowledge is based on working backward, whereas experts work forward. Thus the acquisition of scientific knowledge includes not only adding information to memory but also reorganizing knowledge in coherent and useful ways.

In conclusion, a major conceptual change in science education involves viewing science learning as a process of making conceptual changes in students' knowledge rather than as a process of adding information to students' memories.

SUGGESTED READINGS

Carey, S. (1985). *Conceptual change in childhood.* Cambridge: MIT Press. (Argues for the conceptual-change view of learning and development, using examples from children's conceptions of biology.)

Gabel, D. L. (Ed.). (1994). *Handbook of research on science teaching and learning.* New York: Macmillan. (Reviews many of the central issues in science education.)

Glynn, S. M., Yeany, R. H., & Britton, B. K. (Eds.). (1991). *The psychology of learning science.* Hillsdale, NJ: Erlbaum. (Suggests how science teachers can apply state-of-the-art research in their classrooms.)

References

Adams, A., Carnine, D. & Gersten, R. (1982). Instructional strategies for studying content area texts in the intermediate grades. *Reading Research Quarterly, 18,* 27–55.

Adams, M. J. (1990). *Beginning to read.* Cambridge, MA: MIT Press.

Anderson, R. G., & Freebody, P. (1981). Vocabulary knowledge. In J. T. Guthrie (Ed.), *Comprehension and teaching: Research reviews.* Newark, DE: International Reading Association.

Applebee, A. N. (1982). Writing and learning in school settings. In M. Nystrant (Ed.), *What writers know.* New York: Academic Press.

Ashcraft, M. H., & Stazyk, E. H. (1981). Mental addition: A test of three verification models. *Memory and Cognition, 9,* 185–196.

Ausubel, D. P. (1968). *Educational psychology: A cognitive view.* New York: Holt, Rinehart & Winston.

Baker, L., & Anderson, R. C. (1982). Effects of inconsistent information on text processing: Evidence for comprehension monitoring. *Reading Research Quarterly, 17,* 281–293.

Bangert-Drowns, R. L. (1993). The word processor as an instructional tool: A meta-analysis of word processing in writing instruction. *Review of Educational Research, 63,* 69–93.

Baron, J. (1977). What we might know about orthographic rules. In S. Dornic (Ed.), *Attention and performance VI.* Hillsdale, NJ. Erlbaum.

Baron, J. (1978). The word-superiority effect: Perceptual learning from reading. In W. K. Estes (Ed.), *Handbook of learning and cognitive processes. Vol. 6.* Hillsdale, NJ: Erlbaum.

Bartlett, E. J. (1982). Learning to revise. Some component processes. In M. Nystrand (Ed.), *What writers know.* New York: Academic Press.

Bartlett, E. J., & Scribner, S. (1981). Text and content: An investigation of referential organization in children's written narratives. In C. H. Frederiksen & J. F. Dominic (Eds.), *Writing. Vol. 2.* Hillsdale, NJ: Erlbaum.

Bartlett, F. C. (1932). *Remembering: A study in experimental and social psychology.* Cambridge, UK: Cambridge University Press.

Bean, T. W., & Steenwyk, F. L. (1984). The effect of three forms of summarization instruction on sixth graders' summary writing and comprehension. *Journal of Reading Behavior, 16,* 297–306.

Beck, I. L., Perfetti, C. A., & McKeown, M. G. (1982). Effects of long-term vocabulary instruction on lexical access and reading comprehension. *Journal of Educational Psychology, 74,* 506–521.

Beck, I. L., & McKeown, M. G. (1994). Outcomes of history instruction: Paste-up accounts. In M. Carretero & J. F. Voss (Eds.), *Cognitive and instructional processes in history and the social sciences.* Hillsdale, NJ: Erlbaum.

Beck, I. L., McKeown, M. G., Sinatra, G. M., & Loxterman, J. A. (1991). Revising social studies text from a text-processing perspective: Evidence of improved comprehensibility. *Reading Research Quarterly, 26,* 251–276.

Bereiter, C. (1980). Development in writing. In L. W. Gregg, & E. R. Sternberg (Eds.), *Cognitive processes in writing.* Hillsdale, NJ: Erlbaum.

Berieter, C., & Scardamalia, M. (1987). *The psychology of written composition.* Hillsdale, NJ: Erlbaum.

Bobrow, D. G. (1968). Natural language input for a computer problem solving system. In M. Minsky (Ed.), *Semantic information processing.* Cambridge, MA: MIT Press.

Bradley, L., & Bryant, P. (1978). Difficulties in auditory organization as a possible cause of reading backwardness. *Nature, 271,* 746–747.

Bradley, L., & Bryant, P. (1983). Categorizing sounds and learning to read—a causal connection. *Nature, 301,* 419–421.

Bradley, L., & Bryant, P. (1985). *Rhyme and reason in reading and spelling.* Ann Arbor, MI: University of Michigan Press.

Bradley, L., & Bryant, P. (1991). Phonological skills before and after learning to read. In S. A. Brady & D. P. Shankweiler (Eds.), *Phonological processes in literacy.* Hillsdale, NJ: Erlbaum.

Bransford, J. D., & Johnson, M. K. (1972). Contextual prerequisites for understanding: Some investigations of comprehension and recall. *Journal of Verbal Learning and Verbal Behavior, 11,* 717–726.

Bransford, J. D., Zech, L., Schwartz, D., Barron, B., Vye, N., & The Cognition and Technology Group at Vanderbilt (1996). Fostering mathematical thinking in middle school students: Lessons from research. In R. J. Sternberg & T. Ben-Zeev (Eds.), *The nature of mathematical thinking.* Mahwah, NJ: Elbaum.

Brenner, M. A., Mayer, R. E., Mosely, B., Brar, T., Duran, R., Reed, B. S., & Webb, D. (1997). Learning by understanding: The role of multiple representations in learning algebra. *American Educational Research Journal, 34,* 663–690.

Brononski, J. (1978). *The common sense of science.* Cambridge, MA: Harvard University Press.

Brown, A. L., Campione, J. C. & Barclay, C. R. (1979). Training self-checking routines for estimating test readiness: Generalization from list learning to prose recall. *Child Development, 50,* 501–512.

Brown, A. L., Campione, J. C. & Day, J. D. (1981). Learning to learn: On training students to learn from texts. *Educational Researcher, 10,* 14–21.

Brown, A. L. & Day, J. D. (1983). Macrorules for summarzing texts: The development of expertise. *Journal of Verbal Learning and Verbal Behavior, 22,* 1–14.

Brown, A. L., Day, J. D. & Jones, R. S. (1983). The development of plans for summarizing texts. *Child Development, 54,* 968–979.

Brown, A. L., & Palinscar, A. S. (1989). Guided, cooperative learning and individual knowledge acquisition. In L. B. Resnick (Ed.), *Knowing, learning, and instruction: Essays in honor of Robert Glaser* (pp. 393–452). Hillsdale, NJ: Erlbaum.

Brown, A. L., & Smiley, S. S. (1977). Rating the importance of structural units of prose passages: A problem of metacognitive development. *Child Development, 48,* 1–8.

Brown, A. L., & Smiley, S. S. (1978). The development of strategies for studying texts. *Child Development, 49,* 1076–1088.

Brown, J. S., & Burton, R. R. (1978). Diagnostic models for procedural bugs in basic mathematical skills. *Cognitive Science, 2,* 155–192.

Brown, J. S., McDonald, J. L., Brown, T. L., & Carr, T. H. (1988). Adapting to processing demands in discourse production: The case of handwriting. *Journal of Experimental Psychology: Human Perception and Performance, 14,* 45–59.

Bruce, B., Collins, A., Rubin, A., & Gentner, D. (1982). Three perspectives on writing. *Educational Psychologist, 17,* 131–145.

Bruer, J. T. (1993). *Schools for thought.* Cambridge, MA: MIT Press.

Bryan, W. L., & Harter, N. (1897). Studies in the physiology and psychology of telegraphic language. *Psychological Review, 4,* 27–53.

Caccamise, D. J. (1987). Idea generation in writing. In A. Matsushashi (Ed.), *Writing in real time: Modeling production processes.* Norwood, NJ: Ablex.

Calfee, R., Chapman, R., & Venezky, R. (1972). How a child needs to think to learn to read. In L. W. Gregg (Ed.), *Cognition in learning and memory.* New York: Wiley.

Carey, S. (1985). *Conceptual change in childhood.* Cambridge, MA: MIT Press.

Carey, S. (1986). Cognitive science and science education. *American Psychologist, 41,* 1123–1130.

Carey, S., Evans, R., Honda, M., Jay, E., & Unger, C. (1989). "An experiment is when you try it and see if it works": A study of grade 7 students' understanding of the construction of scientific knowledge. *International Journal of Science Education, 11,* 514–529.

Carpenter, P. A., & Just, M. A. (1981). Cognitive processes in reading: Models based on readers' eye fixations. In A. M. Lesgold & C. A. Perfetti (Eds.), *Interactive processes in reading.* Hillsdale, NJ: Erlbaum.

Carver, R. P. (1971). *Sense and nonsense in speed reading.* Silver Springs, MD: Revrac.

Carver, R. P. (1985). How good are some of the world's best readers? *Reading Research Quarterly, 20,* 389 419.

Case, R., & Okamoto, Y. (1996). The role of central conceptual structures in the development of children's thought. *Monographs of the Society for Research in Child Development, 61(1 & 2),* No. 246.

Cattell, J. M. (1886). The time taken up by cerebral operations. *Mind, 11,* 220–242.

Chall, J. S. (1979). The great debate: Ten years later, with a modest proposal for reading stages. In L. B. Resnick & P. A. Weaver (Eds.), *Theory and practice of early reading.* Hillsdale, NJ: Erlbaum.

Chall, J. S. (1983). *Learning to read: The great debate.* New York: McGraw-Hill.

Chall, J. S. & Squire, J. R. (1991). The publishing industry and textbooks. In R. Barr, M. L. Kamil, P. B. Mosenthal, & P. D. Pearson (Eds.), *Handbook of reading research, Vol. 2* (pp. 120–146). New York: Longman.

Champagne, A. B., Gunstone, R. F., & Klopfer, L. E. (1985). Effecting changes in cognitive structures among physics students. In H. T. West & A. L. Pines (Eds.), *Cognitive structure and conceptual change.* Orlando, FL: Academic Press.

Champagne, A., Klopfer, L., & Gunstone, R. (1982). Cognitive research and the design of science instruction. *Educational Psychologist, 17,* 31–53.

Chi, M. T. H., Feltovich, P. J., & Glaser, R. (1981). Categorization and representation of physics problems by experts and novices. *Cognitive Science, 5,* 121–152.

Chi, M. T. H., Bassok, M., Lewis, M. W., Reimann, P. & Glaser, R. (1989). Self-explanations: How students study and use examples in learning to solve problems. *Cognitive Science, 13,* 145–182.

Clement, J. (1982). Students' preconceptions in elementary mechanics. *American Journal of Physics, 50,* 66–71.

Clymer, T. (1963). The utility of phonic generalizations in the primary grades. *Reading Teacher, 16,* 252–258.

Cognition and Technology Group at Vanderbilt (1992). The Jasper series as an example of anchored instruction: Theory, program description, and assessment data. *Educational Psychologist, 27,* 291–315.

Cohen, H., Hillman, D., & Agne, R. (1978). Cognitive level and college physics achievement. *American Journal of Physics, 46,* 1026.

Crowder, R. G. (1982). *The psychology of reading.* New York: Oxford University Press.

Crowder, R. G., & Wagner, R. K. (1992). *The psychology of reading.* New York: Oxford University Press.

Cubberly, E. P. (1920). *The history of education.* Boston: Houghton Mifflin.

Cunningham, A. E. (1990). Explicit vs. implicit instruction in phonemic awareness. *Journal of Experimental Child Psychology, 50,* 429–444.

DiVesta, F. (1989). Applications of cognitive psychology to education. In W. C. Wittrock & F. Farley (Eds.), *The future of educational psychology* (pp. 37–73). Hillsdale, NJ: Erlbaum.

Dossey, J. A., Mullis, I. V. S., Lindquist, M. M., & Chambers, D. L. (1988). *The mathematics report card.* Princeton, NJ: Educational Testing Service.

Dowhower, S. L. (1994). Repeated reading revisited: Research into practice. *Reading & Writing Quarterly, 10,* 343–358.

Dunbar, K. (1993). Concept discovery in a scientific domain. *Cognitive Science, 17,* 397–434.

Ehri, L. C. (1991). Development of the ability to read words. In R. Barr, M. L. Kamil, P. Mosenthal, & P. D. Pearson (Eds.), *Handbook of research on reading Vol. 2.* White Plains, NY: Longman.

Ehri, L. C., & Robbins, C. (1992). Beginners need some decoding skill to read by analogy. *Reading Research Quarterly, 27,* 13–26.

Ehri, L. C., & Roberts, K. T. (1979). Do beginners learn printed words better in context or in isolation? *Child Development, 50,* 175–685.

Elliot-Faust, D. J., & Pressley, M. (1986). How to teach comparison processing to increase children's short- and long-term listening comprehension monitoring. *Journal of Educational Psychology, 78,* 27–33.

Englert, C. S., Raphel, T. E., Anderson, L. M., Anthony, H. M., & Stevens, D. D. (1991). Making strategies and self-talk visible: Writing instruction in regular and special education classrooms. *American Educational Research Journal, 28,* 337–372.

Erickson, G. L. (1979). Children's conception of heat and temperature. *Science Education, 63,* 222–230.

Eylon, B. & Linn, M. C. (1988). Learning and instruction: An examination of four research perspectives in science education. *Review of Educational Research, 58,* 251–301.

Fitzgerald, J. & Markman, L. R. (1987). Teaching children about revision in writing. *Cognition and Instruction, 41,* 3–24.

Fitzgerald, J. (1987). Research on revision in writing. *Review of Educational Research, 57,* 481–506.

Fleisher, L. S., Jenkins, J. R., & Pany, D. (1979). Effects on poor readers' comprehension of training in rapid decoding. *Reading Research Quarterly, 15,* 30–48.

Flesch, R. P. (1955). *Why Johnny can't read.* New York: Harper.

Flower, L. (1979). Writer-based prose: A cognitive basis for problems in writing. *College English, 41,* 13–18.

Flower, L., & Hayes, J. R. (1981). Plans that guide the composition process. In C. H. Fredericksen & J. F. Dominic (Eds.), *Writing: Volume 2.* Hillsdale, NJ: Erlbaum.

Frase, L. T. (1982). Introduction to special issue on the psychology of writing. *Educational Psychologist, 17,* 129–130.

Fuson, K. C. (1982). An analysis of the counting-on solution procedure in addition. In T. P. Carpenter, J. M. Moser, & T. A. Romber (Eds.), *Addition and subtraction: A cognitive perspective.* Hillsdale, NJ: Erlbaum.

Fuson, K. C. (1992). Research on whole number addition and subtraction. In D.A. Grouws (Ed.), *Handbook of research on mathematics teaching and learning.* New York: Macmillan.

Gagne, R. M. (1968). Learning hierarchies. *Educational Psychologist, 6,* 1–9.

Gagne, R. M. (1974). *Essentials of learning for instruction.* Hinsdale, IL: Dryden Press.

Gardner, H. (1985). *The mind's new science. A history of the cognitive revolution.* New York: Basic Books.

Gentner, D. (1983). Structure mapping: A theoretical framework. *Cognitive Science, 7,* 155–170.

Gentner, D. (1989). The mechanisms of analogical learning. In S. Vosni-adou & A. Ortony (Eds.), *Similarity and analogical reasoning.* Cambridge, England: Cambridge University Press.

Gentner, D., & Gentner, D. R. (1983). Flowing waters or teeming crowds: Mental models of electricity. In D. Gentner & A. L. Stevens (Eds.), *Mental models.* Hillsdale, NJ: Erlbaum.

Gentner, D., & Stevens, A.L. (Eds.) (1983). *Mental models.* Hillsdale, NJ: Erlbaum.

Gernsbacher, M.A. (1990). *Language comprehension as structure building.* Hillsdale, NJ: Erlbaum.

Gernsbacher, M.A. (Ed.) (1994). *Handbook of psycholinguistics.* San Diego: Academic Press.

Glynn, S. M., Britton, B. K., Muth, D., & Dogan, N. (1982). Writing and revising persuasive documents: Cognitive demands. *Journal of Educational Psychology, 74,* 557–567.

Glynn, S. M. (1991). Explaining science concepts: A teaching-with-analogies model. In S. M. Glynn, R. H. Yeany, & B. K. Britton (Eds.). *The psychology of learning science.* Hillsdale, NJ: Erlbaum.

Glynn, S. M., Yeany, R. H., & Britton, B. K. (Eds.) (1991). *The psychology of learning science.* Hillsdale, NJ: Erlbaum.

Goswami, U., & Bryant, P. (1990). *Phonological skills and learning to read.* Hillsdale, NJ: Erlbaum.

Goswami, U., & Bryant, P. (1992). Rhyme, analogy, and children's reading. In P. B. Gough, L. C. Ehri, & R. Treiman (Eds.), *Reading acquisition.* Hillsdale, NJ: Erlbaum.

Goswami, U. (1986). Children's use of analogy in learning to read: A developmental study. *Journal of Experimental Child Psychology, 42,* 73–83.

Gould, J. D. (1978a). How experts dictate. *Journal of Experimental Psychology: Human Perception and Performance, 4,* 648–661.

Gould, J. D. (1978b). An experimental study of writing, dictating, and speaking. In J. Requien (Ed.), *Attention and performance, VII.* Hillsdale, NJ: Erlbaum.

Gould, J. D. (1980). Experiments on composing letters: Some facts, some myths, and some observations. In L. W. Gregg & E. R. Steinberg (Eds.), *Cognitive processes in writing.* Hillsdale, NJ: Erlbaum.

Greeno, J. G. (1980). Some examples of cognitive task analysis with instructional implications. In R. E. Snow, P. Frederico, & W. E. Montague (Eds.), *Aptitude, learning, and instruction, Vol. 2.* Hillsdale, NJ: Erlbaum.

Griffin, S., & Case, R. (1996). Evaluating the breadth and depth of training effects when central conceptual structures are taught. In R. Case & Y. Okamoto (Eds.), The role of central structures in the development of children's thought (pp. 83–102). *Monographs of the Society for Research in Child Development, 61,* Serial No. 246, Nos. 1–2.

Griffin, S.A., Case, R., & Siegler, R.S. (1994). Rightstart: Providing the central conceptual prerequisites for first formal learning of arithmetic to students at risk for school failure. In K. McGilly (Ed.), *Classroom lessons: Integrating cognitive theory and classroom practice.* Cambridge, MA: MIT Press.

Griffin, S.A., Case, R., & Capodilupo, S. (1995). Teaching for understanding: The importance of ventral conceptual structures in the elementary school mathematics curriculum. In A. McKeough, J. Lupart, & A. Marini (Eds.), *Teaching for transfer: Fostering generalization in learning.* Hillsdale, NJ: Erlbaum.

Griffiths, D. (1976). Physics teaching: Does it hinder intellectual development? *American Journal of Physics, 44,* 81–85.

Grinder, R. E. (1989). Educational psychology: The master science. In W.C. Wittrock & F. Farley (Eds.), *The future of educational psychology* (pp. 3–18). Hillsdale, NJ: Erlbaum.

Groen, G. J., & Parkman, J. M. (1972). A chronometric analysis of simple addition. *Psychological Review, 97,* 329–343.

Groen, G. J., & Patel, V. L. (1988). The relationship between comprehension and reasoning in medical expertise. In M.T.H. Chi, R. Glaser, & M.J. Farr (Eds.), *The nature of expertise.* Hillsdale, NJ: Erlbaum.

Grouws, D. A. (Ed.) (1992). *Handbook of research on mathematics teaching and learning.* New York: Macmillan.

Gunstone, R. F., & White, R. T. (1981). Understanding of gravity. *Science Education, 65,* 291–300.

Haberlandt, K. (1984). Components of sentence and word reading times. In D.E. Kieras & M.A. Just (Eds.), *New methods in reading comprehension research.* Hillsdale, NJ: Erlbaum.

Halpern, D. (Ed.) (1992). *Enhancing thinking skills in the sciences and mathematics.* Hillsdale, NJ: Erlbaum.

Halsford, G.S. (1993). *Children's understanding: The development of mental models.* Hillsdale, NJ: Erlbaum.

Hansen, J., & Pearson, P. D. (1983). An instructional study: Improving the inferential comprehension of good and poor fourth-grade readers. *Journal of Educational Psychology, 75,* 821–829.

Hansen, J. (1981). The effects of inference training and practice on young children's comprehension. *Reading Research Quarterly, 16,* 391–417.

Hartley, J. (1984). The role of colleagues and text-editing programs in improving text. *IEEE Transactions on Professional Communication, 27,* 42–44.

Hayes, J. R., & Flower, L. S. (1980). Identifying the organization of writing processes. In L. W. Gregg & E. R. Steinberg (Eds.), Cognitive processes in writing. Hillsdale, NJ: Erlbaum.

Hayes, J. R. (1985). Three problems in teaching general skills. In S. F. Chipman, J. W. Segal, & R. Glaser (Eds.), *Thinking and learning skills: Volume 2, Research and open questions.* Hillsdale, NJ: Erlbaum.

Hayes, J. R., & Flower, L. S. (1986). Writing research and the writer. *American Psychologist, 41,* 1106–1113.

Hayes, J. R. (1996). A new framework for understanding cognition and affect in writing. In C. M. Levy & S. Ransdell, (Eds.), *The science of writing*. Mahwah, NJ: Erlbaum.

Hayes, J. R., Waterman, D. A., & Robinson, C. S. (1977). Identifying relevant aspects of a text problem. *Cognitive Science, 1,* 297–313.

Hegarty, M., Mayer, R.E. & Monk, C.A. (1995). Comprehension of arithmetic word problems: A comparison of successful and unsuccessful problem solvers. *Journal of Educational Psychology, 87,* 18–32.

Hillocks, G. (1984). What works in teaching composition: A meta-analysis of experimental treatment studies. *American Journal of Education, 93,* 133–170.

Hinsley, D., Hayes, J. R., & Simson, H. A. (1977). From words to equations. In P. Carpenter & M. Just (Eds.), *Cognitive processes in comprehension.* Hillsdale, NJ: Erlbaum.

Huey, E. B. (1908). *The psychology and pedagogy of reading.* New York: Macmillan. (Reprinted by MIT Press in 1968).

Huey, E. B. (1968). *The psychology and pedagogy of reading.* Cambridge, MA: MIT Press. (Originally published in 1908).

Hyona, J. (1994). Processing of topic shifts by adults and children. *Reading Research Quarterly, 29,* 76–90.

Inhelder, B., & Piaget, J. (1958). *The growth of logical thinking from childhood to adolescence.* New York: Basic Books. (A. Parson & S. Milgram, Trans.; original French edition, 1955).

James, W. (1958). *Talks to teachers.* New York: Norton. (Originally published in 1899.)

Johnson, R. E. (1970). Recall of prose as a function of the structural importance of linguistic units. *Journal of Verbal Learning and Verbal Behavior, 9,* 12–20.

Johnston, J. C., & McClelland, J. L. (1980). Experimental tests of a hierarchical model of word identification. *Journal of Verbal Learning and Verbal Behavior, 19,* 503–524.

Johnston, J. C. (1978). A test of the sophisticated guessing theory of word perception. *Cognitive Psychology, 10,* 123–153.

Johnston, J. C. (1981). Understanding word perception: Clues from studying the word superiority effect. In O. J. L. Tzeng & H. Singer (Eds.), *Perception of Print.* Hillsdale, NJ: Erlbaum.

Juel, C., Griffith, P. L., & Gough, P. B. (1986). Acquisition of literacy: A longitudinal study of children in first and second grade. *Journal of Educational Psychology, 78,* 243–255.

Just, M. A., & Carpenter, P. A. (1978). Inference process during reading: Reflections from eye fixations. In J. W. Senders, D. F. Fisher, & R. A. Monty (Eds.), *Eye movements and the higher psychological functions.* Hillsdale, NJ: Erlbaum.

Just, M. A., & Carpenter, P. A. (1981). A theory of reading: From eye fixations to comprehension. *Psychological Review, 87,* 329–354.

Kaiser, M. K., Proffitt, D. R., & McCloskey, M. (1985). The development of beliefs about falling objects. *Perception and Psychophysics, 38,* 533–539.

Kameenui, E. J., Carnine, D. W., & Freschi, R. (1982). Effects of text construction and instructional procedures for teaching word meanings on comprehension and recall. *Reading Research Quarterly, 17,* 367–388.

Karplus, R., Karplus, E., Formisano, M., & Paulsen, A. (1979). Proportional reasoning and control of variables in seven countries. In J. Lochhead & J. Clement (Eds.), *Cognitive process instruction: Research on teaching thinking skills.* Philadelphia: Franklin Institute Press.

Kearney, H. (1971). *Science and change.* New York: McGraw-Hill.

Kellogg, R. T. (1987). Effects of topic knowledge on the allocation of processing time and cognitive effort to writing processes. *Memory & Cognition, 15,* 256–266.

Kellogg, R. T. (1988). Attentional overload and writing performance: Effects of rough draft and outline strategies. *Journal of Experimental Psychology: Learning, memory, and Cognition, 14,* 355–365.

Kellogg, R. T. (1994). *The psychology of writing.* New York: Oxford University Press.

Kellogg, R. T., & Mueller, S. (1993). Performance amplification and process restructuring in computer-based writing. *International Journal of Man-Machine Studies, 39,* 33–49.

Kiefer, K. E., & Smith, C.R. (1983). Textual analysis with computers: Tests of Bell Laboratories' computer software. *Research in the Teaching of English, 17,* 201–214.

Kintsch, W. (1976). Memory for prose. In C. N. Cofer (Ed.), *The structure of human memory.* New York: Freeman.

Kintsch, W., & Greeno, J. G. (1985). Understanding and solving word problems. *Psychological Review, 92,* 109–129.

Klahr, D., & Dunbar, K. (1988). Dual space search during scientific reasoning. *Cognitive Science, 12,* 1–48.

Klayman, J., & Ha, Y. W. (1987). Confirmation, disconfirmation and information in hypothesis testing. *Psychological Review, 94,* 211–228.

Kolers, P. A. (1968). Introduction. In E. B. Huey, *The psychology and pedagogy of reading.* Cambridge, MA: MIT Press.

Kolodiy, G. (1975). The cognitive development of high school and college science students. *Journal of College Science Teaching, 5*(1), 20–22.

Koskinen, P. S., & Blum, I. H. (1986). Paired repeated reading: A classroom strategy for developing fluent reading. *Reading Teacher, 40*(1), 70–75.

Kreiger, L. E. (1975). Familiarity effects in visual information processing. *Psychological Bulletin, 82,* 949–974.

Kuhn, D., Amsel, E., & O'Loughlin, M. (1988). *The development of scientific thinking skills.* San Diego: Academic Press.

LaBerge, D., & Samuels, S. J. (1974). Toward a theory of automatic information processing in reading. *Cognitive Psychology, 6,* 293–323.

Lambert, N., & McCombs, B. L. (Eds.). (1998). *How students learn: Reforming schools through learner centered education.* Washington, DC: American Psychological Association.

Lane, H. (1976). *The wild boy of Aveyron.* Cambridge, MA: Harvard University Press.

Larkin, J. H. (1979). Information processing models and science instruction. In J. Lochhead & J. Clement (Eds.), *Cognitive process instruction: Research on teaching thinking skills.* Philadelphia: Franklin Institute Press.

Larkin, J., McDermott, J., Simon, D. P., & Simon, H. A. (1980). Expert and novice performance in solving physics problems. *Science, 208,* 1335–1342.

Larkin, J. H. (1983). The role of problem representation in physics. In D. Gentner & A. L. Stevens (Eds.), *Mental models.* Hillsdale, NJ: Erlbaum.

Larkin, J. H., McDermott, J., Simon, D. P., & Simon, H. A. (1980a). Models of competence in solving physics problems. *Cognitive Science, 4,* 317–348.

Larkin, J. H., McDermott, J., Simon, D. P., & Simon, H. A. (1980b). Expert and novice performance in solving physics problems. *Science, 208,* 1335–1342.

Lawson, A. E., & Snitgen, D. A. (1982). Teaching formal reasoning in a college biology course for preservice teachers. *Journal of Research in Science Teaching, 19,* 233–248.

Lawson, A. E., & Wollman, W. T. (1976). Encouraging the transition from concrete to formal operative functioning: An experiment. *Journal of Research in Science Teaching, 13,* 413–430.

Lawson, A. E. (1983). Predicting science achievement: The role of developmental level, disembedding ability, mental capacity, prior knowledge and beliefs. *Journal of Research in Science Teaching, 20,* 117–129.

Lehrer, R. (1992). Introduction to special feature on new directions in technology—mediated learning. *Educational Psychologist, 27,* 287–290.

Lester, F. K., Garofalo, J., & Kroll, D. L. (1989). Self-confidence, interest, beliefs, and metacognition: Key influences on problem-solving behavior. In D. B. McLeod & V. M. Adams (Eds.), *Affect and mathematical problem solving.* New York: Springer-Verlag.

Levy, C. M., & Ransdell, S. (Eds.) (1996). *The science of writing.* Mahwah, NJ: Erlbaum.

Lewis, A. B., & Mayer, R. E. (1987). Students' miscomprehension of relational statements in arithmetic word problems. *Journal of Educational Psychology, 79,* 363–371.

Lewis, A. B. (1989). Training students to represent arithmetic word problems. *Journal of Educational Psychology, 81,* 521–531.

Liberman, I. Y., Shankweiler, D., Fischer, F. W., & Carter, B. (1974). Explicit syllable and phoneme segmentation in the young child. *Journal of Experimental Child Psychology, 18,* 201–212.

Lipson, M. Y. (1983). The influence of religious affiliation on children's memory for text information. *Reading Research Quarterly, 18,* 448–457.

Loftus, E. F., & Suppes, P. (1972). Structural variables that determine problem-solving difficulty in computer assisted instruction. *Journal of Educational Psychology, 63,* 531–542.

Low, R., & Over, R. (1993). Gender differences in solution of algebraic word problems containing irrelevant information. *Journal of Educational Psychology, 85,* 331–339.

Low, R., & Over, R. (1990). Text editing of algebraic word problems. *Austrailian Journal of Psychology, 42,* 63–73.

Low, R., & Over, R. (1989). Detection of missing and irrelevant information within algebraic story problems. *British Journal of Educational Psychology, 59,* 296–305.

Lundberg, I., Frost, J., & Peterson, O. (1988). Effects of an extensive program for stimulating phonological awareness in preschool children. *Reading Research Quarterly, 23,* 263–284.

Macdonald, N. H., Frase, L. T., Gingrich, P. S., & Keenan, S. A. (1982). The writer's workbench: Computer aids for text analysis. *Educational Psychologist, 17,* 172–179.

Mandler, J. M., & Johnson, N. S. (1977). Remembrance of things passed: Story structure and recall. *Cognitive Psychology, 9,* 111–151.

Markman, E. (1979). Realizing that you don't understand: Elementary school children's awareness of inconsistencies. *Child Development, 50,* 643–655.

Markman, E. M. (1985). Comprehension monitoring: Developmental and educational issues. In S. F. Chipman, J. W. Segal, & R. Glaser (Eds.), *Thinking and learning skills: Vol 2, Research and open questions.* Hillsdale, NJ: Erlbaum.

Markman, E. M., & Gorin, L. (1981). Children's ability to adjust their standards for evaluating comprehension. *Journal of Educational Psychology, 73,* 320–325.

Marks, C. B., Doctorow, M. J., & Wittrock, M. C. (1974). Word frequency in reading comprehension. *Journal of Educational Research, 67,* 259–262.

Marr, M. B., & Gorley, K. (1982). Children's recall of familiar and unfamiliar text. *Reading Research Quarterly, 18,* 89–104.

Matsuhashi, A. (1982). Explorations in the real-time production of written discourse. In M. Nystrand (Ed.), *What writers know.* New York: Academic Press.

Matsushashi, A. (Ed.) (1987). *Writing in real time: Modeling production processes.* Norwood, NJ: Ablex.

Mattingly, I. G. (1972). Reading, the linguistic process and linguistic awareness. In J. Kavanagh & I. Mattingly (Eds.), *Language by ear and by eye.* Cambridge, MA: MIT Press.

Mayer, R. E. (1981a). *The promise of cognitive psychology.* New York: Freeman.

Mayer, R. E. (1981b). Frequency norms and structural analysis of algebra story problems into families, categories, and templates. *Instructional Science, 10,* 135–175.

Mayer, R. E. (1982a). Memory for algebra story problems. *Journal of Educational Psychology, 74,* 199–216.

Mayer, R. E. (1982b). Different problem solving strategies for algebra word and equation problems. *Journal of Experimental Psychology: Learning, Memory and Cognition, 8,* 448–462.

Mayer, R. E. (1984). Aids to prose comprehension. *Educational Psychologist, 19,* 30–42.

Mayer, R. E. (1989). Models for understanding. *Review of Educational Research, 59,* 43–64.

Mayer, R. E. (1992). Cognition and instruction: Their historic meeting within educational psychology. *Journal of Educational Psychology, 84,* 405–412.

Mayer, R. E. (1992). *Thinking, problem solving, cognition,* (2nd ed.). New York: Freeman.

Mayer, R. E. (1993a). Educational psychology—past and future. *Journal of Educational Psychology, 85,* 351–553.

Mayer, R. E. (1993b). Illustrations that instruct. In R. Glaser (Ed.), *Advances in instructional psychology, Volume 4.* Hillsdale, NJ: Erlbaum.

Mayer, R. E. (1996a). Learners as information processors: Legacies and limitations of educational psychology's second metaphor. *Educational Psychologist, 31,* 151–161.

Mayer, R. E. (1996b). Learning strategies for making sense out of expository text: The SOI model for guiding three cognitive processes in knowledge construction. *Educational Psychology Review, 8,* 357–371.

Mayer, R. E., & Gallini, J. (1990). When is an illustration worth ten thousand words? *Journal of Educational Psychology, 82,* 715–726.

Mayer, R. E., & Hegarty, M. (1996). The process of understanding mathematics problems. In R. J. Sternberg & T. Ben-Zeev (Eds.), *The nature of mathematical thinking.* Mahwah, NJ: Erlbaum.

Mayer, R. E., Sims, V., & Tajika, H. (1995). A comparison of how textbooks teach mathematical problem solving in Japan and the United States. *American Educational Research Journal, 32,* 443–460.

McCloskey, M. (1983). Intuitive physics. *Scientific American, 248*(4), 122–130.

McCloskey, M., Caramazza, A., & Green, B. (1980). Curvilinear motion in the absence of external forces: Naive beliefs about the motion of objects. *Science, 210*(No. 4474), 1139–1114.

McConkie, G. W., & Rayner, K. (1975). The span of the effective stimulus during a fixation in reading. *Perception & Psychophysics, 17,* 578–586.

McConkie, G. W. (1976). The use of eye-movement data in determining the perceptual span in reading. In R. A. Monty & J. W. Senders (Eds.), *Eye movements and psychological processes.* Hillsdale, NJ: Erlbaum.

McKeown, M. G., Beck, I. L., Omanson, R. C., & Perfetti, C. A. (1983). The effects of long-term vocabulary instruction on reading comprehension: A replication. *Journal of Reading Behavior, 15,* 3–18.

McKeown, M. G., & Beck, I. L. (1990). The assessment and characterization of young learners' knowledge of a topic in history. *American Educational Research Journal, 27,* 688–726.

McKeown, M. G., Beck, I. L., Sinatra, G. M., & Loxterman, J. A. (1992). The contribution of prior knowledge and coherent text to comprehension. *Reading Research Quarterly, 27,* 79–93.

McKinnon, J. W., & Renner, J. W. (1971). Are colleges concerned with intellectual development? *American Journal of Physics, 39,* 1047–1052.

Meyer, B. J. F., & McConkie, G. W. (1973). What is recalled after hearing a passage? *Journal of Educational Psychology, 65,* 109–117.

Meyer, B. J. F. (1975). *The organization of prose and its effects on memory.* Amsterdam: North-Holland.

Myers, M., & Paris, S. B. (1978). Children's metacognitive knowledge about reading. *Journal of Educational Psychology, 70,* 680–690.

Nagy, W. E., & Anderson, R. C. (1984). How many words are there in printed school English? *Reading Research Quarterly, 19,* 304–330.

Nagy, W. E., & Herman, P. A. (1987). Breadth and depth of vocabulary knowledge: Implications for acquisition and instruction. In M. McKeown & M. Curtis (Eds.), *The nature of vocabulary acquisition.* Hillsdale, NJ: Erlbaum.

Nagy, W. E., Herman, P. A., & Anderson, R. C. (1985). Learning words from context. *Reading Research Quarterly, 20,* 233–253.

Nathan, M. J., Kintsch, W., & Young, E. (1992). A theory of algebra word problem comprehension and its implications for the design of learning environments. *Cognition and Instruction, 9,* 329–389.

National Council of Teachers of Mathematics (1989). *Curriculum standards for teaching mathematics.* Reston, VA: Author.

Nemko, B. (1984). Another look at beginning readers. *Reading Research Quarterly, 19,* 461–467.

Nold, E. W. (1981). Revising. In C. H. Frederiksen & J. F. Dominic (Eds.) *Writing: Vol 2.* Hillsdale, NJ: Erlbaum.

Novick, S., & Nussbaum, J. (1978). Junior high school pupils' understanding of the particle nature of matter: An interview study. *Science Education, 62,* 273–281.

Novick, S., & Nussbaum, J. (1981). Pupil's understanding of the particulate nature of matter: A cross-age study. *Science Education, 65,* 187–196.

Nussbaum, J. (1979). Children's conception of the earth as a cosmic body: A cross-age study. *Science Education, 63,* 83–93.

Nystrand, M. (1982a). Rhetoric's "audience" and linguistic's "speech community": Implications for understanding writing, reading, and text. In M. Nystrand (Ed.), *What writers know.* New York: Academic Press.

Nystrand, M. (1982b). An analysis of errors in written communication. In M. Nystrand (Ed.), *What writers know.* New York: Academic Press.

Nystrand, M. (1986). *The structure of written communication: Studies in reciprocity between writers and readers.* Orlando, FL: Academic Press.

Oakhill, J., & Yuill, N. (1996). Higher order factors in comprehension disability: Processes and remediation. In C. Cesare & J. Oakhill (Eds.), *Reading comprehension difficulties.* Mahwah, NJ: Erlbaum.

Osborne, R. J., & Wittrock, M. C. (1983). Learning science: A generative process. *Science Education, 67,* 489–908.

Paige, J. M., & Simon, H. A. (1966). Cognitive processes in solving algebra word problems. In B. Kleinmuntz (Ed.), *Problem solving: Research, method, and theory.* New York: Wiley.

Palinscar, A. S., & Brown, A. L. (1984). Reciprocal teaching of comprehension-fostering and comprehension-monitoring activities. *Cognition and Instruction, 1*, 117–175.

Palinscar, A. S. (1986). Metacognitive strategy instruction. *Exceptional children, 53*, 118–124.

Paris, S. G., & Lindauer, B. K. (1976). The role of inference on children's comprehension and memory for sentences. *Cognitive Psychology, 8*, 217–227.

Paris, S. G., Lindauer, B. K., & Cox, G. L. (1977). The development of inferential comprehension. *Child Development, 48*, 1728–1733.

Paris, S. G., & Upton, L. R. (1976). Children's memory for inferential relationships in prose. *Child Development, 47*, 660–618.

Parkman, J. M., & Groen, G. J. (1971). Temporal aspects of simple addition and comparison. *Journal of Experimental Psychology, 89*, 333–342.

Pearson, P. D., & Gallagher, M. (1983). The instruction of reading comprehension. *Contemporary Educational Psychology, 8*, 317–344.

Pearson, P. D., Hanson, J., & Gordon, C. (1979). The effect of background knowledge on young children's comprehension of explicit and implicit information. *Journal of Reading Behavior, 11*, 201–209.

Pearson, P. D., & Fielding, L. (1991). Comprehension instruction. In R. Barr, M.L. Kamil, P.B. Mosenthal, & P.D. Pearson (Eds.), *Handbook of reading research, Vol 2.* New York: Longman.

Pedersen, E. L. (1989). The effectiveness of WRITER'S WORKBENCH and MACPROOF. *Computer-Assisted Composition Journal, 3*, 92–100.

Pennington, B. F., Groisser, D., & Welsh, M. C. (1993). Contrasting cognitive deficiets in attention deficit disorder versus reading disability. *Developmental Psychology, 29*, 511–523.

Perfetti, C. A., & Hogaboam, T. (1975). The relationship between single word decoding and reading comprehension skill. *Journal of Educational Psychology, 67*, 461–469.

Perfetti, C. A., & Lesgold, A. M. (1979). Coding and comprehension in skilled reading and implications for reading instruction. In L. B. Resnick & P. A. Weaver (Eds.), *Theory and practice of early reading.* Hillsdale, NJ: Erlbaum.

Pflaum, S. W., Walberg, H. J., Karegianes, M. L., & Rasher, S. P. (1980). Reading instruction: A quantitative analysis. *Educational Researcher, 9*, 12–18.

Piaget, J. (1926). *The language and thought of the child.* London: Kegan Paul, Trench, Trubner and Company.

Piaget, J. (1972). Intellectual evolution from adolescent to adulthood. *Human Development, 15*, 1–12.

Pianko, S. (1979). A description of the composing process of college freshman writers. *Research in the Teaching of English, 13*, 5–22.

Pichert, J., & Anderson, R. C. (1977). Taking different perspectives on a story. *Journal of Educational Psychology, 69*, 309–315.

Polya, G. (1945). *How to solve it.* Princeton, NJ: Princeton University Press.

Polya, G. (1965). *Mathematical discovery.* New York: Wiley.

Posner, G. J., Strike, K. A., Hewson, P. W., & Gertzog, W. A. (1982). Accomodation of a scientific conception: Toward a theory of conceptual change. *Science Education, 66*, 211–227.

Pressley, M. (1990). *Cognitive strategy instruction that really improves children's academic performance.* Cambridge, MA: Brookline Books.

Pressley, M., & McCormick, C. B. (1995). *Cognition, teaching, and assessment.* New York: HarperCollins.

Quilici, J. H., & Mayer, R. E. (1996). Role of examples in how students learn to categorize statistics word problems. *Journal of Educational Psychology, 88,* 144–161.

Rayner, K., & Duffy, S. A. (1986). Lexical complexity and fixation times in reading: Effects of word frequency, verb complexity, and lexical ambiguity. *Memory & Cognition, 14,* 191–201.

Rayner, K., & Pollatsek, A. (1989). *The psychology of reading.* Englewood Cliffs, NJ: Prentice-Hall.

Rayner, K., & Sereno, S. C. (1994). Eye movements of reading: Psycholinguistic studies. In M.A. Gernsbacher (Ed.), *Handbook of psycholinguistics* (pp. 58–81). San Diego: Academic Press.

Rayner, K., Well, A. D., & Pollatsek, A. (1980). Asymmetry of the effective visual field in reading. *Perception and Psychophysics, 27,* 537–544.

Read, C. (1981). Writing is not the inverse of reading for young children. In C. H. Frederiksen & J. F. Dominic (Eds.), *Writing: Volume 2.* Hillsdale, NJ: Erlbaum.

Reed, S. K. (1987). A structure-mapping model for word problems. *Journal of Experimental Psychology: Learning, Memory, and Cognition, 13,* 124–139.

Reed, S. K., Dempster, A. & Ettinger, M. (1985). Usefulness of analogous solutions for solving algebra word problems. *Journal of Experimental Psychology: Learning, Memory, and Cognition, 11,* 106–125.

Reicher, G. M. (1969). Perceptual recognition as a function of the meaningfulness of stimulus material. *Journal of Experimental Psychology, 81,* 275–280.

Resnick, L. B. (1982). Syntax and semantics in learning to subtract. In T. Carpenter, J. Moser, & T. Romberg (Eds.), *Addition and subtraction: A cognitive perspective.* Hillsdale, NJ: Erlbaum.

Resnick, L. B. (1989). Introduction. In L. B. Resnick (Ed.), *Knowing, learning, and instruction: Essays in honor of Robert Glaser* (pp. 1–24). Hillsdale, NJ: Erlbaum.

Resnick, L. B., & Ford, W. W. (1981). *The psychology of mathematics for instruction.* Hillsdale, NJ: Erlbaum.

Richardson, K., Calnan, M., Essen, J., & Lambert, M. (1975). Linguistic maturity of 11-year-olds: Some analysis of the written compositions of children in the National Child Development Study. *Journal of Child Language, 3,* 99–116.

Rieben, L., & Perfetti, C. A. (Eds.) (1991). *Learning to read: Basic research and its implications.* Hillsdale, NJ: Erlbaum.

Riley, M., Greeno, J. G., & Heller, J. (1982). The development of children's problem solving ability in arithmetic. In H. Ginsburg (Ed.), *The development of mathematical thinking.* New York: Academic Press.

Robinson, C. S., & Hayes, J. R. (1978). Making inferences about relevance in understanding problems. In R. Revlin & R. E. Mayer (Eds.), *Human reasoning*. Washington: Winston.

Robinson, F. P. (1941). *Diagnostic and remedial techniques for effective study*. New York: Harper.

Robinson, F. P. (1961). *Effective study*. New York: Harper.

Roller, C. M. (1990). The interaction between knowledge and structure variables in the processing of expository prose. *Reading Research Quarterly, 25,* 79–89.

Rosenshine, B. V. (1980a). Skill hierarchies in reading comprehension. In R. J. Spiro, B. C. Bruce & W. F. Brewer (Eds.), *Theoretical issues in reading comprehension*. Hillsdale, NJ: Erlbaum.

Rumelhart, D. E. (1975). Notes on a schema for stories. In D. G. Bobrow & A. Collins (Eds.), *Representation and understanding*. New York: Academic Press.

Salomon, G., & Perkins, D. (1989). Rocky roads to transfer: Rethinking mechanisms of a neglected phenomenon. *Educational Psychologist, 24,* 113–142.

Samuels, S. J. (1967). Attentional processes in reading: The effect of pictures in the acquisition of reading responses. *Journal of Educational Psychology, 58,* 337–342.

Samuels, S. J. (1979). The method of repeated readings. *The Reading Teacher, 32,* 403–408.

Scandura, J. M., Frase, L. T., Gagne, R. M., Stolorow, K. A., Stolorow, L. M., & Groen, G. (1981). Current status and future directions of educational psychology as a discipline. In F. Farley & N. J. Gordon (Eds.), *Psychology and education*. Berkeley, CA: McCutchan.

Scardamalia, M. (1981). How children cope with the cognitive demands of writing. In C. H. Frederiksen & J. F. Dominic (Eds.), *Writing: Vol 2*. Hillsdale, NJ: Erlbaum.

Scardamalia, M., Bereiter, C., & Goelman, H. (1982). The role of production factors in writing ability. In M. Nystrant (Ed.), *What writers know*. New York: Academic Press.

Schoenfeld, A. H. (1979). Explicit heuristic training as a variable in problem solving performance. *Journal for Research in Mathematics Education, 10,* 173–187.

Schoenfeld, A. H. (1985). *Mathematical problem solving*. Orlando: Academic Press.

Schoenfeld, A. H. (1988). When good teaching leads to bad results: The disasters of "well-taught" mathematics classes. *Educational Psychologist, 23,* 145–166.

Schoenfeld, A. H. (1992). Learning to think mathematically: Problem solving, metacognition, and sense making in mathematics. In D. A. Gouws (Ed.), *Handbook of research on mathematics teaching and learning*. New York: Macmillan.

Schvaneveldt, R., Ackerman, B. P., & Semelar, T. (1977). The effect of semantic context on children's word recognition. *Child Development, 48,* 612–616.

Shavelson, R. J. (1972). Some aspects of the correspondence between content structure and cognitive structure in physics instruction. *Journal of Educational Psychology, 63,* 225–234.

Shavelson, R. J. (1974). Some methods for examining content structure and cognitive structure in instruction. *Educational Psychologist, 11,* 110–122.

Shepherd, D. L. (1978). *Comprehensive high school reading methods.* Columbus, OH: Merrill.

Shulman, L. S., & Quinlan, K. M. (1996). The comparative psychology of school subjects. In D. Berliner & R. Calfee (Eds.), *Handbook of educational psychology.* New York: Macmillan.

Siegler, R. S., & Jenkins, E. (1989). *How children discover new strategies.* Hillsdale, NJ: Erlbaum.

Siegler, R. S. (1987). The perils of averaging data over strategies: An example from children's addition. *Journal of Experimental Psychology: General, 116,* 250–264.

Silver, E. A. (1981). Recall of mathematical problem information: Solving related problems. *Journal for Research in Mathematics Education, 12,* 54–64.

Simon, H. A. (1980). Problem solving and education. In D. T. Tuma & F. Reif (Eds.), *Problem solving and education: Issues in teaching and research.* Hillsdale, NJ: Erlbaum.

Singer, H. (1981). Teaching the acquisition phase of reading development: An historical perspective. In O.J.L. Tzeng & H. Singer (Eds.), *Perception of print.* Hillsdale, NJ: Erlbaum.

Singer, M., Revlin, R., & Halldorson, M. (1990). Bridging inferences and enthymemes. In A. C. Graesser & G. H. Bower (Eds.), *Inferences and text comprehension.* San Diego: Academic Press.

Smith, E. E., & Spoehr, K. T. (1974). The perception of printed English: A theoretical perspective. In B. H. Kantowitz (Ed.), *Human information processing: Tutorials in performance and cognition.* Hillsdale, NJ: Erlbaum.

Soloway, E., Lochhead, J., & Clement, J. (1982). Does computer programming enhance problem solving ability? Some positive evidence on algebra word problems. In R. J. Seidel, R. E. Anderson, & B. Hunter (Eds.), *Computer Literacy.* New York: Academic Press.

Spector, J. E. (1995). Phonemic awareness training: Application of principles of direct instruction. *Reading & Writing Quarterly, 11,* 37–51.

Spoehr, K. T., & Schuberth, R. E. (1981). Processing words in context. In O. J. L. Tzeng & H. Singer (Eds.), *Perception of print.* Hillsdale, NJ: Erlbaum.

Stahl, S. A., & Fairbanks, M. M. (1986). The effects of vocabulary instruction: A model-based meta-analysis. *Review of Educational Research, 56,* 72–110.

Stallard, C. K. (1974). An analysis of the writing behavior of good student writers. *Research in the Teaching of English, 8,* 206–218.

Stanovich, K. E. (1980). Toward an interactive-compensatory model of individual differences in the development of reading fluency. *Reading Research Quarterly, 16,* 32–65.

Stanovich, K. E. (1986). Mathews effects in reading: Some consequences of individual differences in the acquisition of literacy. *Reading Research Quarterly, 21,* 360–407.

Stanovich, K.E. (1991). Discrepancy definitions of reading disability: Has intelligence led us astray? *Reading Research Quarterly, 26,* 7–29.

Steinberg, E. R. (1980). A garden of opportunities and a thicket of dangers. In L. W. Gregg & E. R. Steinberg (Eds.), *Cognitive processes in writing.* Hillsdale, NJ: Erlbaum.

Sterkel, K. S., Johnson, M. I., & Sjorgren, D. (1986). Textual analysis with composites to improve the writing skills of business communication students. *Journal of Business Communication, 23,* 43–61.

Sternberg, R. J. (1985). *Beyond IQ: A triarchic theory of human intelligence.* Cambridge, England: Cambridge University Press.

Stotsky, S. (1990). On planning and writing plans—Or beware of borrowed theories. *College Composition and Communication, 41,* 37–57.

Strike, K. A., & Posner, G. J. (1985). A conceptual change view of learning and understanding. In L. West & L. Pines (Eds.), *Cognitive structure and conceptual change.* San Diego: Academic Press.

Strike, K. A., & Posner, G. J. (1992). A revisionist theory of conceptual change. In R.A. Duschl & R.J. Hamilton (Eds.), *Philosophy of science: Cognitive psychology, and educational theory and practice.* Albany, NY: State University of New York Press.

Tamir, P., Gal-Choppin, R., & Nussinovitz, R. (1981). How do intermediate and junior high school students conceptualize living and nonliving? *Journal of Research in Science Teaching, 18,* 241–248.

Taylor, B. (1980). Children's memory for expository text after reading. *Reading Research Quarterly, 15,* 399–411.

Taylor, B. M., & Beach, R. W. (1984). The effects of text structure instruction on middle-grade students' comprehension and production of expository text. *Reading Research Quarterly, 19,* 134–146.

Thorndike, E. L. (1906). *The principles of teaching based on psychology.* Syracuse, NY: Mason-Henry Press.

Thorndike, E. L. (1913). *Educational psychology, Volume 2: The psychology of learning.* New York: Teachers College, Columbia University.

Thorndike, E. L. (1922). *The psychology of arithmetic.* New York: Macmillan.

Thorndyke, P. W. (1977). Cognitive structures in comprehension and memory for narrative discourse. *Cognitive Psychology, 9,* 77–110.

Thurstone, L. L. (1924). The nature of intelligence. New York: Harcourt, Brace.

Trowbridge, D. E., & McDermott, L. C. (1981). Investigation of student understanding of the concept of acceleration in one dimension. *American Journal of Physics, 49,* 242–253.

Tulving, E., & Gold, C. (1963). Stimulus information and contextual information as determinants of tachistoscopic recognition of words. *Journal of Experimental Psychology, 66,* 319–327.

Van Haneghan, J., Barron, L., Young, M., Williams, S., Vye, N., & Bransford, J. (1992). The Jasper Series: An experiment with new ways to enhance mathematical thinking. In D. F. Halpern (Ed.), *Enhancing thinking skills in the sciences and mathematics*. Hillsdale, NJ: Erlbaum.

Verschaffel, L., De Corte, E., & Pauwels, A. (1992). Solving compare problems: An eye movement test of Lewis and Mayer's consistency hypothesis. *Journal of Educational Psychology, 84,* 85–94.

Vosniadou, S., & Brewer, W. (1992). Mental models of the earth: A study of conceptual change. *Cognitive Psychology, 34,* 535–558.

Vosniadou, S., Pearson, P. D., & Rogers, T. (1988). What causes children's failures to detect inconsistencies in text? Representation versus comparison difficulties. *Journal of Educational Psychology, 80,* 27–39.

Voss, J. F., & Bisanz, G. L. (1985). Knowledge and processing of narrative and expository texts. In B. K. Britton & J. R. Black (Eds.), *Understanding expository text.* Hillsdale, NJ: Erlbaum.

Wagner, R. K., & Torgesen, J. K. (1987). The nature of phonological processing and its causal role in the acqustion of reading skills. *Psychological Bulletin, 101,* 192–212.

Wagner, S., & Kieran, C. (Eds.) (1989). *Research issues in the learning and teaching of algebra.* Reston, VA: National Council of Teachers of Mathematics.

Weaver, C.A., & Kintsch, W. (1991). Expository text. In R. Barr, M.L. Kamil, P.B. Mosenthal, & P.D. Pearson (Eds.), *Handbook of reading research, Vol. 2.* New York: Longman.

Weaver, P. A., & Resnick, L. B. (1979). The theory and practice of early reading: An introduction. In L. B. Resnick & P. A. Weaver (Eds.), *Theory and practice of early reading.* Hillsdale, NJ: Erlbaum.

West, R. F., & Stanovich, K. E. (1978). Automatic contextual facilitation in readers of three ages. *Child Development, 49,* 717–727.

Westfall, R.S. (1977). *The construction of modern science.* Cambridge, England: Cambridge University Press.

Whaley, J. F. (1981). Readers' expectations for story structures. *Reading Research Quarterly, 17,* 90–114.

Wheeler, A. E., & Kass, H. (1978). Student misconceptions in chemical equilibrium. *Science Education, 62,* 223–232.

White, B. (1993). ThinkerTools: Causal models, conceptual change, and science education. *Cognition and Instruction, 10,* 1–100.

White, R., & Gunstone, R. (1992). *Probing understanding.* London: Falmer Press.

Winne, P.H., Graham, L., & Prock, L. (1993). A model of poor reader's text-based inferencing: Effects of explanatory feedback. *Reading Research Quarterly, 28,* 53–66.

Wittrock, M. C., Marks, C., & Doctorow, W. (1975). Reading as a generative process. *Journal of Educational Psychology, 67,* 484–489.

Wollman, W. T., & Lawson, A. E. (1978). The influence of instruction on proportional reasoning in seventh graders. *Journal of Research in Science Teaching, 15,* 227–232.

Woodring, P. (1958). Introduction. In W. James (Ed.), *Talks to teachers* (pp. 6–17). New York: Norton.

World Book Encyclopedia (1990). Chicago: Author.

Yuill, N. M., & Oakhill, J. V. (1988). Effects of inference awareness training on poor reading comprehension. *Applied Cognitive Psychology, 2,* 33–45.

Zbrodoff, N. J. (1985). Writing stories under time and length constraints. *Dissertation Abstracts International, 46,* 1219A.

Credits and Acknowledgments (continued from p ii)

p. 52: From Tulving, E. & Gold. C. (1963). Stimulus information and contextual information as determinants of tachistoscopic recognition of words. *Journal of Experimental Psychology 66,* 322. Copyright 1963 by the American Psychological Association. Reprinted with permission.

p. 53: From West, R. F. & Stanovich, K. E. (1978). Automatic contextual facilitation in readers of three ages. *Child Development 49,* 721. © Society for Research in Child Development, Inc. Reprinted by permission.

pp. 59 and 60: From McConkie, G. W. & Rayner, K. (1975). The span of effective stimulus during a faxation in reading. *Perception & psychophysics, 17,* 578-586. Reprinted by permission of Psychonomic Society Publications and G. W. McConkie.

p. 61: From Carpenter, P. A. & Just, M. A. (1981). Cognitive processes in reading: Models based on readers' eye fixations. In A. M. Lesgold & C. A. Perfetti (Eds.), *Interactive process in reading* (pp. 177-213). Copyright 1981 by Lawrence Erlbaum Associates, Inc. Reprinted by permission.

pp. 70 and 72: From Barlett, F. C. (1932). Remembering. Cambridge, England: Cambridge University Press. Copyright 1932 by Cambridge University Press. Reprinted by permission.

p. 78: From Bransford, J. D. & Johnson, M. K. (1972). Contextual prerequisites for understanding: Some investigations of comprehension and recall. *Journal of Verbal Learning and Verbal Behavior, 61,* 722. Reprinted with permission of Academic Press.

p. 79: From Pichert, J. & Anderson, R. C. (1977). Taking different perspectives on a story. *Journal of Educational Psychology, 69,* 309–315. Coypright © 1977 by the American Psychological Association. Reprinted by permission.

pp 86, 87, 91, and 92: From Brown, J. S. & Smiley, S. S. (1978). The development of strategies for studying texts. *Child Development, 49,* 1082. By permission of the Society for Research in Child Development.

p. 90: Excerpt from Appendix from Ilyona, Jukka. (1994, January). Processing of topic shifts by adults and children. *Reading Research Quarterly, 29* (1), 76–90. Reprinted by permission of the International Reading Association.

p. 93: From Taylor, Barbara M., and Beach, Richard. (1984, Winter). The Effects of text structure instruction on middle-grade students' conprehension and production of expository text. *Reading Research Quarterly, 19* (2), 134–146. Reprinted by persmission of the International Reading Association.

pp. 111–112: From Palinscar, A. S. (1986). Metacognitive stratetgy instruction. *Exceptional Children, 53,* 118-124. By permission of the Council for Exceptional Children.

pp.118–20: From Piaget, J. (1926). *The language and thought of the child.* London: Kegan Paul, Trench, Trubner and Company.

p. 127: From Matsuhashi, A. (1982). Explorations in real-time production of written discourse. In N. Nystrand (Ed.), *What writers know* (pp. 269-324). San Diego: Academic Press. By permission of Academic Press.

p. 147: From Macdonald, N. H., Frase, L. T., Gingrich, P. S., Keenan, S. A. (1982). The writer's workbench: Computer aids for text analysis. *Educational Psychologist, 17,* 172-179.

p. 153: From Englert, C. S., Raphael, T. E., & Anderson, L. M. (1989). *Cognitive strategy instruction in writing project.* East Lansing, MI: Institute for Research on Teaching.

p. 167: From Lewis, A. B. (1989). Training students to represent arithmetic word problems. *Journal of Educational Psychology, 81,* 523. Copyright © 1989 by the American Psychological Association. Reprinted with permission.

pp. 170–71: From Hinsley, D. A., Hayes, J. R., & Simon, H. A. (1977). From words to equations: Meaning and representation in algebra word problems. In M. A. Just and P. A. Carpenter (Eds.), *Cognitive processes in comprehension* (pp. 89-106). Hillsdale, NJ: Erlbaum. By permission of publisher.

p. 174: From Mayer, R. E. (1982). Memory for algebra story problems. *Journal of Educational Psychology, 74,* 199-218. Copyright © 1982 by the American Psychological Association. Adapted by permission.

p. 194: From *Thinking, problem solving, cognition* (2nd ed.) by Mayer © 1992 by W. H. Freeman and Company. Used with permission.

p. 195: From Groen, G. J., & Parkman, J. M. (1972). A chronometric analysis of simple addition. *Psychological Review, 97*, 329–343.

p.198: From *The promise of cognitive psychology* by Mayer © 1981 by W. H. Freeman and Company. Used with permission.

pp. 206 and 207: Reprinted with permission from McCloskey, M., Caramazza, A., & Green, B. (1980). Curvilinear motion in the absence of external forces: Naive beliefs about the motion of objects. *Science, 210,* 1139, 1140. Copyright 1980 American Association for the Advancement of Science.

pp. 210 and 212: From McCloskey, M. (1983). Intuitive physics. *Scientific American, 248,* 123, 126. Michael Goodman. © 1983. Scientific American. Reprinted by permission.

pp. 213–15: Reprinted with permission from Clement, J. (1982). Students' preconceptions in introductory mechanics. *American Journal of Physics, 50,* 66-71. Copyright 1982 American Association of Physics Teachers.

pp. 224 and 226: From White, B. J. (1993). Thinker Tools: Causal models, conceptual change, and science education. *Cognition and Instruction, 10,* 12. Copyright 1993 by Lawrence Erlbaum Associates, Inc. Reprinted by permission.

pp. 228 and 230: From Karplus, R., Karplus, E., Formisano, M., & Paulsen, A. (1979). Proptional reasoning and control variables in seven countries. In J. Lochhead & J. Clement (Eds). *Cognitive process instruction: Research on teaching thinking skills* (pp. 47-107). Philadelphia: Franklin Institute Press. Copyright 1979 by Lawrence Erlbaum Associates, Inc. Reprinted by permission.

p. 233: From Dunbar, K. (1993). Concept discovery in a scientific domain. *Cognitive Science, 17,* 397–434. Copyright, Cognitive Science Society, Inc., used by permission.

p. 242: From *Thinking, problem solving, cognition* (2nd ed) by Mayer © 1992 by W. H. Freeman and Company. Used with permission.

p. 244: From Larkin, J. H. (1983). The role of problem representation in physics. In D. Gentner & A. L. Stevens (Eds.), *Mental modes* (pp. 75-98). Hillsdale, NJ: Erlbaum. Copyright 1983 by Lawrence Erlbaum Associates, Inc. Reprinted by permission.

pp. 245: From Chi, T. H. Feltovich, P. J., & Glaser, R. (1981). Categorization and representation of physics problems. *Cognitive Science, 5,* 121-152.

AUTHOR INDEX

SUBJECT INDEX

The *f* and *t* following the page numbers indicate the figures and tables included in the text.

4080